DEATH
and the
Afterlife

About the Author

Dr. Morey is the Executive Director of the Research and Education Foundation and the author of over 20 books, some of which have been translated into French, German, Spanish, Italian, Finnish, Norwegian, Polish, and Chinese. He is an internationally recognized scholar in the field of comparative religions, the cults, and the occult. His other books in include:

The Battle of the Gods
Death and the Afterlife
An Examination of Exclusive Psalmody
Fearing God
Here Is Your God
Horoscopes and the Christian
How to Answer a Jehovah's Witness
How to Keep Your Faith While in College
How to Answer a Mormon
How to Keep Your Kids Drug Free
An Introduction to Defending the Faith
The Islamic Invasion
The New Atheism and the Erosion of Freedom
Reincarnation and Christianity
Studies in the Atonement
The Truth About Masons
When Is It Right to Fight?
Worship Is All of Life
Satan's Devices

Dr. Robert A. Morey

DEATH
and the
Afterlife

BETHANY HOUSE PUBLISHERS
MINNEAPOLIS, MINNESOTA 55438
A Division of Bethany Fellowship, Inc.

Published by Bethany House Publishers
A Ministry of Bethany Fellowship International
11400 Hampshire Avenue South
Bloomington, Minnesota 55438
www.bethanyhouse.com

Printed in the United States of America by
Bethany Press International
Bloomington, Minnesota 55438

ISBN 0-7642-2686-X (Trade paper)
ISBN 0-87123-433-5 (Hardcover)

Library of Congress Cataloging-in-Publication Data

Morey, Robert A., 1946-.
  Death and the afterlife.
ISBN 0-7642-2686-X (Trade paper)
ISBN 0-87123-433-5 (Hardcover)
  Bibliography: p.
  Includes indexes.
    1. Future punishment. 2. Future life—Christianity. 3. Intermediate
state. I. Title.
BT836.2.M67   1984   236   84-15682

Dedicated to Mrs. Ruth Morey, my grandmother, who, like Timothy's grandmother, prayed and labored that her children and grandchildren might come to a saving knowledge of Christ.

World Religions and Cults Resources
From Bethany House Publishers

General
> *The Compact Guide to World Religions*—Halverson, ed.
> *The Kingdom of the Cults* (Updated 1997)—Martin
> *The Many Faces of Deception*—Bulle
> *Operation World*—Johnstone/Mandryk

Islam
> *Sharing Your Faith With a Muslim*—Abdul-Haqq

Jehovah's Witnesses
> *How to Answer a Jehovah's Witness*—Morey
> *Jehovah's Witnesses*—Martin

Mormonism
> *Answering Mormons' Questions*—McKeever
> *How to Answer a Mormon*—Morey
> *Letters to a Mormon Elder*—White
> *Out of Mormonism*—Robertson
> *Questions to Ask Your Mormon Friend*—
>   McKeever/Johnson

Occult and Astrology
> *The Dark Side of the Supernatural*—Myers/Wimbish
> *Demon Possession*—Montgomery

Dr. R. A. Morey received a B.A. in philosophy and his M.Div. and D.Min. from Westminster Theological Seminary. He is presently Pastor of New Life Bible Church and Professor of Apologetics and Hermeneutics at Perry Bible Institute. He has also written the following books:

Reincarnation and Christianity
Horoscopes and the Christian
How to Answer a Jehovah's Witness
How to Answer a Mormon
A Christian Handbook for Defending the Faith
The Bible and Drug Abuse
The Dooyeweerdian Concept of the Word of God
Worship Is All of Life
Is Sunday the Christian Sabbath?
An Examination of Exclusive Psalmody
The Saving Work of Christ
The New Life Notebook

FOREWORD

The soul or the spirit of mankind has occupied the minds of philosophers and theologians of all religious persuasions for thousands of years.

King Solomon asked the question, "If a man die, shall he live again?" This statement, in the context of the book of Ecclesiastes, mirrors the cynical pessimism of the skeptical philosopher as well as the ultimate solution which, by nature, must be theological. The world of non-Christian religions and pseudo-Christian cults has created a "semantic swamp" on the subject of the afterlife, almost always ignoring the resurrection of the body while arguing for a permanent state of existence for the spirit. For more than 150 years, liberal Protestant theology has fostered this in the United States and Europe. The intermediate state has, in the minds of a great many people, become a shadowy world of universal salvation at the expense of classic biblical theology.

There has been a great absence of sound, scriptural scholarship in the important area of the intermediate state of man, pending the resurrection of the body, as well as the concept of eternal, conscious punishment for those who have finally rejected the grace of God.

Fortunately for evangelical Christianity, this has now been remedied with the publication of this volume by Dr. Robert Morey, a well-educated Christian theologian whose scholarship and careful analysis reflects his reformation theology.

Dr. Morey ably deals with the original languages of Scripture, paying careful attention to the laws of hermeneutics. He is particularly effective when exegeting difficult passages which are often perverted by cultic and liberal theology. The book is also noteworthy for its recognition of a wide range of literature, Jewish sources in particular, seldom discussed in contemporary literature.

The command of apocryphal and pseudopegriphal materials and the careful attention to the cultural and theological background of the sources he utilizes gives this volume the authentic ring of careful scholarship and attention to those details necessary to arrive at ultimate truth.

However, Dr. Morey is not content to merely quote sources; he carefully integrates biblical and nonbiblical details to show both contrast and an essential pattern of revealed truth consistent in both the Old and New Testaments.

The scholarship of this volume will impress those who have studied the subject with any degree of thoroughness. At the same time, he communicates many great and profound truths in language that the average layman will both appreciate and profit from.

There can be little doubt that the subjects of conditional immortality, eternal punishment, the annihilation of the wicked, and the teaching of "soul sleep" have seldom been dealt with so completely as in this work. It not only is a condensation of a tremendous breadth of literature, but a major landmark in addressing these very important areas of Christian theology.

In a world which delights in analysis of "out of body experiences," ESP, psychic phenomena, and alleged reincarnational and spiritistic manifestations, Dr. Morey's book directs the light of Scripture, once again, into this murky area of human confusion and dispels the darkness and uncertainty that such speculations create and promote. It is a clear, cool breath of fresh air in the midst of a vacuum of doubt and unbelief. The first major work on the subject in this century, *Death and the Afterlife* will for many years be a standard reference work in this sorely neglected field.

—Walter Martin
Founder and Director,
Christian Research Institute,
San Juan Capistrano, California

PREFACE

Dr. Robert Morey's work provides an extensive examination of the biblical language related to human destiny beyond death (including reference to apocryphal and other Jewish literature in instances where they can shed light on the meaning of terms) and a careful discussion of the passages of canonical Scripture in which the future condition of the lost is referred to.

Universalism and annihilationism (as well as materialism and occultism) are the object of this searching critique, in which the main arguments of their supporters are examined and refuted. The lucid style and the very careful organization of the material make the work readily understandable to lay people as well as useful for pastors and other scholars. From the helpful bibliography, it is obvious that Dr. Morey has achieved a high degree of familiarity with the literature in English dealing with this subject and has made good use of the sources.

—Dr. Roger Nicole
Professor of Theology
Gordon Conwell Theological
Seminary

TABLE OF CONTENTS

INTRODUCTION

There is a discernible historical cycle to the Christian Church's attitude toward the doctrine of hell. The cycle begins with a long period of time during which it is acknowledged that the Scriptures clearly teach the intermediate and eternal punishment of the wicked. It is assumed by all that this was and always shall be the doctrinal position of historic Christianity.

After acknowledgment comes indifference. The "negative side" of the gospel in which sinners are warned to "escape" and "flee" from "the wrath to come" (Matt. 23:33; Luke 3:7) is ignored and often downplayed, while the "positive side" of God's love in Christ is overemphasized to the exclusion of anything else. The doctrine of hell is acknowledged to be true but rarely preached.

After indifference comes ignorance. Because the biblical theme of God's judgment is ignored, the people in the pew do not know *why* they are expected to believe in hell. There is no instruction given on the subject, and the issue is avoided because no one wants to be characterized as a "hell-fire and brimstone" preacher.

After ignorance comes doubt. Since no one is told why he should believe that there really is a hell, doubts begin to creep into people's minds. It becomes fashionable to speak of the doctrine of hell as being "unkind," "unloving," or "negative."

After doubt comes denial. The cults are quick to put forth either Universalism or annihilationism as the answer to the "horrible" doctrine of hell. Many books are published and distributed which directly attack the orthodox position. Since orthodox teachers have not instructed their people on the subject, the Universalists and annihilationists succeed in convincing many people and generating controversy in many churches.

After denial comes irritation. When the pressure from the Universalists and annihilationists is first felt by orthodox theologians, they respond by saying or thinking, "I don't have time to deal with this issue right now," "Wasn't this issue solved one hundred years ago?" or "If we ignore them, maybe they will go away."

After irritation comes affirmation. When the Universalists and annihilationists don't go away but multiply drastically, the orthodox theologians take up the defense of historic Christianity and demonstrate that the Bible does indeed teach the doctrine of eternal punishment. God's people are once again instructed as to why they should believe that there is a hell to shun and a heaven to gain. The subject is preached and taught with boldness. The Universalists and annihilationists are thoroughly discredited and refuted.

After affirmation comes acknowledgment. The Christian Church reaffirms its historic position, and it is universally acknowledged that the Scriptures do teach the intermediate and eternal, conscious torment of the wicked. The controversy passes and the church returns to its dogmatic slumbers.

Then the cycle starts all over again! After a long period of acknowledgment, indifference will set in and the other phases will follow.

In terms of this cycle, Bible-believing Christians have passed through the acknowledgment, indifference, ignorance, doubt, denial and irritation phases and are now entering the affirmation phase. The Universalists and the annihilationists have invaded the Christian Church just as the Philistines invaded Israel. It is once again necessary to defend the gospel truth that unbelief results in God's wrath (John 3:36) and that this wrath is eternal (Matt. 25:46).

May God be pleased to use this study to equip His people with biblical truth in order to give a reason for what they believe (1 Pet. 3:15).

PART 1

EXPOSITION

Chapter 1

THE HERMENEUTICS OF DEATH

As we approach the subject of what the Bible teaches concerning death and an afterlife, we must emphasize the importance of hermeneutics. What is hermeneutics?

Hermeneutics is the discovery, understanding and use of those linguistic and literary principles or rules of interpretation which should be followed when one seeks to understand the Bible. Exegesis is the practical application of hermeneutical principles to a specific text in order to discover the intent and mind of the author. It is the opposite of eisegesis, which is reading into a text our own ideas with little or no regard for what the author meant.

Why bother with hermeneutics? First, the Bible comes to us as literature (prose, poetry, historical narrative, apocalyptic literature, letters, dialogue, theological treatises, biography, etc.). Since it is literature, we must treat it as such.

Second, hermeneutics is simply a reflection on the unconscious principles which we all follow when reading any piece of literature in general. When we pick up a newspaper or novel we (1) observe grammar and syntax; (2) observe literary units such as paragraph and chapter; and (3) seek to understand what the author was saying. These same things apply to reading the Bible.

Third, the Scriptures themselves warn us there are wrong ways as well as right ways to interpret the Bible (2 Pet. 3:16; cf. 2 Tim. 2:15).

Some of the wrong ways are (1) partial quotation of a text; (2) not observing who said it or wrote it; (3) bringing together unrelated proof texts; (4) taking the verse out of context; and (5) taking a mystical approach to the Bible in which it is allowed to fall open at random and then a verse is picked by "chance."

This means it is erroneous to say the Bible can be interpreted any way one pleases. God has given us a library of literature which we call "The Bible," and we must avoid misinterpreting it or reading into it our own theological biases. Hermeneutics is the attempt to curb or bridle invalid ways of interpreting the Scriptures and to set forth those positive literary principles which should govern everyone's interpretation of the Bible.[1]

Where should we get our hermeneutical principles? The foundational principle is that the same basic linguistic and literary rules which we must follow when interpreting any historic literature should be utilized when seeking to interpret the Bible. Since the Bible does not contain any unique literary forms but uses those forms found in the surrounding culture of that time, we cannot develop a unique hermeneutic which is applicable only to the Bible.

Our foundational principle reveals the basic error of liberal and neo-orthodox hermeneutics, which cannot be applied to any historic or contemporary literature but are applied to the Bible. These hermeneutics are based on "special pleading" in that they apply rules of interpretation to the Bible which are obviously erroneous if applied to any other piece of literature. For example, The Wellhausen Documentary Hypothesis which rejects the Mosaic authorship of the Pentateuch and then proposes that it was a "scissor and paste" work of multiple authors (J.E.D.P.) is based on principles which are obviously erroneous if applied to the works of Homer, Plato, Shakespeare, or any historic or contemporary author.[2]

The same accusation can be validly raised against the nearsighted and artificial hermeneutics of Barth, Bultmann, Fuchs, Ebeling, Dillenberger, Buri, Ogden, etc. To follow their hermeneutical systems when reading any piece of literature, historic or contemporary, would be disastrous. Why then should we follow their method of interpretation when reading the Bible?[3]

Our foundational principle also means we cannot follow the typical method of interpretation which is utilized by such groups as the Jehovah's Witnesses, Seventh-Day Adventists, Christian Scientists, the Unification Church, the Mormons, etc. The "cultic" hermeneutic is based on the assumption that the cultic leader or founder is especially inspired of God to give a "secret" or "inner" meaning to Scripture which cannot be found in the grammar, syntax or context of the passage. Thus cultic leaders can and do read into the Bible their own theological aberrations without the constraint of context or grammar.[4]

The cultic hermeneutic is a modern revival of the medieval hermeneutic which saw four levels of interpretation in each passage. Each text supposedly had (1) a literal meaning which could be discerned by the uneducated masses, (2) a moral meaning which could be understood by the educated and cultured, and (3) an anagogical and (4) mystical meaning which only the clergy could discern. The clergy usually resorted to a highly allegorical methodology which produced eisegetical interpretations.

The Protestant Reformers rightly ridiculed the medieval Catholic hermeneutic and emphasized in opposition that since the Bible was written in normal everyday language and not in mystical symbols, and since it was written for normal everyday people and not just for theologians or clergyman, the only way to interpret the Bible is in a normal everyday way. In other words, a plain Bible written for a plain people needs a plain interpretation.

The Reformers were correct in their thinking, because there are no secret or mystical insights in the Bible which only the specially gifted or enlightened few may see. There are no secret "keys" to unlock the mysteries of the Bible, because the Bible does not come to us as a locked book but it is open and plain to the honest reader. And, we hasten to add, neither has the Church of Jesus Christ been anxiously waiting for that one "special" interpreter to come along who will develop a special hermeneutic which would at last open the meaning of the Bible.

We must therefore beware of all the secret hermeneutics which depend on some "new" principle of interpretation which is proclaimed as "the key" to unlock the mysteries of the Bible. The history of theology is littered with the corpses of past hermeneutical systems which were, at one time, thought to be the key to Scripture. Despite these clear lessons of history, we are still being confronted today by individuals who claim that they, and they alone, have discovered the key to interpretation. We must beware of all such "key" mentalities.

As we approach the subject of the Bible's view of death and the afterlife, hermeneutics become very important. Various false interpretations have arisen through the constant violation of basic hermeneutical principles. This is why we were surprised to see that, of the over one thousand books which we surveyed on the subject, only a few authors paid any attention to hermeneutics whatsoever.[5] As we investigated the so-called "biblical" interpretation of the vast majority of those who ignored hermeneutics, the consequences became self-evident in their absurd interpretations of Scripture.

There are several hermeneutical principles which are crucial to our understanding of the biblical teaching on death. Since our approach to Scripture is governed by these principles, a brief review of them will be given at this time.

PRINCIPLE 1—THE CLARITY OF SCRIPTURE

The Bible was written to be understood by the normal person who would take the words of the Bible in their simplest and most natural meaning. When the prophets, apostles and Christ spoke to the common people of their day, they spoke in the common language using those words, figures of speech, idiomatic expressions, etc., which would most likely make plain their meaning.[6] They did not seek to use mystical or occultic terminology in order to hide their message from everyone. The exact opposite was true. The whole purpose of preaching was to proclaim the message loud and clear to the common man on the street. Thus, the apostles stated in Acts 26:26 that their message was not something done "in a corner" but "in the world."

Nowhere more clearly does this principle apply than to the issue of the biblical teaching on an afterlife. When an annihilationist or Universalist gives an elaborate and esoteric interpretation of those biblical texts which speak of endless punishment, they go to great lengths to demonstrate that "everlasting" does not mean everlasting and "torment" does not mean torment! It never seems to occur to them that if the biblical authors wanted to express clearly the idea of the extinction or ultimate salvation of the wicked, there were words available to them in the Hebrew and Greek languages which could have been used. But the biblical authors did not use those words.

On the other hand, if the biblical authors wished to express clearly to their hearers the idea of unending, conscious torment, there were words in the Greek and Hebrew language which would express that idea. As we shall see, the biblical authors used those words which were the only ones available to them which would indicate endless punishment to the average person of their day. To think that they would use the Greek and Hebrew words which would mean endless punishment to the common hearer in order to teach annihilation or Universalism is to label them either deceptive or ignorant.[7]

As we approach the text of Scripture, we will seek to discern its natural and most obvious meaning as it would have been understood by the person of that day because we cannot accept the notions that the authors of Scripture were willfully deceptive in teaching the opposite of what their words imply.

PRINCIPLE 2—PROGRESSIVE REVELATION

The author of Hebrews stated in 1:1, 2 that God spoke to the fathers through the prophets in bits and pieces and in many different ways. The entirety of God's revelation was not given to humanity in a single instant but was dispersed in different ways to different people over several thousand years. Each new revelation was like a piece of a cosmic puzzle. Even when the last of the Old Testament prophets had all the pieces which were given to those before him, he still could not understand the total picture. It was only after the coming of Christ that the last remaining pieces were supplied and the puzzle completed.

The progressive character of revelation can also be understood in terms of a gradual unfolding of biblical truths which began quite vague, but slowly, little by little, came to be understood in absolute clarity. Revelation is thus progressive in a theological sense as well as in a historical sense. Each new revelation was like a turn of the knob on a pair of binoculars which would eventually change the initial blurred vision of the seer to the point of crystal clarity.[8]

The implications of the progressive character of God's revelation has direct bearing on the issue of what the Bible says about death and an afterlife.

First, this means that we cannot base our understanding of death and an afterlife solely upon passages found in the Old Testament. Since the Old Testament prophets awaited the coming of the New Testament to supply them with the last pieces of the puzzle before the whole picture could be seen, we must recognize that the vision of the Old Testament prophets was intrinsically blurred and, as a result, was vague on most of the details.[9]

This point directly applies to such groups as the Adventists and Jehovah's Witnesses. A survey of their literature reveals an almost total dependence on Old Testament texts to support their theory of soul sleep and annihilationism.[10] If one brings up New Testament texts which clearly teach the contrary, they are dismissed on the basis of an assumed priority of the Old Testament as over against the New Testament. They do not see any progress from the Old Testament to the New Testament but flatten out the distinction between the testaments. Instead of giving priority to the clarity of the New Testament, they feel safer staying with the blurred vision found in the Old Testament. We must beware of those theological positions which depend primarily on Old Testament texts.

Second, the principle of progressive revelation also means that biblical words will change in their meaning as the understanding of God's people deepens. Each new revelation meant a deeper understanding of some aspect of divine truth. Thus, we must not assume that a biblical word will have only one meaning which transcends the division between the Old and the New Testaments.

Two errors are commonly made in this regard. Some read the vagueness of the Old Testament into the New Testament and fail to appreciate the final clarity of the New Testament. They state that the meaning of Sheol in the Old Testament determines the meaning of Hades in the New Testament. Thus there is no further or deeper meaning in the New Testament. Once one discovers the meaning of the Old Testament meaning of the concept of Sheol, this is to be transported in its entirety into the New Testament with no deletions or additions.

This is the fundamental error of both Chambers and Kester.[11] They assumed that the New Testament meaning of Hades must be limited to the Old Testament Sheol. Because in the Old Testament all men went to Sheol, they concluded that the New Testament must teach that all men go to Hades. They stressed that the terms must have the same meanings. In this way they failed to observe the clarity and priority of the New Testament as well as the progressive nature of revelation.

On the other extreme, one encounters authors who read the New Testament meaning of Hades into the Old Testament concept of Sheol. Whatever Hades means in the New Testament is assumed to be the exact meaning of Sheol in the Old Testament. The vagueness and incompleteness of the Old Testament is completely ignored as the New Testament is read into the Old Testament wholesale.

This is the fundamental error of W.G.T. Shedd. His working assumption throughout *The Doctrine of Eternal Punishment* is that the Old Testament meaning of Sheol must conform to the New Testament meaning of Hades. He takes this position out of fear that if the meaning of Sheol is not conformed to the New Testament concept of Hades, "this would imperil the doctrine of the final judgment."[12] Throughout his book, he ignores any concept of progressive revelation but reads the Hades of the New Testament into the Sheol of the Old Testament without hesitation.

Both of the above approaches ignore the principle of progressive revelation and actually assume that the Bible is one book given at one time with words which admit only one meaning from the beginning to the end of the book. They assume that if the Old Testament teaches something which is not exactly like what the New Testament teaches, the Bible would be contradicting itself. But the Bible is a library of sixty-six books, written by forty or more authors over a period of two thousand years or more. It must be viewed as progressive in nature. But this does not and indeed cannot mean it is contradictory. Just as our understanding of ourselves and the world around us deepened as we grew from children to adults without contradiction, even so the understanding of God's people grew and developed without contradiction. The integrity of the Old Testament and New Testament is preserved only by the principle of progressive revelation, and, we must point out, the principle of progressive revelation does not lead to biblical contradictions, but *solves* the problem of apparent contradiction.

Third, we will expect to find that the Old Testament will be unclear and vague in its teaching on death and an afterlife. We will not expect or demand that the Old Testament will be precise in its usage of such words as "soul," "spirit," or "sheol." The clarity of the New Testament need not be eisegetically read back into the Old Testament. Neither should we read the vagueness of the Old Testament into the New Testament and declare with some modern liberal theologians, such as Jungel, that the New Testament as well as the Old Testament is vague about death.[13] Instead, we should appreciate the distinctive vagueness of the Old Testament and the distinctive clarity of the New Testament. We should avoid leveling the distinction between the testaments.

PRINCIPLE 3—THE IMPORTANCE OF THE ORIGINAL LANGUAGES

The importance of the original languages for the serious interpreter of Scripture cannot be overemphasized.[14] That someone would write a book in which he dogmatically stated what certain Greek and Hebrew words meant when he had never studied such languages is unthinkable. While the English text is basically clear to the average modern reader, the biblical scholar seeks to understand what a particular word meant in the original language in which it was written.

Biblical words must be studied, first of all, etymologically. Thus, we must refer to the lexicons or dictionaries which define words in their original meanings. In this way, some mistaken views are, at once, revealed. For example, while conversing with a Jehovah's Witness, he informed us that the word Hades in the Greek language meant "the grave." He was quite dogmatic about this and said that the Watchtower had great Greek scholars who could prove this.

You can imagine his confusion when we pointed out that the word Hades is a compound of two Greek words, one being the negative "not" and the other "seen." The word simply means "unseen" or "invisible." As Ramm pointed out, since graves are seen and are visible, it is quite erroneous to say that the word Hades in the Greek language means "the grave." As a matter of fact, Hades as a Greek word refers to the unseen or invisible underworld where the spirit or soul of unregenerate man goes after the death of the body.[15]

Any theological position which ignores the lexicographical material and gives arbitrary definitions to words which contradict their basic meaning in the original languages should be avoided. It only stands to reason that we must approach biblical interpretation with the initial assumption that the words found in the Bible will be understood in their everyday "street" meaning. This, of course, does not rule out those few instances where biblical authors used a word in a new way or coined a new word. But these instances are very rare and are easily discerned by their usage in Scripture.

Not only must a word be studied etymologically but also comparatively. To be accurate in defining what a given biblical word means, one must discover and compare all the usages of the word in the Bible. Because of the progressive character of revelation, a word will have different meanings depending on where, why and how it is used in other Scripture passages. For example, the words "soul" and "spirit" are used to describe different functions or aspects of man, and one definition will not cover all the occurrences of these words. That a word develops and evolves in meaning should not be viewed as contradictory but as progressive.

Biblical words must also be understood in their historical context (*zeitgeist*). We must seek to discover what the words of Scripture meant in the context of the social, cultural, economic, political and religious situations. This is why the famous Baptist Greek scholar, Dr. A. T. Robertson, called his Greek grammar, *The Greek New Testament in the Light of Historical Research*.

This principle entails a comparative study of the meaning of biblical words and extra-biblical literature such as the Apocrypha, rabbinic writings and Greek literature.

Once the meaning of a word is clear in terms of its usage in extra-biblical literature, we should begin with the strong assumption that this is more than likely what the word means in Scripture.

This principle also reveals the biased approach of those cultic and neo-orthodox interpreters who deny that the Bible teaches that the soul or spirit of man is conscious after death, while, at the same time, readily admitting that the Apocrypha, apocalyptic, rabbinic and Greek extra-biblical literature understand the word "soul" to refer to that conscious part of man which survives the death of the body. In other words, they totally ignore what the word "soul" meant in contemporary Jewish and Greek religion and culture.[16]

Some cultic groups, such as the Jehovah's Witnesses, go so far as to teach that the word "soul" cannot refer to some immortal part of man which survives death because that was the contemporary meaning of the word soul in all extra-biblical literature.[17]

If we assumed that the biblical words always had a meaning which was opposite to the meaning of the word as it was used in extra-biblical literature and culture, all interpretation would cease. There must be clear and necessary reasons for abandoning the common meaning of a word. Otherwise, the common meaning must prevail.

PRINCIPLE 4—GRAMMATICAL INTERPRETATION

Grammar and syntax has to do with an understanding of the nature of words and how they function in sentences to convey the mind of the author. The importance of interpreting a verse in harmony with its grammatical structure can be crucial in theological controversy. All languages have a grammatical structure whether or not an author is conscious of using it. A noun is a noun and a verb is a verb regardless of one's theological bias. There can be no disagreement over such things as identifying the subject and predicate in a simple sentence because grammar is not a matter of religious prejudice.

The issue of the Bible's view of death cannot be resolved without close attention to the grammar of the Greek and Hebrew languages. Some of the major cultic errors concerning death can be refuted simply by observing the meaning of Greek tenses. For example, the conditional immortalitists teach that no one has "everlasting life" *now* as a present possession, but go on to say that everlasting life must be viewed as the reward of future bodily immortality obtained at the resurrection. Yet, when one turns to the Greek New Testament, one discovers numerous instances where believers are grammatically said to have everlasting life *as a present possession*.[18] Thus in 1 John 5:11-13, the Apostle uses the present indicative tense in the Greek which means that the believer has everlasting life now because he possesses Jesus Christ now.

> And the witness is this, that God has given us eternal life, and this life is in his Son. He who has the Son *has* the life; he who does not have the Son of God does not have the life. These things have I written to you who believe in the name of the Son of God, in order that you may know that you *have* eternal life.

We must observe the grammatical structure of a passage in order to discern the intent and mind of the author. No amount of special pleading can remove the significance of grammar and syntax in the interpretation of Scripture.

PRINCIPLE 5—THE PRINCIPLE OF CONTEXT

As we approach the Scriptures, we must begin with the primary assumption that each text must be understood in the light of its own literary context. This means that we do not begin with the assumption that a text should be interpreted literally or figuratively. It is the context and the context alone which decides how we are to interpret the words of the author.[19]

What do we mean by "context"? First, there is the literary context of the immediate paragraph or chapter in which the text is found. The verses before and after a text should be read to get the immediate context.

Just observing this point alone removes ninety percent of the so-called "biblical" arguments utilized by the cults. For example, the Mormons teach that the "stick of Joseph" and "the stick of

Judah" mentioned in Ezek. 37:19 refer to the book of Mormon and the Bible. Yet, when we read the verses before and after verse 19, we discover that the uniting of the sticks refers to the reuniting of the tribes as they return to their homeland (vv. 15–23).

Any text taken out of context is a pretext. This principle alone ultimately robs most of the cultic arguments of any biblical validity.

Second, there is the literary context of the entire book in which the text is found. This means that we must remember that the Bible is a library of sixty-six books with each book having its own theme, focus and concern. For example, this principle is particularly important when interpreting passages from Ecclesiastes. The failure to interpret its statements in the light of its overall theme and focus is the most common error of those who deny a conscious afterlife. Such groups as the Adventists and Jehovah's Witnesses constantly refer to the book of Ecclesiastes as "proving" the doctrine of soul sleep. Their interpretation of Ecclesiastes is erroneous because they fail to deal with the subject and purpose of the book.

Third, there is the context of the analogy of faith. This refers to the principle that a valid interpretation of a text will not produce a doctrine that is elsewhere in Scripture clearly condemned. Apparent contradictions arise from defects in the interpreter and his methods rather than out of the text itself.

Fourth, there is the historical, cultural, religious, and linguistic context. Great benefit can be derived from understanding what a word meant to the people of biblical times. This principle relates directly to understanding such biblical words as Gehenna. As we shall see, erroneous views often arise due to ignorance of the historical meaning of a word.

The principle of context means that we must interpret a text in the light of its own literary and cultural surroundings. The failure to observe this principle is one of the foundational problems in the hermeneutics of liberal and cultic theologians.

PRINCIPLE 6—FIGURES OF SPEECH

Once we approach the Bible without initially assuming that we must interpret everything literally, we discover that the biblical authors used the richness of figurative language to convey biblical truth. The variety of the kinds of figurative language used in the Bible include such things as metaphor, simile, symbolism, parable, allegory, analogy, idiom, cliché, proverb, metonymy, synecdoche, hyperbole, and irony. Terry, in his classic *Biblical Hermeneutics*, devotes no less than 250 pages to discussing how to interpret the figures of speech found in the Bible.

The principle of observing figurative language will play an important part in our investigation of the biblical teaching on the afterlife. Many Christians have literalized what was intended to be taken figuratively. As a result, they have caused confusion among themselves and unnecessarily opened themselves up to the severest criticism of clear-thinking unbelievers. Because of the sad neglect of this principle, we will pause at this point to clarify what we mean by figurative language.

We can think with or without mental images. A mental image takes place when we picture something, someone, or some activity in our mind. Those with vivid imaginations do this easier and more often than do others. A mental image is the theater of the mind in which we mentally picture something.

Figurative language can also be likened unto the film that is used to project pictures on a movie screen. The film is often composed of people, places, objects and activities which come from our own experiences.

In the above paragraph, we used the simile of a film and theater in order to convey the function of figurative language. We did not intend to be interpreted in a literal sense. There is no literal film or movie theater in the mind. We used a figure of speech to illustrate our point. Just because the mental image of a film and theater in the mind is "false," i.e. not literal, does not mean that what we were saying was not true or that it should be dismissed because it is figurative language.

The purpose of figurative language is to create mental images or pictures to illustrate ideas. The mental pictures need not be true or real. Thus when Psalm 1 speaks of a believer as a "tree firmly planted by streams of water," it is understood that while this is neither true nor real, literally speaking, it is, nevertheless, helpful to create a mental picture of the security and stability of the righteous. While the security of the righteous is a true concept and a real experience, David used a simile to enable his readers to picture this in their minds.

The mental images created by such figurative language as symbol or analogy are always inferior to the reality which they try to picture. Hence, the reality is always far greater than the mental image created by the figurative language. The security of the righteous is far greater than the mental image of the security of a tree planted by streams of water.

This brief overview of the function of figurative language will be extremely important in our study of death. The failure to observe the presence and function of figurative language is perhaps the most common error in the literature on the subject.

First, there are those who do not recognize the presence of figurative language. The biblical authors used the mental image of the gnawing worms and smoldering fires in the city dump called Gehenna, which was right outside Jerusalem, in order to produce a vivid and striking picture of future judgment. They did not intend to be understood as saying that there will be a literal garbage dump with literal worms and fire.[20] When Christ referred to hell as the place where the "worm does not die and the fire is not quenched" (Mark 9:48), He was using a rabbinic figure of speech which was well known at the time. The rabbinic literature before and during the life of Christ used the mental picture of the worms and fire connected with the city dump in the valley of Gehenna to illustrate the doctrine of everlasting punishment. Christ was not teaching that hell will involve literal worms gnawing at literal bodies.

Second, there are those who assume that the presence of figurative language means the absence of any meaning. They are ignorant of the fact that doctrine can come from figures of speech.[21] Once they grasp that "hell fire" is used in a metaphorical sense, they dismiss the concept which fire tries to picture. Thus, the typical Universalist and annihilationist will dismiss the idea of everlasting, conscious torment because of the figures of speech which were used to create a mental image of it. For example, it is very common for such writers to dismiss Christ's teaching in Luke 16:19–31 because they feel it is a "parable."[22] Evidently, they assume that if it is a parable, it can be dismissed as not teaching anything. This is the result of a gross ignorance of the most basic understanding of the use of figurative language. Figurative language is used to create mental images to enable people to understand some aspect of a past, present or future reality.

Third, there are those who correctly understand that figurative language illustrates some kind of reality, but they incorrectly assume that the reality is of a lesser nature or power than what the figure portrays. Thus "hell fire" becomes temporary remorse or grief. But this assumption is due to ignorance of the function of figurative language. The reality is always greater than the mental image created by figurative speech.[23] Thus hell will be more horrible than the mental image of eternal worms gnawing on eternal bodies or being lost in an eternal lake of sulfuric fire. Hell will be greater than all the weak and feeble metaphors which human language can provide.

Since hell is a future reality which no one has yet seen, the authors of Scripture and the Master himself used what was available in the situation to describe the awfulness of ultimate separation from God.

This explains how and why mixed metaphors are used to describe hell. Jude can use the rabbinic metaphor of the horror, loneliness and despair of being lost in "the black darkness forever" in

Jude 13, while John can speak of being cast into the anger of God by the rabbinic metaphor of a "lake of fire and brimstone" (Rev. 20:10). There is no need to solve the literalist's riddle of how can hell be dark and yet be fire, by locating hell in a black hole in space. Neither the darkness nor fire are literal.

Hell is described by many different figures of speech, each emphasizing a different aspect of ultimate alienation from God. None are to be taken in a literal sense. But all are to be viewed as weak and feeble attempts to mentally picture something so horrible that the most awful situations here on earth cannot adequately describe it.

In this light, it becomes clear that the literalists who demand literal darkness and fire have actually done the opposite of what they intended to do by demanding a literal interpretation. They refuse to accept the literary fact that metaphors are used in Scripture to describe hell because they are afraid that this would make hell less than what it was intended to be. They are zealous to guard the truth of future perdition. But by hanging on to the metaphors and claiming that they should be understood literally, they have made hell *less* than what it was intended to be.[24] Hell will be far more terrifying than being thrown alive into a lake of sulfuric fire.

The annihilationists are just as guilty here as well. When they take the position that the wicked will pass into nothingness, they fail to see that nothingness is less in nature and power than the figures of endless torment given in Scripture. Thus, the concept of annihilation would never generate such terrifying mental images as given in Scripture.

As a matter of fact, annihilation is an idea which makes hell less than what it was intended to be by having it mean nothingness. In fact, if hell is nothingness, what mental images can be called upon to conceive of it? There is no mental image for "nothing." Whence came all the terrifying mental images of hell given in Scripture? Evidently the authors of Scripture attempted to depict hell as *something*, not nothing. If annihilation were true, then there would be no need for the terrifying mental images of figurative speech used in the Bible to describe hell.

CONCLUSION

The study of Scripture is an exciting and rewarding task. The rules and principles of hermeneutics are meant to strengthen the joy of interpretation by teaching people how to avoid those linguistic and literary mistakes which would lead to a misunderstanding of the Scriptures. There would be a great deal more uniformity among Christians on doctrinal matters if they would avoid eisegesis and interpret Scripture according to sound hermeneutical principles. With these basic principles in mind, we will now begin our investigation of the biblical teaching on death.

NOTES

1. L. Berkhof, *Principles of Biblical Interpretation* (Grand Rapids: Baker Book House, 1950); B. Mickelsen, *Interpreting the Bible* (Grand Rapids: Wm. B. Eerdmans Pub. Co., 1979); B. Ramm, *Protestant Biblical Interpretation* (Boston: W.A. Wilde Co., 1956); M. Terry, *Biblical Hermeneutics* (Grand Rapids: Zondervan Pub. Co.).

2. R. Wilson, *A Scientific Investigation of the Old Testament* (Chicago: Moody Press, 1959); O.T. Allis, *The Five Books of Moses* (Philadelphia: Presbyterian and Reformed Pub. Co., 1964); J. McDowell, *More Evidence Which Demands a Verdict* (Campus Crusade for Christ International, 1975).

3. G. Clark, *Karl Barth's Theological Method* (Philadelphia: Pres. & Ref. Pub. Co., 1963); C. Henry, *Frontiers in Modern Theology* (Chicago: Moody Press, 1965); D. Guthrie, *New Testament Introduction* (Chicago: InterVarsity Press, 1966), Vol. I; C. Van Til, *Christianity and Barthianism* (Nutley, N.J.: Pres. & Ref. Pub. Co., 1965); ibid., *The New Hermeneutic*, loc. cit., 1974.

4. J. Sire, *Scripture Twisting—20 Ways the Cults Misread the Bible* (Downers Grove, Ill.: InterVarsity Press, 1980).

5. Hellwig and Coons were virtually alone in this concern for hermeneutics in their discussions of death.

6. *The Infallible Word* (ed. Paul Wooley; Philadelphia: Pres. & Ref. Pub. Co., 1946), pp. 204–205.

"The writers of Scripture were under the necessity of using words in the common meaning attached to them at the time. . . . The Bible was written to be intelligible to contemporaries. It was not something essentially esoteric which could have no immediate usefulness to the people of the times when its various parts were being written."

7. A. Hodge, *Evangelical Theology* (London: Banner of Truth Trust, 1976), p. 390.

8. B. Ramm, *Hermeneutics* (Grand Rapids: Baker Book House, 1980), p. 21f.; B. Ramm, *Protestant Principles of Interpretation*, ibid., p. 111f.; Terry, ibid., p. 566f.; G. Vos, *Biblical Theology* (Grand Rapids: Wm. B. Eerdmans Pub. Co., 1969).

9. E. Plumtre, *The Spirits in Prison* (New York, Thomas Whittaker, 1885), p. 31; E. Young, *The Study of Old Testament Theology Today* (London: James Clarke and Co., Ltd., 1958).

10. E. White, *The Great Controversy Between Christ and Satan*

(Washington, D.C.: Review and Herald Pub. Assoc., 1911), p. 617; *Let God Be True* (New York: Watchtower Bible and Tract Society, Inc., 1946), pp. 76–80; *Make Sure All Things* (New York: Watchtower Bible and Tract Society, Inc., 1965), pp. 142–144; L. Froom, *The Conditionalist Faith of Our Fathers* (Washington, D.C.: Review and Herald Pub., 1966), Vol. I, p. 76f.

11. A. Chambers, *Our Life After Death* (Philadelphia: George Jacobs & Co., 1897); J. Kester, The Life Beyond Death (Nashville: Southern Baptist Convention, 1930).

12. W.G.T. Shedd, *The Doctrine of Endless Punishment* (Minnesota: Klock & Klock Christian Pub., 1980), p. 29.

13. E. Jungel, *Death: The Riddle and the Mystery* (Philadelphia: Westminster Press, 1974).

14. Mickelsen, ibid., pp. 114–177; Terry, ibid., pp. 175–180.

15. B. Ramm, *Protestant Principles of Interpretation*, loc. cit., p. 129.

16. Kittel's *Theological Dictionary of the New Testament*, clearly guilty of this error in its treatment of the word "soul" in Vol. IX, p. 608f.

17. *Is This Life All There Is?* (New York: Watchtower Bible and Tract Society, Inc., 1974).

18. John 5:24; 6:47; 11:25, 26; etc.

19. Mickelsen, ibid., pp. 99–113.

20. Ramm, ibid., p. 110.

21. Terry, ibid., p. 593.

22. R. Whitelaw, *Hell the Abode of the Dead* (Virginia: G.A.M., 1981), pp. 19–26.

23. C.S. Lewis, *Miracles* (New York: The Macmillan Co., 1947), pp. 46–53; Mickelsen, ibid., pp. 318–322.

24. Terry, ibid., p. 591.

Chapter 2

BODY, SOUL, AND SPIRIT

"What is man?" is one of the most practical questions that anyone could possibly consider. It is practical because its answer forms the basis of our self-image. And our self-image influences to a great degree how we act. The great Jewish philosopher, King Solomon, put it this way:

> As [a man] thinks within himself, so he is. (Prov. 23:7)

THE NATURE OF MAN

The question of the nature of man has been a consistent problem in the history of Western thought from the days of the pre-Socratic philosophers to the present time. While a complete discussion of this subject is not permissible within the limits of this volume, nevertheless, a few remarks should be made in order to clear the way for an explanation of the biblical position on the nature of man.

Beginning with the Enlightenment, the attempt has been made to view man as a machine. As such, he is viewed as being part of the giant cosmic machine and is hopelessly trapped within a deterministic universe because there is no part of man which transcends the material. All man does and thinks is mechanistically determined by such irrational forces as genetic factors, chemical secretions, environmental conditioning, and class consciousness. He does not have a soul or mind, i.e., something which is not of a material nature and which transcends or escapes the determinism of the cosmic machine.

The end result of such depressing views as described above reduced man to being merely an animal or a machine. Whereas in historic Christianity man was viewed as standing uniquely outside of the cosmic machine because he had been made in the image of God, now he was viewed as being only a part of the cosmic machine and no different from any other machine or animal. Instead of being "like God," man was reduced to being "like a dog."

Since the materialist's answer to the great question of man's nature is reductionistic and self-refuting, as we shall outline later in our chapter on the subject, many people in the late 20th century have turned to various modern revivals of ancient pagan mythologies in which man is neither "like a dog" nor "like God" but is God. There is an explosion of pseudo-pagan cults in the West which all deify man. This represents a violent swing of the pendulum from the extreme of materialism to the extreme of mystic deification.

In the context of modern society, most people are thus confronted with two choices: Either man is nothing but a machine, or he is God. The Christian answer that man is neither machine nor God is completely ignored. It is for this reason that a brief overview of the Christian answer to the question of man's nature must be presented at this point.

THE CHRISTIAN ANSWER

The Christian answer is found in the Holy Scriptures which form the basis of historic Christianity. When we turn to the Bible with the question of man's nature in mind, we find that the biblical authors wrestled directly with the question "What is man?"

> When I consider Thy heavens, the work of Thy fingers, the moon and the stars, which Thou hast ordained; what is man, that Thou dost take thought of him? And the son of man, that Thou dost care for him? Yet Thou hast made him a little lower than God, and dost crown him with glory and majesty! Thou dost make him to rule over the works of Thy hands; Thou hast put all things under his feet, all sheep and oxen, and also the beasts of the field, the birds of the heavens, and the fish of the sea, whatever passes through the paths of the seas. (Ps. 8:3–8)

In giving the biblical answer to the question of the nature of man, we must first recognize that the question is incomplete because the Scriptures view all of life in terms of the creation, the radical fall of man into sin, and God's plan of redemption.[1] These three concepts are foundational to the biblical explanation of the existence and form of the universe. They are foundational presuppositions which make up the biblical world view. To understand anything correctly is to view it in the light of these basic truths of the Scriptures.

Chronologically, these are the first truths we encounter in the Bible because they are foundational to all that follows. For example, in Genesis 1 through 3, we find that Moses unfolds the three truths of creation, fall, and redemption. Also, thematically, everything else in Scripture is a development of these three themes. In the Old Testament and in the New Testament, we are constantly reminded of these three great events. Also, exegetically, these three truths serve as spectacles, or glasses, through which we can understand and deal with present problems and issues.

When Jesus dealt with the issue of marriage and divorce, He approached it in terms of what marriage ought to be on the basis of what it was at the creation. Then He looked at marriage from the perspective of the fall, because sin explains why divorce was granted to man (Matt. 19:1–8).

The Apostle Paul also used creation, fall, and redemption as the glasses through which he could examine from the biblical perspective: (1) the respective role and function of male and female in the context of the home and the church (1 Cor. 11:3–12; 1 Tim. 2:12–14); (2) whether certain foods are evil and should not be eaten by Christians (1 Tim. 4:1–5); (3) why the universe is in a state of groaning and travailing; and (4) why the Christian has the hope that the creation itself will be delivered from the effect of Adam's fall into sin (Rom. 9:19–23).

Starting with the given presuppositions of creation, fall, and redemption, we can develop a distinctively Christian position on the issues which confront us on every side. This Christian position will be seen as being in direct opposition to the opposing non-Christian concepts.

Viewing the question of man's nature from the biblical perspective of creation, fall, and redemption, we see at once that the question "What is man?" must be broken into three separate questions.

What was man at the creation? (past)
What is man after the fall? (present)
What is man after redemption? (future)

"What is man?" is a complicated question. It involves three separate questions and answers. Failure to recognize this has led to all kinds of reductionistic answers from Christians and non-Christians alike. To assume that what man is today is what he was in the past and will be in the future is an unwarranted assumption which the biblical authors directly contradict. A "Christian" anthropology will therefore take into consideration what man was at creation, what he is after the fall, and what he is after redemption if it is to be a biblically complete anthropology.

Creation: An Image-Bearer

The biblical teaching on creation explains the noble side of man. Man is not a part of the cosmic machine, because he is a special creation of God. Thus he is not a dog or a god, but man was made in "the image of God."

> Then God said, "Let Us make man in Our image, according to Our likeness; and let them rule over the fish of the sea and over the birds of the sky, and over the cattle and over all the earth, and over every creeping thing that creeps on the earth." And God created man in His own image, in the image of God He created him; male and female He created them. (Gen. 1:26, 27)

As the image-bearer of God, man was created with true free will and was not mechanistically determined by internal or external factors, because he was created to reflect God's free and sovereign will in subduing the world.

> And God blessed them; and God said to them, "Be fruitful and multiply, and fill the earth, and subdue it; and rule over the fish of the sea and over the birds of the sky, and over every living thing that moves on the earth." (Gen. 1:28)

Thus the world was not made to control man in some mechanistic or deterministic way, but man was made to control the world in a personal and rational way.

What is the "image of God" in which man was created? Despite all the elaborate attempts to read highly technical, theological, and philosophical concepts into the biblical words "the image of God," we should take them in their simplest meaning as they would have been understood by the people to whom Moses wrote. In this sense, "the image of God" simply meant that man was created to be and do on a finite level what God was and did on an infinite level.

Man was created to reflect God in the created order. Thus, we do not need to divide up the image of God into such categories as "inner and outer," "higher and lower," etc. Neither should we reduce the image-bearing capacity of man to one of his functions such as reason, language, or emotion. The "image of God" simply means that man reflects his creator in those capacities and capabilities which separate him from the rest of the creation. The nobility, uniqueness, meaning, worth and significance of man all rest on his being made in the image of God and being placed over the world as God's prophet, priest, and king (Gen. 1:26, 27). This is why the Apostle Paul could refer to Jesus as the messianic image-bearer of God (Col. 1:15). As the second Adam, Christ was the full and complete image-bearer. This is why Christ could say that to see Him was to see the Father (John 14:9). Christ reflected on a finite level as the second Adam what the Father was like on an infinite level.

In terms of our self-image, we must view ouselves as uniquely wonderful, intrinsically valuable and richly invested with meaning, significance and purpose. Man was created to glorify God and to enjoy Him and His creation. Man is not worthless.

In the light of the dignity and worth of man as the unique

image-bearer of God, we cannot accept, therefore, the idea of the conditional immortalitists that man's death can be reduced to the death of brute beasts. What they fail to realize is that man is far too wonderful to die like a dog. A conscious afterlife is exactly what we would expect of such a wonderful creation as man.

The Fall: A Rebel Sinner

The biblical account of man's historic fall out of a state of righteousness and holiness into a state of sin and condemnation explains the dark side of man (Gen. 3). After his creation, man was God's image-bearer. After the fall, man became Satan's image-bearer as well. This is why the biblical authors used such language as "the children of the devil" to describe sinners. They used a rabbinic metaphor which simply meant that sinners were Satan's image-bearers in that they did on a human level what Satan did on a demonic level. Christ himself used this rabbinic metaphor in John 8:38–44.

> "I speak the things which I have seen with My Father; therefore you also do the things which you heard from your father." They answered and said to Him, "Abraham is our father." Jesus said to them, "If you are Abraham's children, do the deeds of Abraham. But as it is, you are seeking to kill Me, a man who has told you the truth, which I heard from God; this Abraham did not do. You are doing the deeds of your father." They said to Him, "We were not born of fornication; we have one Father, even God." Jesus said to them, "If God were your Father, you would love Me; for I proceeded forth and have come from God, for I have not even come on My own initiative, but He sent Me. Why do you not understand what I am saying? It is because you cannot hear My word. You are of your father the devil, and you want to do the desires of your father. He was a murderer from the beginning, and does not stand in the truth, because there is no truth in him. Whenever he speaks a lie, he speaks from his own nature, for he is a liar, and the father of lies."

This is not to say that man is no longer God's image-bearer. In James 3:9, man is still viewed as being made in the image of God. But this image has been marred and defaced by man's sin. While man is still *man*, he is now a *sinful* man.

The fall revolved around man's rebellion against God and focused on his attempt to become as God. Satan's lie was to tell them that if they ate of the fruit, they would become like God himself (Gen. 3:5). The temptation to self-deification proved effective on Adam and Eve and they ate the fruit.

This lie of self-deification is at the base of all Eastern religions which view man as "God" or a part of God. It is also the driving force behind all the cultic and occultic Western groups which promise us deification. The "mind" cults tell us that we are God. The Mormons and Armstrongites promise that we will become gods. They are all based on Satan's lie that man can escape his creatureliness and become deity.

The radical nature of the fall explains on a finite level why we have a problem with evil. People lie, cheat, steal, murder and rape because they are sinners by nature, i.e., "children of wrath" (Eph. 2:3). In the wake of Adam's sin and guilt (Rom. 5:12), all men are constituted rebel sinners (Rom. 3:23). God is never the author or agent of evil (James 1:13–17). Man is his own worst enemy.

In terms of our self-image, we should view ourselves as rebel sinners as well as image-bearers. In fact, it is man's capacity as God's image-bearer that makes sin so awful. Man's creation purpose magnifies his sin and rebellion.

It is at this point that many modern theologians fail. They are all in favor of viewing man as God's image-bearer. But they don't want anything to do with the fall. They attempt to mythologize it or to turn it into a poem. But this approach fails to explain how and why men do the evil that they do. The liberal view tries desperately to view men as good and perfectable through humanistic means. But all such attempts have failed.

The biblical teaching on a real fall allows us to escape the Pollyanna world of liberal theology. It corresponds to what is there. When we look in a mirror, we see our dark side as well as our noble side. In all we do, there is evil present (Rom. 7:21). There is no way to escape the reality of man's sin and its tragic effects. Without a real historic fall, there is no explanation for the present condition of man.

The fall is also the basis of the biblical understanding of death. While the creation does not explain why or how man dies or what happens after death, the radical nature of man's fall into sin and guilt explains it.

First, the Bible speaks of the fact of death (Heb. 9:27). The inescapable reality of death faces all of us and removes all the vain humanistic hopes for immortality in this life.

Science may make many discoveries, but it will never conquer death. The occult arts may promise a way to avoid death, but in the end they fail. The cults, such as Christian Science, may deny it as a teaching, but they all experience it as a reality. God has ordained the hour of our death, and no one can hinder or hurry His plan (Job 14:1–5; Eccles. 3:1, 2; Heb. 9:27).

Second, the Bible describes the origin of death. Death is a divine punishment for man's disobedience. Through the consequences of the fall and our own personal sins, the Grim Reaper comes to harvest our souls for judgment (Rom. 5:12–17; 6:23; Heb. 9:27; James 1:14, 15). This means that death is not "natural," "normal," or "human." It is unnatural and subnormal. All the humanistic concepts about death being "natural" or part of human nature are false. Death is the terrible and unnatural ripping of the soul out of man's body. Death tears man in half. Man was made to live, not to die.

Christian Attitude	Humanist Attitude
1. Death is unnatural.	1. Death is natural.
2. Death flows from sin.	2. Death is part of life.
3. Death is a time of sorrow (John 11:33–39).	3. Death should mean little or nothing to us.
4. Death will be done away with when Jesus returns (Rev. 21:4).	4. Death will always be here.

Third, the Bible explains the nature of death in terms of separation, not annihilation. It is the leaving of the soul or spirit from the body that causes death.

> And it came about as her soul was departing (for she died), that she named him Ben-oni; but his father called him Benjamin. (Gen. 35:18)
> Remember Him before the silver cord is broken and the golden bowl is crushed, the pitcher by the well is shattered and the wheel at the cistern is crushed; then the dust will return to the earth as it was, and the spirit will return to God who gave it. (Eccles. 12:6, 7)
> For just as the body without the spirit is dead, so also faith without works is dead. (James 2:26)

While we will discuss soul sleep in our chapter on annihilationism, we must point out that the concept of death as a state of nonexistence is patently absurd.

The day on which Adam and Eve ate the fruit was the day of their death (Gen. 2:17; 3:3). They were separated from God and cut off from His fellowship (Gen. 3:8, 23). Their death meant separation, not annihilation.

Is it any wonder that physical death is used to describe man's spiritual death. Thus man is "dead" in sin (Eph. 2:1). This spiritual death is defined as being separated from the grace and gifts of God in Eph. 2:12, 13. Later in 1 Tim. 5:6, Paul described wanton widows as "dead even while she lives." Surely he did not mean "nonexistent."

Jesus said, "Let the dead bury their dead." It is obvious that Jesus was not saying, "Let the nonexistent ones bury the nonexistent ones or the unconscious ones bury the unconscious ones." He was simply referring to those who were separated from God as being dead while they yet lived.

Lastly, the Bible speaks of the character of death in that it is called the "last [great] enemy" (1 Cor. 15:26, 54–56; Heb. 2:14–18). Death is viewed as being a mixture of good and evil. Death can mean release from this life to be with Christ which is far better than being in the body (Phil. 1:21–24), while, at the same time, death can be viewed as the last great enemy which will be destroyed when Jesus comes back.

Redemption: A Child of God

The biblical concept of redemption explains the hopeful side of man because man is not only viewed as redeemable but worth redeeming.

Man's intrinsic worth and significance as the image-bearer of God is magnified by the lengths to which God went to redeem him. That God would himself undertake the task of personally atoning for the sins of His people is astounding. No other religion in history ever conceived of a vicarious atonement performed by incarnate deity as the full and complete salvation from sin and its effect.[2]

In the Scriptures, God's work of redemption is viewed as climaxing in the act of adoption by which rebel sinners became the children of God by faith in Christ Jesus (John 1:12; Gal. 3:26). In the resurrection, the children of God will be publicly revealed and enthroned as the heirs of the cosmos (Rom. 8:17–23).

The biblical teaching on the sufficiency of Christ's atonement completely undercuts the theory of reincarnation or transmigration. Since Christ's death cleanses us from "all sin" (1 John 1:7) and purges the believers from all moral evil (Heb. 1:3), there is no need for a Karmic cycle of rebirths by which a person is eventually purged of evil by his or her own suffering. Since Christ has suffered in our place and nailed our sins to His cross (1 Pet. 2:24), we do not need to make any other sacrifices to atone for our sins. By His one sacrifice for all time and eternity, Christ Jesus has perfected forever those who come to God through Him (Heb. 10:10, 12, 14).

In terms of our self-image, if we have accepted Jesus Christ as our prophet, priest, and king, we should not only view ourselves as image-bearers and redeemed sinners, but also as the children of God and the heirs of the cosmos.

When we look in a mirror and meditate on what we think, say and do, we find that our experience is understandable only if we view ourselves through the biblical glasses of creation, fall, and redemption. It is the failure to grasp all three principles that leads to dire psychological as well as philosophical and theological consequences. The degree to which we embrace our threefold self-image will determine the degree to which we will have a healthy and holistic self-image.

UNITY AND DIVERSITY

Another aspect of man's nature which confronts us in our experience, as well as in Scripture, is that just as God's nature must be understood in terms of unity and diversity, even so man's nature must be understood in terms of unity and diversity.

The Scriptures describe God in terms of unity and diversity. Thus Christians believe in one God eternally existing in three persons or centers of consciousness which the Scriptures call the Father, the Son and the Spirit. To reduce God only to the Father or to the Son is a biblical error which is the basis of many cultic and occultic groups today.[3] Both errors reflect the philosophic tendency to place unity in opposition to diversity and to affirm one over the other. The root of this tendency can be traced back to the problem of the One and Many in early Greek philosophy.

The problem of the One and Many, or unity and diversity, directly applies to man as well as to God. Does man's nature reflect unity and diversity or must we restrict man's nature to being either unity or diversity?

All secular and religious materialists assert that life is wholly physical. They deny that man has an invisible and immortal mind, soul or spirit. They argue that the unity of man implies that man's nature is wholly physical. They stress the unity of man as an argument against his having an immortal soul.

Various Eastern religions and modern Western cults stress that man's nature is wholly spiritual or mental. They deny that man has a material body or they downgrade the body as evil and look upon it as not really part of man but only as the receptacle which the mind or soul indwells.

Man is thus viewed as being a spiritual or mental being. The Christian Science cult is an example of this kind of reasoning. Mrs. Eddy put it this way:

> Man is not matter. He is not made up of brains, blood, bones, and other material elements. . . . Man is spiritual and perfect . . . he is not physique. (*Science and Health*, p. 475, vv. 6–12)

We are thus left with two extreme positions. Man is viewed as either wholly material or wholly spiritual. Both positions are reductionistic and reflect the tendency to deny diversity and to overemphasize unity. As such, they both fail to adequately explain man.

To deny the physical or spiritual aspects of man is to deny reality because human experience cannot be reduced exclusively to one or the other.

The Biblical Picture

The Scriptures do not commit the reductionistic fallacy of limiting human nature to either the physical or the spiritual side of man. Just as it views God in terms of unity and diversity, it describes man as manifesting unity and diversity as well. Thus man's nature is not simply material or nonmaterial but both. Man cannot be reduced to being physical or psychical, but must be viewed as both. He is not just body *or* soul but body *and* soul.

The biblical picture of man avoids the errors of denying the existence of the material or nonmaterial side of man, downgrading either side as evil or viewing the body as only a receptacle and not an essential part of human nature.

The Two Sides of Man

In the context of the unity and diversity of human nature, the Scriptures speak of man as having two sides, or participating in two levels of reality. As C. S. Lewis put it, man cannot simply be reduced to being either wholly a material or immaterial being. He is both, and the Christian Church has always viewed man as being comprised of two sides.[4]

The material side of man is his body. Man was created as a material being in order to be able to interreact with the other material beings and objects around him in this world (Gen. 2:7). The human body and all material objects as such are not to be viewed as being intrinsically evil but are to be viewed as being intrinsically good (Gen. 1:31; 1 Tim. 4:4). This is why the resurrection is essential to Christian thinking. While some Eastern and Western religions view salvation as the soul being set free from an evil body, the Scriptures view salvation as ultimately resulting in a perfected soul returning to a perfected body at the resurrection. Salvation in the Bible is consistently viewed in a holistic sense as involving both sides of man. Thus the Apostle Paul could look forward to the time when both sides of man would be entirely sanctified, preserved completely, without blame at the coming of the Lord Jesus Christ (1 Thess. 5:23).

Man's immaterial side is given many different names in Scripture. No attempt was ever made by the authors of the Scriptures to define the metaphysical or philosophical nature or essence of the invisible side of man. It is always described in terms of how man functions, or how he relates to God, the world around him or the next life. Thus these terms should not be viewed as referring to separate entities in man but as simply describing man's multi-dimensional functions and relationships.

The biblical authors used whatever words or terms were available to them in their historical and linguistic situation to describe the immaterial side of man. They used the same words which all the religions around them were using to describe man's immortal and immaterial self, or ego.

If the biblical authors did not believe that man had an immaterial side, they would not have used such terms as "soul," which would indicate this to the hearer of their day. Thus the mere presence of such terms in the Bible as "soul" reveals the absurdity of those who claim that the authors did not believe that man had an immaterial side or soul. After all, it only stands to reason that if the authors did not believe there was more to man than his body, they would not have used those exact words in the cultural context which would directly refer to man's immaterial and immortal side.

The following are the terms used by the authors of Scripture to describe the immaterial side of man. These terms are not technical words in the sense that they have one consistent meaning throughout Scripture. They display unity and diversity by being synonymous at times when referring to the immaterial side of man, and at other times, referring to different functions or ways of relating. It is obvious that we should not impose 20th-century standards of consistency and linguistic preciseness to a book which was written thousands of years ago. Each term may have a dozen different meanings, depending on the context and the progressive nature of revelation.

The failure to avoid reductionistic and simplistic definitions is based on the hidden assumption that once the meaning of a word is discovered in a single passage, this same meaning must prevail in every other occurrence of the word. For example, it has become quite fashionable to restrict the meaning of the word "soul" to "physical life" because this was probably what it meant when it was used by Moses to refer to the immaterial life principle within animals (Gen. 1:20) or within man (Gen. 2:7).

Once the annihilationists and some neo-orthodox writers demonstrated that the word "soul" in Gen. 2:7 (KJV) probably means "living beings," they then pronounce that this is the *only* definition of soul which is allowed. Whenever other passages are presented where the context demands another definition of the word "soul," they lay these passages aside and retreat to Gen. 2:7.

As long as they fail to understand the progressive character revelation and the resulting deepening understanding of words and concepts, they will be stuck in Gen. 2:7. The resistance to the idea that what soul meant to Moses was probably not what it meant to David or Paul is based on their unconscious assumption that the Bible is one book written at one time. Thus as we approach the biblical term which describes the immaterial side of man, we will not attempt to develop artificial definitions based upon the absolutizing of the meaning of a word in a single passage but recognize that a contextual approach will reveal a wide range of meanings.

OLD TESTAMENT TERMS

Nephesh: Soul

The word *nephesh* is found in the Hebrew Bible 754 times. It is translated in the King James Version as follows:

Soul: 472 times	Me: 3 times
Life: 118 times	Lust: 2 times
Person: 30 times	Ghost: 2 times
Self: 20 times	Appetite: 2 times
Heart: 16 times	They: 2 times
Mind: 15 times	You: 1 time
The dead: 12 times	Them: 1 time
Creature: 8 times	We: 1 time
He, him, her: 8 times	Discontent: 1 time
Desire: 5 times	Breath: 1 time
Will: 4 times	Mortality: 1 time
Man: 4 times	Fish: 1 time
Any or one: 4 times	Dogs: 1 time
Pleasure: 3 times	Deadly: 1 time
Beast: 3 times	Tablet: 1 time

THE LEXICOGRAPHICAL MATERIAL

Brown, Driver, and Briggs point out in *A Hebrew and English Lexicon of the Old Testament* (p. 659) that *nephesh* has three basic meanings: the life principle, figurative usage, and the inner being, or soul, of man which "departs at death and returns with life at the resurrection." Langenscheidt's *Hebrew-English Dictionary to the Old Testament* (p. 220) defines *nephesh* as referring to the self, or mind, as well as life. No lexicographical material was found which restricted *nephesh* to the principle of physical life.

THE EXEGETICAL EVIDENCE

First, the word *nephesh* refers to that invisible and immaterial life principle which animates the bodies of animals and man. In

Gen. 1:20, 21, 24, 30; 2:19; 9:10, etc., an animal is call a *nephesh* as long as it is living. A dead animal is never called a *nephesh* because its body would be devoid of the life principle. In this sense, once the life principle was breathed into the body of Adam, he became a *nephesh*, i.e., a living creature (Gen. 2:7).

When the life principle departs from the bodies of animals or men, they die. Thus, the Old Testament used *nephesh* to refer to the principle of physical life approximately 150 times.

That *nephesh* is an immaterial and invisible life principle is seen from the fact that Adam's body was complete yet unanimated until God placed in it "the spirit of life," i.e., the life principle (Gen. 2:7). The idea of spontaneous generation (i.e., life arises out of non-life) is demonstrably false on every account. Adam did not become alive when his body was complete. His body awaited the introduction of the invisible and immaterial life principle before he could become a *nephesh*, that is, a living creature.

Second, the word *nephesh* is used in figurative language. The biblical authors often used synecdoches; i.e., they used a part to represent the whole in a figurative sense. Thus *nephesh* sometimes meant the whole person, as in Gen. 36:6 where the people in the household were called *nepheshim*.[5] It is in this sense that the Jews were told not to touch dead people (Lev. 21:1, 11). Even though the life principle was gone, the word *nephesh* was used in a figurative sense to speak of a person as a whole. Or again, since blood is used as symbol of life, *nephesh* is figuratively spoken of as "life blood" (Lev. 17:10, 11).

Third, *nephesh* is used to describe the part of man which transcends the life principle, separates him from animals and likens him unto God.

God is a self-conscious being who as a cognitive ego can say, "I am." Thus God swears by His *nephesh*, i.e., His soul, or "self" in Jer. 51:14 and Amos 6:8. In this sense, God is said to possess a "mind," "will," "heart," "emotions," "self," etc. (Job 23:13). The *nephesh*, or soul, of God is His transcendent self which hates sin (Ps. 11:5). In no way can God's *nephesh* be reduced to the principle of physical life, because God does not have a physical body.

When *nephesh* is used of God, it obviously transcends the mere life principle of animals who do not have self-awareness. In the same way, *nephesh* is used to describe that part of man which transcends the life principle.

Man, as God's image-bearer, is a cognitive ego who can say, "I am." Thus *nephesh* was translated to indicate that man possesses mind, emotions, will, heart, ego, self, etc.

It is this transcendent self that is traditionally called "the soul." At death the transcendent self as well as the life principle leaves the body. The word *nephesh* was often used in the Old Testament to describe activities and relationships which were sustained in this present world. However, when a person died and his transcendent self, or ego, went to Sheol, he was said to be "cut off" from the living. This does not logically imply that the person was not now functioning on a different level in another world. Being cut off from this world cannot logically be used to argue that the person cannot consciously exist in another world.

Those who teach "soul sleep," i.e., man is extinguished at death or passes into an unconscious state, have always sought to restrict the meaning of the word *nephesh* to the principle of physical life. They have emphasized that animals as well as man have the life principle. They resist any idea that man has a transcendent self, or ego, which can be distinguished from his physical life. They take the verses where man's physical life is cut off or "destroyed" and then state that there is nothing in man which survives death. The fate of a man and a dog are viewed as being the same.

First, we must point out that this position fails to take into account that *nephesh* has more than one meaning. It is used in a figurative sense in many different ways. Second, this position goes too far in making man's soul no more than the soul of animals. They have obviously reduced man's soul to the soul of animals in order to argue that a man and a dog experience the same fate at death, that is, extinction. That man may be resurrected one day does not alleviate the fact that man's death is reduced to the death of a dog.

That man has a soul which transcends the mere principle of physical life which is shared by animals and by man is clear from the following points:

1. If man's soul is to be solely understood as being no more or no less than the soul of animals, why should the Scriptures speak of the necessity of making an atonement to redeem man's soul? (Lev. 16). The blood atonement makes no sense whatsoever if man's soul is reduced to that of physical life shared by animals. Man's soul obviously transcends the mere principle of physical life. The infinite value of man's soul makes no sense if it is reduced to the same level as the "souls" of animals (Mark 8:36).

2. When the people were told to afflict their soul (Lev. 16:29; 23:27, 32, etc.), this cannot mean that they were expected to torment the body or life principle, but it must refer to experiencing grief and sorrow in their transcendent self.

3. If we use the words "life principle" or "physical life" and insert them into every passage where *nephesh* is found, it becomes obvious that *nephesh* has more than one meaning. It also becomes clear that *nephesh* cannot be simply reduced to the principle of phys-

ical life. For example, there is no way that the principle of physical life could be understood as being that part of man which worships God (Deut. 10:12), sorrows (Lev. 26:16), feels bitterness (1 Sam. 1:10), misery (Judg. 10:16), grief (1 Sam. 2:33) or alienation (Ezek. 23:17, 18). Can the life principle shared by man and animals "thirst after God"? (Ps. 42:2).

The Old Testament Scriptures are clear that there is a *nephesh* in man that transcends the life principle and to which is attributed reason, emotion, will, and worship. Unless one is willing to attribute such things to animals, it must be concluded that man's nature ultimately transcends the animal principle of physical life.

4. There are passages where physical life is contrasted to the higher *nephesh*, or soul of man (2 Sam. 11:11). They echo Isa. 1:14 (KJV) where God is said to have a soul. That God's soul must be interpreted as referring to His immaterial and invisible transcendent self and that it cannot mean physical life or life principle is obvious. In the same way, man's self is also transcendent and cannot be reduced to the life of the body. This is why man's body is called a house of clay in which the transcendent self, or soul, dwells (Job 7:10). The body was thus viewed as the place where man's soul dwelled. But the body was never equated with the soul.

5. The importance of the kind of phraseology used in the Old Testament to describe death and resurrection must not be overlooked at this point. Writers who argue for soul sleep speak of death in terms of extinction. They use such metaphors as the turning off and on of an electric switch to explain death and resurrection. In their view, the soul does not leave the body at death and it does not return to dwell in the body at resurrection. The soul is restricted to the life principle within the body and this is switched off at death and on at resurrection.

The orthodox speak of death in terms of the transcendent self or conscious soul leaving the body to dwell elsewhere and returning back to dwell in the body at the resurrection. The soul's leaving and returning explains death and resurrection.

In the Old Testament, death and resurrection are consistently spoken of in terms of the leaving and returning of the soul. In the following Old Testament passages death and resurrection are spoken of in terms of the departure and return of the soul.

> And it came about as her soul was departing (for she died), that she named him Ben-oni; but his father called him Benjamin. (Gen. 35:18)
> And he stretched himself upon the child three times, and cried unto the Lord, and said, O Lord my God, I pray thee, let this child's soul come into him again. And the Lord heard the voice of Elijah; and the soul of the child came into him again,

and he revived. (1 Kings 17:21, 22, KJV)

If the authors of Scripture did not believe that the soul left the body at death and would return to the body at resurrection, they would not have used such phraseology. Their manner of speaking reveals they believed that man ultimately survived the death of the body.

6. The continuing problem of necromancy in Israel's history has been noted by many scholars as clear evidence that the Jews did not believe in soul sleep.[6] Necromancy is the attempt to communicate with the departed conscious souls in Sheol. For example, Saul attempted to contact Samuel's soul by having the medium of Endor call him up from Sheol (1 Sam. 28:7–25).

Without getting into the debate of whether or not it was Samuel or a demon who answered the medium at Endor, what is absolutely clear is that Saul believed Samuel was still consciously alive in Sheol. That the King of Israel would believe in an afterlife while the rest of the nation did not is totally unreasonable. While the Old Testament prophets condemned necromancy as something which was "forbidden," they never stated that it was impossible because the dead were unconscious (Deut. 18:9–14). The silence of the Old Testament prophets on this point cannot be explained any other way than to mean that Israel did believe in a conscious afterlife. While they were forbidden to be engaged in séances, they did not believe that man was extinguished at death.

THE SEPTUAGINT

The Septuagint uses the word *psuche* 810 times. In the majority of these instances the authors of the Septuagint used the word *psuche* as the Greek equivalent for *nephesh* except in 25 cases. In those cases, they translated the word *nephesh* as "living people" (Gen. 14:21; Josh. 10:28–39). They also took the instances where God was spoken of as having a *nephesh* and translated them to refer to God's transcendent "self" by which He thinks, wills, and feels (Amos 6:8; Job 23:13, etc.) Thus, man's *nephesh* is also translated to refer to his transcendent "self" which feels, thinks and wills (see Deut. 21:14).

The word *psuche* is found 41 times as the Greek equivalent for Hebrew words other than *nephesh*. It is used twice for *ruach*, which is the Hebrew word for spirit (Gen. 41:8; Ex. 35:21); and in the majority of remaining cases, it is the Greek equivalent for *lev*, the Hebrew word for heart (1 Chron. 12:38; Isa. 7:2, 4, etc.).

Interestingly, the translators of the Septuagint never used *bios*, the Greek word for physical life, as the equivalent for *nephesh*. If the conditional immortalists were correct in their position that *nephesh* only means physical life, why didn't the authors of the Septuagint translate *nephesh* as *bios*? Since they used *bios* many times in the Septuagint, their avoidance of using it as an equivalent for *nephesh* must be viewed as a deliberate choice on their part. Because they wished to avoid the idea that man's soul could be reduced to mere physical life, they avoided using *bios* which would have given people that idea.

This observation highlights once again the linguistic burden under which the conditional immortalitists labor. The translators of the Septuagint did not use a term such as *bios* which a conditional immortalitist would have chosen. The translators used *psuche*, which culturally and linguistically referred to the immortal soul of man. If the authors of Scripture and the translators of the Septuagint wanted to teach that man did not have a transcendent self which survived death and that man was composed only of physical life, then they would have avoided all words which would have indicated that position. The linguistic fact that they used those words which were everywhere understood to refer to the immortal and invisible soul of man reveals that they did so because they believed in the immortality of the soul.

THE RABBINIC MATERIAL

The rabbinic literature is clear that the soul of man was understood to be invisible and immortal (Bab. Tal. Ber. 59, AZ 21). At death, the soul leaves the body and remains conscious.

Mid. Gen. 409, 516, 549; Num. 733; Ecc. 83, 229

Ba. Tal. Shab. 777–779

PT Mo'ed Ketan 111. 5,826, Yeb amoth XVI.3,157, Bereshath Rabba C.7, Vayyakra Rabba XVIII.1

The righteous go to "The Throne of Glory" or Paradise (Bab. Tal. Shab. 779), while the wicked "recline in anguish and rest in torment till the last time come, in which they shall come again and be tormented still more" (2 Baruch 36:12). Thus the wicked experience conscious torment (Apocalypse of Ezra VII, 78–101; Book of Enoch 103:7).

The righteous in paradise are exhorted to worship God (Song of Three Children, 64). This obviously requires that they are still conscious after death.

The rabbis interpreted Eccles. 9:5, "the dead do not know anything," as referring to the living wicked who are called "dead" in a spiritual sense (Mid. Ecc. 229). The word "sleep" is used to describe the body at rest awaiting the resurrection while the soul is conscious in the afterlife (Mid. Gen. 549).

At the resurrection, the soul returns to the body according to

The Apocalypse of Baruch. Early Christian apocalpytic literature such as *The Apocalypse of Paul* described the angels carrying the righteous away at death (14) and evil spirits coming to carry away the souls of the wicked to torment (15–19). *The Apocalypse of Peter* graphically described the conscious torment of the wicked in the hereafter (390, 508, 514, 523, etc.).

Josephus states that the Essenes and all Jews except the Sadducees believed in the immortality of the soul (Wars II, 154–159, 163, 166).

The early church historian Eusebius (E.H. VI, C37) stated that the doctrine of "soul sleep" was invented by third-century heretics.

The exact nature of the belief of the Essenes is still under investigation and there is conflicting material in the Dead Sea Scrolls. There seems to be a mixture of the teaching of annihilationism and eternal torment in the literature coming from the Essenean community. Thus writers can quote sources to support either position.

Ruach: Spirit

The word *ruach* is found 361 times in its Hebrew and Chaldee forms in the Old Testament. It is translated in the KJV as follows:
The Spirit of God: 105 times
The spirit (in man): 59 times
The wind: 43 times
Spirit (attitude or emotional state): 51 times
Spirits (angels): 23 times
Breath: 14 times
Mind: 6 times
Side (of wind): 7 times
Blast: 4 times
Vein: 2 times
Air: 1 time
Tempest: 1 time

THE LEXICOGRAPHICAL EVIDENCE

A Hebrew and English Lexicon of the Old Testament (pp. 924–925) defines *ruach* as having nine different meanings, depending on the context. *Ruach* may refer to (1) God's spirit, i.e., the Holy Spirit, (2) angels, good and evil, (3) the principle of life in men and animals, (4) disembodied spirits, (5) breath, (6) wind, (7) disposition or attitude, (8) the seat of emotions, or (9) the seat of mind and will in men. Langenscheidt defines *ruach* as referring to breath, wind, air, animal life, spirit, ghost, soul, mind, intellect, passion, etc. (p. 314). No lexicographical material could be found which restricted *ruach* to the mere principle of physical life or the breath of the body.

THE SEPTUAGINT

The translators of the Septuagint always used the word *pneuma* as the Greek equivalent for the word *ruach* except in approximately 75 instances. Most of these instances were cases where *ruach* referred to the wind and the translators used the Greek words for wind such as *anemas* or *notos* instead of *pneuma*.

The word *pneuma* is used 388 times in the Septuagint. The times it is used when it is not the equivalent for *ruach*, it is the translation of such words as *nephesh*.

THE RABBINIC LITERATURE

As with the soul, the talmudic literature speaks of the spirit of man departing at death to dwell either in conscious bliss or sorrow. Death itself was understood as resulting from the departure of the spirit from the body.

THE EXEGETICAL EVIDENCE

The word *ruach*, like *nephesh*, has a wide range of meanings.

First, it seems originally to have referred to the wind which was viewed as being invisible and immaterial (Gen. 8:1).

Second, since God is invisible and immaterial like the wind, He is described as "spirit" (Isa. 63:10).

Third, since the angels of God are invisible and immaterial, they are called "spirits" (Ps. 104:4, KJV; cf. Heb. 1:14).

Fourth, since the life principle which animates man and animals is invisible and immaterial, it is also called "spirit" (Gen. 7:22). In this sense it was viewed as the "breath" of life which departs at death.

Fifth, since man has an invisible and immaterial self or soul which transcends the life principle by its self-consciousness, man's "mind" or "heart" is called his "spirit" (Ps. 77:6; Prov. 29:11, KJV).

The invisible side of man which is called "spirit" cannot be reduced to the mere principle of physical life or the breath of the body because man's transcendent self is contrasted to those things in such places as Isa. 42:5. Also, man's self-awareness as a cognitive ego obviously transcends the life principle which operates in animals.

At death, this transcendent ego or disincarnate mind is called a "spirit" or a "ghost" (Job 4:15).[7] This is parallel to *rephaim* or disembodied spirit (Job 26:5). Thus at death, while the life principle or breath of life ceases to exist in man or animals, the higher self or spirit of man ascends at death to the presence of God (Ps. 31:5; Eccles. 12:7).

The *ruach* of animals is never said to ascend to God's presence at death, but it is said to descend to the earth. Thus, the writer of Ecclesiastes 3:21 asks, "How do we know that the spirit of man ascends to God at death while the spirit of animals descends to the earth?" (author's paraphrase). The wording of his question reveals that it was assumed in his day that man's soul or spirit ascended to God and continued to exist after death while the mere life principle of animals went down into the earth into extinction.

Sixth, since attitudes and dispositions such as pride, humility, joy, or sorrow are invisible and immaterial, they are described as being someone's "spirit" (Prov. 11:13; 16:18). The Holy Spirit is described as the "sevenfold Spirit" in the sense that He gives people the disposition, attitude or spirit of wisdom, understanding, counsel, might, knowledge, fear and holiness (Isa. 11:2; cf. Rom. 1:4; Rev. 3:1).

METAPHORS FROM THE BODY

The Hebrews used various bodily organs or parts as metaphors for the invisible or immaterial side of man. When we say today, "I love you with all my heart," it is understood that we are not referring literally to the organ in our body which pumps blood, but the word "heart" is used in a metaphorical sense to refer to our soul or transcendent self. In the same way, the Hebrews used parts of the body to speak of the emotional, volitional and intellectual function of man's immaterial side or soul.

1. *Heart:* The Hebrews had five different words which were commonly translated as "heart."

Lev: 548 times
Lib-bab: 8 times
Levav: 6 times (Chaldee)
Sech-vee: 1 time
Bahl: 1 time (Chaldee)

The word "heart" was metaphorically used to describe that part of man which transcended mere physical life. Brown, Driver, and Briggs pointed out (p. 523) that *lev* refers to "the inner man, mind, will, heart . . . the inner man in contrast to the outer (Ps. 73:26) . . . , i.e., the soul, comprehending mind, affections, and will." While *nephesh* can mean physical life at times, *lev* is never used in that sense. It always refers to the transcendent self or soul of man.

2. *Bowels:* The word *kerev* is used 24 times in the metaphorical

sense as referring to man's transcendent self. It is translated: "self" (Gen. 18:12), "heart" (Ps. 39:3; 55:4), "soul" (1 Kings 17:21, 22, KJV; "life" in NASB), "spirit" (Ps. 51:10; Zech. 12:1), "thoughts" (Ps. 49:11).

Under the new covenant, God will write His law upon the *kerev* and place His Spirit in it (Jer. 31:33; Ezek. 36:27). It is used in an all-inclusive sense to refer to all the psychical functions of man in Ps. 103:1 where David says, "And all that is within me, bless his holy name."

3. *Kidneys:* The word *klayoth* is used 13 times in a metaphorical sense. It is often used as a parallel to *lev* in poetic literature (Ps. 7:9 and 26:2).

4. *Liver:* The word *kabhedh* is used in a metaphorical sense in Lam. 2:11 (KJV; "Spirit" in NASB) to refer to the soul or heart of man.

5. *Loins:* The word *halac* is used to describe the spirit or soul of man in Job 38:3; 40:7.

6. *Innermost parts of the body:* In Prov. 18:8; 20:27; 26:22 the word *hedher* is used to describe the transcendent self.

7. *Inward parts:* The word *tuhoth* is used metaphorically in Job 38:36 and Ps. 51:6 (KJV; "Innermost being" in NASB) to refer to the soul or mind of man.

One important observation must be pointed out at this time. The Old Testament consistently views man's spirit, soul, mind, heart, etc., as residing in the body. Nowhere does the Old Testament say that "man is kidney" or "man is spirit." The body is "the house of clay" in which man's conscious and transcendent self resides (Job 7:10). At no point is it possible to reduce man's self to his body or to the mere principle of physical life.

In this light, it becomes obvious that those who chant, "Man does not have a soul but is soul," are guilty of the grossest kind of reductionism. To say that "man is soul" is as absurd as saying "man is heart" or "man is spirit."

We must also point out that all the terms are used interchangeably and are all synonyms which refer to man's invisible side. At no point does the Old Testament speak of man's "soul" and "spirit" as being separate metaphysical entities. Therefore they must be viewed in a functional and relational sense instead of a substantial sense.

NEW TESTAMENT TERMS
Psuche: Soul

The word *psuche* is found 104 times in the New Testament. It is translated in the KJV as:

Soul: 59 times
Life: 39 times
Mind: 3 times
Heart: 2 times
You: 1 time
Us: 1 time

THE LEXICOGRAPHICAL MATERIAL

Arndt and Gingrich in *A Greek-English Lexicon of the New Testament* (pp. 901, 902) define *psuche* as (1) physical life, i.e., the life principle in man and animals, (2) earthly life itself, (3) the soul or inner self which transcends physical life and is the seat of intellect, emotion and will. "It stands in contrast to the body. . . . There is nothing more precious than *psuche* in this sense. . . . The soul is the center of both the earthly and the supernatural life," and (4) used in a figurative sense as a metonymy to refer to living people in general. It is used as a synechdoche, i.e., a part is put for the whole. Thayer's *Greek-English Lexicon of the New Testament* (p. 677) views *psuche* as meaning (1) "the vital force which animates the body" of men and animals, (2) a figure of speech for living persons, (3) the soul as the seat of emotion, intellect and will, "the soul regarded as a moral being destined for everlasting life . . . as an essence which differs from the body and is not dissolved by death . . . a disembodied soul."

THE EXEGETICAL EVIDENCE

The word *psuche* like *nephesh* has several different meanings. First, it refers to the invisible and immaterial principle of physical life which animates the bodies of animals and man (Rev. 8:9; 16:3; Matt. 2:20). Second, it is used in a relational or functional sense to refer to earthly life (Matt. 6:25). Third, it is used as a figure of speech to refer to people in general (Acts 2:41). Fourth, it is used of God in Matt. 12:18 and Heb. 10:38 in the sense of God's transcendent self. That *psuche* cannot mean physical life when used of God is obvious. It is used to refer to the seat of emotion, intellect, and will in God. Fifth, as the image-bearer of God, man also possesses a *psuche* which transcends the physical life of the body (Matt. 10:28).

The Apostle John clearly contrasts the physical life of the body to the condition of man's transcendent soul in 3 John 2. As a result, man's soul, or ego, is the center of his intellect (Acts 14:2), emotion (Matt. 26:38), and will (Eph. 6:6).

Psuche is also used to describe disincarnate souls which worship at God's throne in Rev. 6:9. In Acts 2:26, 27, Luke clearly states that the conscious *psuche* of Christ went to the underworld (Hades), while His body went to the grave. It is used as a synonym in connection with such words as heart, mind, and understanding (Matt. 22:37; Mark 12:33; Acts 4:32).

COMPARATIVE STUDIES

The word *psuche* was already clearly understood to refer to the invisible and immortal part of man which survives the death of the body in Greek literature before the 5th century B.C.

Aesch. Sept. c. Theb. 571–596;
Simonides Fr. 542, 27–30;
Eur. Hepp., 173; Demon. Fr. 170F.;
Isoc. OR., 15, 180, etc.

That Plato and Socrates believed that man's soul, or self, survived after death is no longer debated.

> The soul on her release from the body goes to give account
> of herself before the judgment seat. The righteous are sent to
> The Isles of the Blessed; the wicked go to Tartarus and there
> suffer punishment.[8]

The Septuagint clearly "presupposed that the *psuche* will be separate from the body and will spend some time in the underworld."[9] The same is clearly seen in the apocalyptic and pseudepigraphical works. "The soul lives on after death" (Ps. Phocyledes, 105 ff.). It then returns to God (Apc. Esr. 7:3; 6:4), is received by angels (Test. A. 6:5; Test. Tobi 52), where it goes to the underworld (S. Bar. 21:23; Apc. Esr. 4:12; Saphoneas Apc. 1:1).

The Talmudic sources have already been listed in connection with *nephesh*. While the rabbinic literature clearly sets "the soul and the body in antithesis, however, there is no disparagement of the body."[10] At death, the soul leaves the body (4 Esr. 7:78) and awaits its return to its resurrection body at the end of time (Bab. Sanh. 91 a b).

THE PATRISTIC MATERIAL

One question which bears on the biblical understanding of the nature of man and the word "soul" is, what did the Christians believe in the first and second centuries? While the early church fathers were not inspired, their writings do give us an indication of what the church taught during the time immediately following the apostles. It is only reasonable to assume that if the apostles taught annihilationism or Universalism, these unique teachings would have been magnified in the Greco-Roman world where the immortality of the soul and eternal punishment were everywhere believed. On the other hand, if the earliest Christian literature taught a conscious afterlife and eternal punishment, we must assume that they probably received such teaching from the apostles themselves.

It is on this point that the annihilationists are greatly inconsistent. First, they disagree among themselves as to what the patristic literature teaches. One affirms and the other denies that the literature reveals a belief in the immortality of the soul. Second, those who admit that the early fathers believed in a conscious afterlife and eternal punishment attribute such beliefs solely to the influence of pagan philosophy. They downgrade the importance of church history and emphasize that it is the Bible, and the Bible alone, which should influence our beliefs. On the other hand, there are those who claimed that all the early church fathers believed in annihilationism and soul sleep. They stress that the early fathers must have received their beliefs from the apostles. Thus, Leroy Froom claims "The Apostolic Fathers were all conditionalists" (*The Conditionalist Faith of our Fathers,* Vol. I, p. 803).

At the outset of our investigation, there are several practical principles which should be observed in regard to interpreting early Christian literature. First, we must realize that not much literature survives from the first two centuries of the church. Most of the important fragments and manuscripts were gathered together in Volume I of the Library of Christian Classics, which has been published as a 397-page book entitled *Early Christian Fathers* (Macmillan Pub. Co., N.Y., 1970). For convenience sake, all page references will be made in reference to this edition.

Second, since some of the existing material for a patristic author is only a fragment of his work, there are instances where his statements can be interpreted either for or against annihilationism. Vague statements should not be capitalized upon by any position.

Third, the annihilationists are guilty of circular reasoning when they arbitrarily assume that if an author describes the fate of the wicked as "being cast into fire," this automatically means the wicked pass into nonexistence. Instead of arriving at the text with preconceived definitions, we should try to see how an author uses his terms and if he explains himself in another passage. Even though an author may use such words as "destroy" or "perish," this does not mean that he taught annihilationism. The author may simply be using biblical phrases and words which do not exegetically in Scripture imply annihilationism.

Fourth, it must be granted by everyone that the language employed by the early fathers to describe the nature of man at death and judgment is the language more conducive and natural to the orthodox position than that of annihilationism or Universalism.

When a writer speaks of "eternal fire," the orthodox would have phrased his belief in those exact words, while an annihilationist or Universalist would have opted for "temporary fire" or "fire which consumes." Thus, the burden of proof rests on the annihilationist and the Universalist as to why we should not understand the words of the early fathers in their simplest meaning.

In the light of these observations, we will limit our investigation of early Christian literature to those texts found in *Early Christian Fathers*. This is necessary in order not to lose the interest of the reader and to avoid going off on a tangent at this point.

The early fathers did not hesitate to speak of man as being composed of a body and a soul in a scripturally dualistic sense. They had to differentiate their belief from the materialists who denied that man's soul was more than physical life and the spiritualists who denied that man's body was real. Thus, they faced attacks from the Gnostics, who viewed the body as evil and the soul as inherently immortal and preexistent, and from the Stoics and others, who believed that when a man died he simply ceased to exist (*Early Fathers*, p. 24f.). The annihilationists, at this point, do great damage to their own credibility when they take the statements which were contextually aimed at refuting the Gnostic idea of inherent divinity, immortality, and preexistence, and then set forth those passages as an attack on the orthodox position. This is a favorite device of Leroy Froom in his *The Conditionalist Faith of Our Fathers* and is a classic example of building straw men and misapplying texts.

We invite the readers at this point to examine what the early fathers said about the body and the soul at death. There are several questions which the reader should keep in mind.

First, did the fathers speak of the soul as something separate and distinct from the body?

Second, was the soul only physical life or was it viewed as being immortal and invisible?

Third, did man pass into nonexistence or a state of unconsciousness at death?

Fourth, do the righteous experience conscious bliss after death, while the wicked experience conscious suffering?

> Thus no devils' weed will be found among you: but thoroughly pure and self-controlled, you will remain body and soul united to Jesus Christ. (Ignatius to Ephesians, p. 91)
>
> The reason you have a body as well as a soul is that you may win the favor of the visible world. (Ignatius to Polycarp, p. 116)
>
> The outside like the inside means this: The inside means the soul and the outside means the body. Just as your body is visible,

so make your soul evident by your good deeds. (Clement's Second Letter, p. 149)

What the soul is in the body, that Christians are in the world. The soul is dispersed through all the members of the body, and Christians are scattered through all the cities of the world. The soul dwells in the body, but does not belong to the body, and Christians dwell in the world, but do not belong to the world. The soul which is invisible, is kept under guard in the visible body; in the same way Christians are recognized when they are in the world, but their religion remains unseen. . . . The soul is shut up in the body, and yet itself holds the body together; while Christians are restrained in the world as in a prison, and yet hold the world together. The soul, which is immortal, is housed in a mortal dwelling. . . . (Letter to Diognetus, p. 218)

Look at the end of each of the former emperors, how they died the common death of all; and if this were merely a departure into unconsciousness, that would be a piece of luck for the wicked. But since consciousness continues for all who lived, and eternal punishment awaits, do not fail to be convinced and believe that these things are true. . . . Souls are still conscious after death. (First Apology of Justin Martyr, p. 253)

When we say that all things have been ordered and made by God we appear to offer the teaching of Plato–in speaking of a coming destruction by fire, that of the Stoics; in declaring that the souls of the unrighteous will be punished after death, still remaining in conscious existence, and those of the virtuous, delivered from punishment, will enjoy happiness, we seem to agree with poets and philosophers; in declaring that man ought not to worship the works of their hands we are saying the same things as the comedian Menander and others who have said this, for they declared that the Fashioner is greater than what he has formed. (First Apology of Justin Martyr, p. 255)

Moses was earlier than Plato and all the Greek writers. And everything that philosophers and poets said about the immortality of the soul, punishment after death, contemplation of heavenly things, and teachings of that kind—they took hints from the prophets and so were able to understand these things and expounded them. So it seems that there were indeed seeds of truth in all men, but they are proved not to have understood them properly since they contradicted each other. (First Apology of Justin Martyr, p. 271)

We are convinced that when we depart this present life we shall live another. It will be better than this one, heavenly not earthly. We shall live close to God and with God, our souls steadfast and free from passions (lusts). Even if we have flesh, it will not seem so: we shall be heavenly spirits. Or else, if we fall along with the rest, we shall enter one worse life and one in flames. For God did not make us like sheep and oxen, a bywork to perish and be done away with. In the light of this it is not likely that we would be purposely wicked, and deliver ourselves up to the great Judge to be punished. (Athenagoras' Plea, p. 336)

Those who deny they will have to give account of the present life, be it wicked or good, who reject the resurrection and count on the soul's perishing along with the body and, so to say, flickering out, are likely to stop at no outrage. (Athenagoras' Plea, p. 339)

Ignatius spoke of his death throughout his letters in terms of his finally "gathering to God or Christ" (pp. 91, 101, 103, 104, 105, 106, 118, 120). He described his death in terms of "the pangs of being born," i.e., "my coming to life" (p. 105). That he believed in the underworld, i.e. the place of disincarnate souls, is clear from his saying that Christ died "in the sight of heaven, and earth and the underworld" (p. 100). The annihilationists seize upon one statement of Ignatius which says, "When I have fallen asleep, I shall be a burden to no one" (p. 104, v. 2a). That Ignatius uses "sleep" as a metaphor for the state of the body at death is clear from the context, for he actually goes on to say, "When the world sees *my body* no more" (p. 104, v. 26).

Then there are those who think life is this: "Eat and drink for tomorrow we shall die." They view death as a deep sleep and a forgotten—"sleep and death, twin brothers," and men think they're religious! (Athenagoras' Plea, p. 311)

Were we convinced that this life is the only one, then we might be suspected of sinning, by being enslaved to flesh and blood and by becoming subject to gain and lust. (Athenagoras' Plea, p. 335)

From the material given above, it is obvious that annihilationists such as Froom greatly overstate their case when they claim that there is no evidence in the literature of the first two centuries of the church that any of the fathers believed that man possessed an immortal soul and was consciously in bliss or torment after death. Froom does not deal with the above passages and does not make his readers aware of their existence. While we freely admit that there are indications that some of the early fathers believed in the final annihilation or salvation of the wicked, it is clear that the majority of fathers believed in a conscious afterlife and eternal punishment.

Pneuma: Spirit

The word *pneuma* in its various forms is found 406 times in the New Testament. It is translated in the KJV as follows:

Spirit (Holy): 165 times
Ghost (Holy): 88 times

Spirits (good/evil, angels): 55 times
Spirit (man's): 45 times
Spirit (attitude): 22 times
Spirits or ghosts (man's disincarnate soul): 7 times
Spiritual (adjective use): 23 times
Life: 1 time (Rev. 13:15)
Wind: 1 time (John 3:8)

THE LEXICOGRAPHICAL MATERIAL

Thayer (pp. 520–524) defines *pneuma* as meaning (1) air or wind, (2) the life principle which animates the body, (3) "a spirit, i.e. a simple essence, devoid of all or at least all grosser matter, and possessed of the power of knowing, desiring, deciding and action." In this sense, it refers to angels and a "human soul that has left the body," (4) "Spirit as in God's essence, person and power," (5) disposition and attitude as in a "spirit of humility."

Arndt and Gingrich (pp. 680–685) define *pneuma* as meaning (1) wind or air, (2) that which gives life to the body, (3) disincarnate souls, "after a person's death, his *pneuma* lives on as an independent being . . . *pneuma* is that part of Christ which, in contrast to (flesh) did not pass away at death, but survived as an individual entity at death," (4) human personality or ego which is the center of emotion, intellect and will, (5) state of mind or disposition, (6) an independent immaterial being such as God or angels, (7) as God, as in the Holy Spirit, the spirit of Christ, etc.

THE EXEGETICAL EVIDENCE

First, the New Testament writers carry on the precedent set by the translators of the Septuagint by using the Greek words for wind such as *animas* instead of *pneuma*. The only instance where *pneuma* definitely refers to the wind is in John 3:8 where there is a poetic play upon the sovereign movement of the divine Spirit and the wind.

Second, *pneuma* refers to the life principle which animates the body. This is actually a very rare usage in the New Testament. For example, the false prophet who accompanied the Antichrist in the last days will make an idol "alive" (Rev. 13:15).

Third, *pneuma* is used to describe the immaterial nature of God and angels (John 4:24; Heb. 1:14). Christ defined a "spirit" or "ghost" as an immaterial being (Luke 24:39).

Fourth, *pneuma* refers to the disposition which characterizes a person, such as pride, humility, fear, etc. (1 Pet. 3:4).

Fifth, *pneuma* is used to describe the disincarnate spirit or soul of man after death (Matt. 27:50; Luke 24:37, 39; John 19:30; Acts 7:59; Heb. 12:23; 1 Pet. 3:19).

It is obvious that the Jews during the first century as well as during the Old Testament age believed in the survival of man's mind or soul after the death of the body because they clearly believed in "ghosts" (Luke 24:37). The departed are pictured as perfected spirits consciously worshiping at God's throne (Heb. 12:23). Before they ascended to heaven at Christ's resurrection, they were described as "spirits in prison" who dwelt in Hades to whom Christ came and proclaimed the finished atonement (1 Pet. 3:19).

Sixth, man's transcendent self, or ego, is also called *pneuma* because of its immaterial and invisible nature (1 Cor. 2:11). It is described as the center of man's emotions, intellect and will (Mark 8:12; Mark 2:8; Matt. 26:41).

Since man's *pneuma* transcends his mere physical life, it is frequently contrasted to his body, or flesh (Matt. 26:41; Mark 14:38; Luke 24:39; John 3:6; 6:63; 1 Cor. 5:5; 7:34; 2 Cor. 7:1; Gal. 5:17; 6:8, 9; James 2:26). It is man's *pneuma* which ascends to God at death (Acts 7:59).

It is exegetically impossible to reduce *pneuma* to mere physical life. Man's transcendent spirit, or self, survives the death of his body.

Kardia: Heart

The New Testament speaks of man's transcendent self as his "heart" 162 times. Arndt and Gingrich (p. 404) point out that *kardia* is the word frequently used in the Septuagint for the center of man's emotion, intellect, and will. Thayer (p. 325) defines it as "the soul or mind, as it is the fountain and seat of the thoughts, passions, desires, appetite, purposes, endeavors, etc."

The *kardia* of man is that part of him which feels, thinks and decides (Mark 9:24; Luke 24:25; John 14:1). It is used with *psuche* as the center of worship (Mark 12:30; John 4:24). It cannot be reduced to the mere principle of physical life which animates the body of animals as well as man. It everywhere refers to the supernatural or invisible part of man which is his transcendent ego or self.

Mind

The New Testament authors referred to the "mind" of man by several different words.

They used *dianoia* 13 times, translating it as "mind" 9 times, "understanding" 3 times, and "imagination" once. It is used in connection with "soul" in Matt. 22:37 and "heart" in Luke 1:51. It is contrasted to "the flesh" in Eph. 2:3.

The word *phroneena* is translated as "mind" 4 times. It is even used to describe the rational center in the divine Spirit in Rom. 8:27, where Paul speaks of the "mind of the spirit."

The Greek word *noeema* is used five times to describe that part of man which sin blinds and corrupts and which the grace of Christ redeems. It refers to the damaging effect of the fall upon man's intellectual capabilities in such places as 2 Cor. 4:4; 10:5; Phil. 4:7.

The classic Greek word *nous* is used 24 times in the New Testament. It is translated as "mind" 17 times and as "understanding" 7 times. Both Thayer (p. 429) and Arndt and Gingrich (p. 546) point out that *nous* had an established meaning in Greek literature which meant the immaterial and invisible "mind" or "reason" of man which was transcendent above mere physical life. As Arndt and Gingrich stated, *nous* refers to "the higher mental part of natural man which initiates his thoughts and plans." It is also used to describe the "mind" of God in Rom. 11:34 and the "mind" of Christ in 1 Cor. 2:16. In the Greek literature before the New Testament, *nous* was viewed as surviving the death of the body. That the New Testament writers would use such a term indicates that they were not uncomfortable with the concept of life after death.

Eso, Esosthen: Inner Man

The New Testament authors clearly believed that man had a dual nature. They referred to the body as "the outer man" and the soul/spirit as "the inner man" in such places as Rom. 7:22 and Eph. 3:16.

The contrast is so clearly embedded in the mind of the Apostle Paul that he even described "the outer man" as decaying, while "the inner man" or soul was being renewed day by day (2 Cor. 4:16). The contrast between the physical life of the body which was decaying and the onward progressive life of the soul could not be clearer.

The Apostle Paul did not hesitate to speak of the body as the tabernacle or the house of clay in which man's transcendent soul indwells. In 2 Cor. 12:2–4, he could describe a person as being completely conscious while out of the body as well as when the person was in the body. The man in the passage did not cease to exist while out of his body. The man's transcendent soul or spirit could leave his body and ascend to the third heaven and be conscious in the presence of God. In 2 Cor. 5:1–4, the body is "an earthly tent" in which we dwell. In Phil. 1:22–24, Paul could speak of himself as an "I am" which could choose between being "in" a body or "departing" from that body to be with Christ. Paul viewed his approaching death as "the time of my departure," not extinction (2 Tim. 4:6).

The Apostle Peter spoke of himself as dwelling for a while in his earthly tabernacle until the time came for him to lay aside his body and depart (2 Pet. 1:13–15).

With both Peter and Paul there is no indication that they equated their self or soul with their body. Their "I-ness" dwells in an earthly tabernacle. Just as it would be absurd to equate someone who lived in a tent with the tent itself, there is no way to equate man's soul with the body in which it dwells.

The conditional immortalitists have never wrestled with the patently clear passages which speak of a dualism or contrast between the physical life of the body and the transcendent life of the soul or spirit.

Nephroi: Kidneys

In Rev. 2:23, the New Testament uses the Greek word for kidneys in the metaphorical sense as referring to the mind or heart of man in order to reflect the Hebraic text which it is utilizing (Jer. 17:10). It represents the invisible side of man which is discernible by God alone.

Summary

When the New Testament writers sought to explain what they believed about the nature of man, they consistently spoke of man as having a dual nature. Thus, man cannot be reduced to being just a physical or spiritual being but is a combination of both. The authors of the New Testament used those Greek words found in the common language of the day. They used the Greek terms utilized by the Septuagint. They deliberately chose these terms because they refer to the immortal and invisible soul of man which survived the death of the body. The mere presence of such terms in the New Testament reveals the error of the secular and religious materialists who deny that the New Testament teaches that man has a dual nature.

SOUL AND SPIRIT

Since some biblical expositors have taught that man is made up of three separate entities—body, soul and spirit—we shall pause at this point to demonstrate that the words "soul" and "spirit" are actually synonyms and are just different names for the same invisible side of man.

Man's immaterial side is given several different names in Scripture. It has been called the "spirit," "soul," "mind," "heart," "inward parts," etc., of man. The names should not be viewed as referring to separate entities but as descriptions of different functions or relationships which man's immaterial side has. Thus "spirit" and "soul" should not be viewed as separate entities but as describing higher and lower functions and the relationship of man's immaterial side to God and the world. Indeed, spirit and soul are used interchangeably in various passages (Isa. 26:9; Luke 1:46, 47). The fact that they are listed side by side in 1 Thess. 5:23 should not be viewed in a "substantial sense" but in a "functional sense." After all, does Deut. 6:5 or Mark 12:30 mean that man is made up of five parts or entities: heart, soul, mind, strength and understanding? That man's spirit and soul refer to his immaterial side can be seen from the following points:

1. Man's soul/spirit is viewed as being separate from his body (Eccles. 12:7; Isa. 10:18; Matt. 10:28; 1 Cor. 5:5).

2. Death is said to occur when man's soul/spirit leaves the body (Gen. 35:18; 1 Kings 17:21, 22, KJV—"life" in NASB; Eccles. 12:7; James 2:26).

3. Man's soul/spirit is the seat of his intellect (Prov. 23:7; 29:11; Mark 2:8; 1 Cor. 2:11; 14:15; Acts 4:2; Phil. 1:7, 27; Heb. 12:3).

4. Man's soul/spirit is the seat of his will (Ex. 35:21; Ps. 103:1; Matt. 26:41; Eph. 6:6).

5. Man's soul/spirit is the seat of his emotions (Gen. 26:35; 41:8; Ps. 42:1–6; 2 Cor. 2:13, cf. Matt. 26:38; Mark 8:12; Luke 1:46, 47; 2:35; Acts 4:32; 17:16; 18:25; Eph. 6:6; 2 Pet. 2:8).

6. Man's soul/spirit is the place of inner worship (Ps. 51:10, 17; 103:1; 146:1; Luke 1:46, 47, cf. Matt. 22:37; John 4:24; Rom. 1:9; Phil. 3:3; Heb. 12:22–24; Rev. 6:9).

Since man is created in God's image, he is distinct from the animals. While their "life force" or "soul" perishes, man's "ego," or "self," continues after death. Any view which states that man is no different from the brute beasts is labeled "under the sun" or humanistic thought in Eccles. 1:3; 3:19–21; 4:1; 9:3, etc.

Humanistic thought has a view of man which is too low because it reduces him to the level of brute beasts. If humanistic thought were true, then hedonism should be pursued (Eccles. 5:18; 10:19) because everything is meaningless in the end (Eccles. 1:2; 2:10, 11, etc.). But man is not an animal. He is uniquely created in God's image, and his "ego," "soul," "spirit," etc., survives after his body crumbles. Thus his spirit/soul returns to the Creator for judgment (Eccles. 12:6, 7).

A UNIVERSAL CONCEPT

One of the great issues which arose in the 19th century concerning a conscious afterlife was whether or not belief in immortality was universal in an anthropological and historical sense. This issue brought historians, linguists, and anthropologists into the debate which up until that time was the sole concern of theologians and philosophers.

The materialists were determined to find evidence that man in his evolutionary beginnings did not possess a concept of an afterlife. Thus the concept of immortality was a later evolutionary refinement of man's ability to think abstractly. They also tried to find a civilization or nation in history which was not committed to a belief in an afterlife. They were even willing to settle for a primitive tribe which believed that man passed into extinction at death.

The driving force behind the materialists' search was that they were haunted by the fact that belief in a conscious afterlife seemed to be universal. That all of humanity, no matter where and when it is found, believed in an afterlife implied that the concept was somehow tied into man's nature. They were also disturbed because it seemed that the greatest thinkers in every civilization embraced the concept. This implied that the concept was virtually self-evident.

If immortality is a universal belief, then certain questions naturally arise. Is the denial of immortality a denial of something which is an essential part of our humanity? Is the denial of immortality a psychological aberration? Is it caused by a desire to not live beyond the grave? Could the modern rejection of immortality be rooted in a fear of hell? Does a rejection of immortality arise out of a guilt-ridden conscience? Must we judge the present rejection of immortality as an "oddity" born in an age of irrationality?

In the debates over immortality during the 19th century, those who believed in an afterlife presented archeological and literary evidence that immortality was a universal concept. The materialists, in turn, tried to find a civilization or tribe which did not believe in immortality. The debate lasted for several decades as charges and counter-charges were given on both sides. When the dust finally settled, it was granted by all sides that the concept of immortality was indeed a universal idea.[11] Modern research and scholarship since the 19th century have only confirmed the universality of the concept of conscious life after death.

The earliest human artifacts indisputably demonstrate that man from the very beginning believed in an afterlife.[12] The arthritic Neanderthal "cave people" buried their dead with bowls of food and weapons of war. The mere fact that man has always carefully buried his dead instead of merely leaving the bodies to be consumed by animals or the elements reveals his commitment to an afterlife. This is one of the great differences between mankind and the animal kingdom. Animals do not bury their dead, and frequently, they will even cannibalize them. But man, from the beginning, had a reverence for the dead because he understood in some way that while the grave received the body, the mind or soul went somewhere else.

When we turn to the literary evidence, we find that the oldest extant literature abounds with references to a life after death. The *Egyptian Book of the Dead* reveals the elaborate views of that great civilization which arose along the Nile. The earliest Chinese literature spoke eloquently of man's afterlife. *The Tibetan Book of the Dead* reveals the ancient beliefs of those who lived at "the top of the world." The Babylonian and Assyrian belief in an afterlife is indisputable. The *Vedas* of the Hindus stress that death does not end all. The Greeks, Romans, North Europeans, Greenlanders, Eskimos, North and South American Indians, African tribes, and even Australian Aborigines all believed in a conscious afterlife.[13]

In the history of humanity, belief in an afterlife is so universal and natural that the few individuals such as Epictetus who denied it were always viewed as an aberration. Emerson remarked:

> Here is the wonderful thought, whenever man ripens, this audacious belief presently appears. . . . As soon as thought is exercised, this belief is inevitable. . . . Whence came it? Who put it in the mind?

Since the concept is universal, Emerson concluded that it was "not sentimental but elemental"—elemental in the sense that it is "grounded in the necessities and forces we possess."[14]

While it is true that we cannot simply say that something is logically valid just because it is believed by the vast majority of humanity, nevertheless, it is still logically valid that the burden of proof rests on those individuals who reject the majority's position. In any debate, the majority always has the strongest position. We must begin with what is historically accepted. The minority position must do two things. It must first refute the majority position and then, secondly, establish its own theory.

When we turn to find any clear evidence against an afterlife, we find nothing. The materialists usually simply deny it as "unthinkable" and wave it aside. They fail to see that the burden of proof rests on their shoulders. Mere denials are not enough. On the basis of our survey of the issue today, modern materialists do not reject an afterlife on the basis of any convincing or solid evidence.[15] Why then is it rejected?

We find ourselves in the area of psychology when we try to discern the motives for a denial of immortality. One writer, Robert Sproul, in *The Psychology of Atheism* (Bethany House Pub., 1974) points out that such denials, no doubt, arise out of a psychological trauma which leads to a repression of any ideas which are threatening.

When someone has a lifestyle which the very concept of God, an afterlife, or hell threatens, either the lifestyle or the threatening concepts must go. Thus a person will jettison those ideas which threaten his preferred lifestyle.

The Apostle Paul pointed out in his epistle to the Romans that the root cause of man's denial of divine truth is the attempt to evade conviction of sin.

> And just as they did not see fit to acknowledge God any longer, God gave them over to a depraved mind, to do those things which are not proper, being filled with all unrighteousness, wickedness, greed, malice, full of envy, murder, strife, deceit, malice; they are gossips, slanderers, haters of God, insolent, arrogant, boastful, inventors of evil, disobedient to parents, without understanding, untrustworthy, unloving, unmerciful; and, although they know the ordinance of God, that those who practice such things are worthy of death, they not only do the same, but also give hearty approval to those who practice them. (Rom. 1:28–32)

We must also point out that not only must the materialists come up with solid evidence against a conscious afterlife, but they must also give a plausible explanation as to why and how this belief is anthropologically and geographically universal. As of yet, no plausible theories have been developed.

When we turn to the history of philosophy to see what the best of human minds have discerned, we find that from the classic Greek philosophers to the present time, the immortality of the soul has been accepted as immediately reasonable and virtually self-evident. The list of these philosophers who believed in a conscious afterlife would include the greatest thinkers from Socrates to the present time. The same can be said for the great scientists of the past and present who believed in immortality. The list would reach from Aristotle to many modern scientists. It goes without saying that the best of the human race would be on these lists.

Now, it may be objected that this line of reasoning is a veiled appeal to authority. And, of course, we are aware that some logicians label all appeals to authority as invalid. Yet, when we ask them how they know that all appeals to authority are invalid, they appeal to their own authority or the authority of someone else! Evidently, they must appeal to authority to demonstrate that all such appeals are invalid! We fail to be convinced by such self-refuting clichés. Authority and faith lie at the basis of all knowledge because all systems begin with faith assumptions based on authority.

In light of the history of philosophy and science, it is appalling to hear in our day such statements as: "Only ignorant and uneducated people believe in an afterlife." "Science has disproved immortality." "Philosophers can never accept the concept of an afterlife."

Are we really expected to believe that all the philosophers and scientists who looked forward to an afterlife were ignorant and uneducated people? Would such people accept a concept which had no evidence for it? Are the materialists of our day more intelligent than nearly all of humanity who preceded them? On what grounds do they rashly wave aside all the arguments for immortality which have been developed over the entire length of humanity's history?

The only reasonable response is to begin where man began, i.e., with a basic orientation to and belief in an afterlife. Until solid evidence is presented to the contrary, we shall begin with the assumption that some part of man survives death.

When it comes to the history of the Christian Church, C. S. Lewis and others have pointed out that "the earliest Christian documents give ascent to the belief that the supernatural or invisible part of man survives the death of the body."[16]

No one denies that for nearly two thousand years, with rare exceptions, Christians have generally believed in the immortality of the soul. The classic European and American theologians defended it as a biblical concept. Not only have the Roman Catholic and classic Protestant theologians defended it, but most clergy of all denominations have preached it from the pulpit.

It was only after the materialists had gained control of secular higher education that some modern theologians began to teach a religious form of materialism in which they denied that man has a transcendent soul or spirit.

Seeking to gain the approval and acceptance of the secular materialists, some modern theologians have become religious materialists by stripping the supernatural—first from the Bible by denying its miracles and then from man by denying his immortal soul. They have adopted the same anti-supernatural attitude which characterizes secular materialists. They have developed special hermeneutical principles which enable them to de-mythologize the Scriptures and man. Just as the Bible has been reduced to be just one book among many, man has been reduced to being just one animal among many. Once they denied the supernatural in God, they denied it in the Bible. Once they denied the supernatural in the Bible, they denied it in man. In effect, God, the Bible and man all have "died."

What can we say to these modern theologians? First, the marriage of religion and materialism is impossible because materialism can never generate morals, values or meaning which are essential for any religion. Second, they should stop reading materialism into the Bible. Instead, they should let the biblical authors speak for themselves. Third, they should be honest. Without the supernatural element in man or the Bible, religion becomes meaningless. Fourth, they should not use religious words to manipulate people. Modern thinkers delight in redefining words and giving them a meaning directly opposite to what those words historically denoted.

CONCLUSION

The Scriptures view man as the unique image-bearer of God who, in reflecting unity and diversity, has a material and immaterial side. This invisible or immaterial side of man is called various names such as soul, heart, spirit, and mind. At death, man's two sides are separated, and his conscious mind survives the death of the body and experiences either bliss or torment in the hereafter. This is the consistent picture of the nature of man and the nature of death which is found in the Old Testament as well as the New Testament.

NOTES

1. In *A Christian Handbook for Defending the Faith*, we give a presentation of this approach and an application of it to history, psychology, ethics, art and marriage. We then give a detailed application to drug abuse in *The Bible and Drug Abuse*, to reincarnation in *Reincarnation and Christianity*, and to astrology in *Horoscopes and the Christian*.

2. Morey, *The Saving Work of Christ* (Sterling, Virginia: G.A.M., 1980).

3. Morey, *How to Answer a Jehovah's Witness* (Minnesota: Bethany House Pub., 1979).

4. C.S. Lewis, *Miracles*, pp. 175–179, 27.

5. Terry, ibid., p. 250.

6. See: Berkhof, *Systematic Theology*, p. 673; F. Grant, *Facts and Theories as to a Future State*, p. 128; *I.S.B.E.*, Vol. VI, p. 2761; Shedd, *The Doctrine of Endless Punishment*, p. 50, etc.

7. A few modern commentaries have translated *ruach* in Job

4:15 as "a breath or wind" instead of "a spirit." That this is in error is seen from the facts that all the ancient versions translated *ruach* as referring to the disembodied spirit and the rabbinic literature follows the same interpretation. For a full discussion of this point see *Lange's Commentary*, Vol. IV, p. 331.

8. *The Dialogue of Plato* (ed. B. Jorvett; New York: Random House, 1937), Vol. II, p. 922.

9. *Theological Dictionary of the New Testament* (eds. Kittel, Friedrich; Grand Rapids: Wm. B. Eerdmans Pub. Co., 1974), Vol. IX, p. 632.

10. Ibid., p. 637.

11. There is no modern objection to the universality of the concept of immortality. It is fully documented by such writers as Baillis, Baily, Holmons, Salmond, etc., whose works are listed in the bibliography.

12. S. Brandon, *The Judgment of the Dead* (New York: Charles Scribner's Sons, 1907), p. 1; J. Fyfe, *The Hereafter* (Edinburgh: T. & T. Clark, 1980), p. 27; J. Hick, *Philosophy of Religion* (New Jersey: Prentice-Hall, Inc., 1963), p. 48.

13. The following authors whose books are listed in the bibliography give the literary and archeological evidence in minute detail: Charles, Fyfe, Gill, Salmond, Strong, and Warfield. The classic work is Alger's *A Critical History of the Doctrine of a Future Life*. He presents the evidence for Aborigines, Africans, Buddhists, Chinese, Greeks, Egyptians, Essenes, Etruscans, Druids, Greenlanders, Indians of North and South America, Persians, Polynesians, Romans and Scandinavians. His bibliography covers over 5,000 titles.

14. Quoted in *A Modern Introduction to Philosophy* (eds. Edwards and Pap; New York: The Free Press, 1965), pp. 239, 240.

15. The older arguments such as the conservation of energy were fully answered by C.D. Broad in his *The Mind and Its Place in Nature*, and by F. Grant in *Can We Still Believe in Immortality?* Modern attempts to restate the old arguments have been dealt with by W. Penfield, *The Mystery of the Mind;* Popper & Eccles, *The Self and Its Brain*; and Koestler, *The Ghost in the Machine*.

16. C.S. Lewis, *Miracles*, p. 29.

Chapter 3

SHEOL, HADES, AND GEHENNA

One of the most crucial issues which determines our understanding of what the Bible teaches about death and the afterlife is the proper interpretation of such key terms as Sheol, Hades and Gehenna. No study of death is complete without a thorough understanding of these terms.

SHEOL

The Hebrew word Sheol is found 66 times in the Old Testament. While the Old Testament consistently refers to the body as going to the grave, it always refers to the soul or spirit of man as going to Sheol. The nature of Sheol and the condition of those in it is crucial to our understanding of what the Bible teaches about what happens to man after death.

The Lexicographical Material

The first step in understanding any ancient or foreign word is to check the lexicons, dictionaries, encyclopedias, etc., which deal with that language. Brown, Driver and Briggs based their *A Hebrew and English Lexicon of the Old Testament* on the work of Gesenius, one of the greatest Hebrew scholars who ever lived. They define Sheol as: "the underworld . . . whither man descends at death" (p. 982). They trace the origin of Sheol to either *sha-al*, which means the spirit world to which mediums directed their questions to the departed, or *sha-al*, which refers to the hollow place in the earth where the souls of men went at death. Langenscheidt's *Hebrew/ English Dictionary to the Old Testament* (p. 337) defines *Sheol* as: "netherworld, realm of the dead, Hades." *The International Standard Bible Encyclopedia* in Vol. IV, p. 2761, defines Sheol as: "the unseen world, the state or abode of the dead, and is the equivalent of the Greek: Hades." Keil and Delitzsch state that "Sheol denotes the place where departed souls are gathered after death; it is an infinitive form from *sha-al*, to demand, the demanding, applied to the place which inexorably summons all men into its shade."[1]

The lexicographical evidence is so clear that the great Princeton scholar, B. B. Warfield, stated that with modern Hebrew scholars, there is no "hesitation to allow with all heartiness that Israel from the beginning of its recorded history cherished the most settled conviction of the persistence of the soul in life after death. . . . The body is laid in the grave and the soul departs to Sheol."[2] George Eldon Ladd in *The New Bible Dictionary* (p. 380), comments:

> In the Old Testament, man does not cease to exist at death, but his soul descends to Sheol.

Modern scholarship understands the word Sheol to refer to the place where the soul or spirit of man goes at death.[3] None of the lexicographical literature defines Sheol as referring to the grave or to passing into nonexistence.

Comparative Studies

In order to understand what a certain word meant in an ancient language, it is sometimes helpful to find any parallel words in the other languages of that time. Thus comparative studies of Sheol have been done which demonstrate that Sheol's parallels in other languages meant the place where the soul of man goes at death. No research has found a place where Sheol's parallel means the grave or nonexistence. For example, The Ugaritic *ars* and Accadian *su alu* clearly refer to the netherworld.[4] The Babylonians, Assyrians, Egyptians, and Greek parallels to Sheol clearly meant the place of departed spirits.[5] The Ethiopian *Si'ol* cannot mean anything other than the netherwold, the place of conscious life after death.[6]

The Historical Context

What is important about comparative studies is that they place biblical words in their historical context. The word Sheol should thus be understood in terms of what it meant in the Hebrew language and by its parallel in the other languages of that time. Why?

When God wanted Israel to believe something which was unique and contrary to what the surrounding cultures believed, He always clearly condemned and forbade the pagan beliefs and then stressed the uniqueness of the new concept. For example, in order to establish monotheism, God repeatedly and clearly condemned the pagan concept of polytheism and stressed monotheism.

While God clearly condemned polytheism in the Old Testament, at no time did He ever condemn belief in a conscious afterlife. At no time did God ever put forth the concept of annihilation or nonexistence as the fate of man's soul at death.

Also, when Israel had a unique and contrary belief, the pagan societies around Israel would use this belief as the grounds to persecute the Jews. Thus the Jews were persecuted for rejecting polytheism and believing in monotheism. Daniel's three friends who were thrown into a fiery furnace are an excellent example of such persecution.

Yet, where in recorded history did pagan religions or societies persecute the Jews because they denied a conscious afterlife? To think that the Jews could go against the universally held concept of a conscious afterlife and that the pagans would not seize upon this as a pretense for persecution is absurd.

Since the universality of belief in a conscious afterlife is irrefutable, and there is no evidence that Israel deviated from this belief, we must assume that the Old Testament taught a conscious afterlife in Sheol as the fate of man's soul or spirit.

The Rabbinic Literature

It is universally recognized by modern Talmudic scholars that *Sheol* never meant the grave or unconsciousness in rabbinic literature. Ginzburg states that in rabbinic writings one finds a consistent conviction that "there exists after this world a condition of happiness or unhappiness for an individual."[7] Guttman adds, "The Talmud, like the Apocryphal literature, knows of a kind of intermediate state of the soul between death and resurrection; true retribution will be dispensed only after the resurrection of the body. But along with this, we also find the fate in a retribution coming immediately after death and in a life of blessedness for the soul in the beyond."[8]

The rabbinic tradition before, during, and after the time of Christ describes the soul departing the body and descending into *Sheol* at death.[9] The rabbis consistently pictured both the righteous and the wicked as conscious after death.[10] The evidence is so overwhelming that the classic Princeton theologian, Charles Hodge, stated, "That the Jews believed in a conscious life after death is beyond dispute."[11]

The annihilationists have never discovered any evidence that the majority of Jews believed that the soul was extinguished at death. There is no conflict in the rabbinic literature over this issue.[12]

Sheol and the Grave

The KJV translates Sheol as "hell" 31 times, "grave" 31 times, and "pit" three times. Because of this inconsistency of translation, such groups as the Adventists, Armstrongites, and Jehovah's Witnesses have taught that Sheol means the grave. All the conditional immortalitists have traditionally capitalized on the KJV's translation of Sheol as the "grave." For example, in *The Conditionalist Faith of Our Fathers* (Vol. I, pp. 162 and 298), Froom emphatically stated that both Sheol and Hades meant the grave. It is to be regretted that even some modern versions have carried on the tradition of translating Sheol as grave.

Since the conditional immortalitists stress that Sheol means the grave, we will pause at this point to demonstrate that Sheol cannot mean the grave.

First, exegetically speaking, the initial occurrence of Sheol in the Old Testament cannot mean the grave. The word Sheol is first found in Gen. 37:35. After the brothers had sold Joseph into slavery, they informed their father that Joseph had been killed and devoured by a savage beast. As Jacob held the bloodied and tattered remains of Joseph's coat in his hands, he declared:

> "A wild beast has devoured him: Joseph has surely been torn to pieces." (v. 33)

As a result of the shock of the death of Joseph, Jacob cried:

> "Surely I will go down to Sheol in mourning for my son." (v. 35, lit. Heb.)

There are several things about this first occurrence of Sheol which should be pointed out.

1. Jacob assumed that his son was still alive and conscious after death and that he would eventually reunite with his son after his own death. The German commentator Lange comments:

> One thing is clear: [Joseph's death] was not a state of non-being. . . . Jacob was going to be with his son; he was still his son; there was yet a tie between him and his son; he is still spoken of as a personality; he is still regarded as having a being somehow and somewhere.[13]

2. Whatever else Sheol may mean, in this passage it cannot mean Joseph's grave, for Jacob believed that Joseph had been devoured by an animal and had no grave. Since Joseph had no grave, it is impossible for Jacob to be referring to being buried in a common grave with his son.[14]

3. According to the context, Jacob is clearly speaking of reuniting with his favorite son in the underworld, here called Sheol. He even speaks of "going down" to reunite with his son, because it was assumed that Sheol was the place of departed spirits, probably a hollow place in the center of the earth.

The second reason for not identifying Sheol as the grave is that when the biblical authors wanted to speak of the grave, they used the word *kever*. That they did not view *kever* and Sheol as synonymous is clear from the way these words are used throughout the Old Testament. For example, in Isa. 14:19, the king is cast out of his grave (*kever*) in order to be thrown into Sheol where the departed spirits can rebuke him (vv. 9, 10). In this passage, Sheol and *kever* are opposites, not synonyms.

Third, in the Septuagint, Sheol is never translated as *mneema*, which is the Greek word for grave. It is always translated as Hades which meant the underworld. *Kever* is translated as *mneema* 36 times and as *taphos* 45 times. But *kever* is never translated as Hades just as Sheol is never translated as *mneema*.

Fourth, *kever* and Sheol are never used in Hebrew poetic parallelism as equivalents. They are always contrasted and never equated. *Kever* is the fate of the body, while Sheol is the fate of the soul (Ps. 16:8–11).

Fifth, Sheol is "under the earth," or "the underworld," while graves were built as sepulchres above the earth, or caves, or holes in the earth. Sheol is called the underworld in Isa. 14:9. It is also called "the lower parts of the earth" (KJV) in Ps. 63:9; Isa. 44:23; Ezek. 26:20; 31:14, 16, 18; 32:18, 24. Sheol is the opposite of heaven (Ps. 139:8). One must go "down" to get to Sheol (Gen. 37:35).

Sixth, while bodies are unconscious in the grave, those in Sheol are viewed as being conscious (Isa. 14:4–7; 44:23; Ezek. 31:16; 32:21).

Seventh, an examination of the usages of *kever* and Sheol reveals that Sheol cannot mean the grave. The following twenty contrasts between *kever* and Sheol demonstrates this point:

1. While the *kabar* (to bury) is used in connection with *kever*, it is never used in connection with Sheol. We can bury someone in a grave but we cannot bury anyone in Sheol (Gen. 23:4, 6, 9, 19, 20; 49:30, 31, etc.).

2. While *kever* is found in its plural form "graves" (Ex. 14:11), the word Sheol is never pluralized.

3. While a grave is located at a specific site (Ex. 14:11), Sheol is never localized, because it is everywhere accessible at death no matter where the death takes place. No grave is necessary in order to go to Sheol.

4. While we can purchase or sell a grave (Gen. 23:4–20), Scripture never speaks of Sheol being purchased or sold.

5. While we can own a grave as personal property (Gen. 23:4–20), nowhere in Scripture is Sheol owned by man.

6. While we can discriminate between graves and pick the "choicest site" (Gen. 23:6), nowhere in Scripture is a "choice" Sheol pitted against a "poor" Sheol.

7. While we can drop a dead body into a grave (Gen. 50:13), no one can drop anyone into Sheol.

8. While we can erect a monument over a grave (Gen. 35:20), Sheol is never spoken of as having monuments.

9. While we can, with ease, open or close a grave (2 Kings 23:16), Sheol is never opened or closed by man.

10. While we can touch a grave (Num. 19:18), no one is ever said in Scripture to touch Sheol.

11. While touching a grave brings ceremonial defilement (Num. 19:16), the Scriptures never speak of anyone being defiled by Sheol.

12. While we can enter and leave a tomb or grave (2 Kings 23:16), no one is ever said to enter and then leave Sheol.

13. While we can choose the site of our own grave (Gen. 23:4–9), Sheol is never spoken of as something we can pick and choose.

14. While we can remove or uncover the bodies or bones in a grave (2 Kings 23:16), the Scriptures never speak of man removing or uncovering anything in Sheol.

15. While we can beautify a grave with ornate carvings or pictures (Gen. 35:20), Sheol is never beautified by man.

16. While graves can be robbed or defiled (Jer. 8:1, 2), Sheol is never spoken of as being robbed or defiled by man.

17. While a grave can be destroyed by man (Jer. 8:1, 2), nowhere in Scripture is man said to be able to destroy Sheol.

18. While a grave can be full, Sheol is never full (Prov. 27:20).

19. While we can see a grave, Sheol is always invisible.

20. While we can visit the graves of loved ones, nowhere in Scripture is man said to visit Sheol.

Sheol and Its Inhabitants

Given the principle of progressive revelation, it is no surprise that the Old Testament is vague in its description of Sheol and the condition of those in it. While the Old Testament prophets stated many things about Sheol, they did not expound in any measure of depth on this subject. Another reason for this vagueness is that a conscious afterlife was so universally accepted that it was assumed by the biblical authors to be the belief of anyone who read the Scriptures. Since it was not a point of conflict, no great attention was given to it.

The following things are stated about Sheol with the caution that figurative language was used by biblical authors in their description of Sheol and the conditions of those in it. Much harm has been done by literalizing what was intended to be figurative.

First, Sheol is said to have "gates" by which one enters and "bars" which keep one in (Job 17:16; Isa. 38:10). Such figurative language conveys the idea that Sheol is a realm from which no escape is possible.

Second, the Old Testament describes Sheol in the following ways:

1. Sheol is a shadowy place or place of darkness (Job 10:21, 22; Ps. 143:3). Evidently, it is another dimension which is not exposed to the rays of the sun.

2. It is viewed as being "down," "beneath the earth," or in "the lower parts of the earth" (Job 11:8; Isa. 44:23; 57:9; Ezek. 26:20; Amos 9:2). These figures of speech should not be literalized into an absurd cosmology. They merely indicate that Sheol is not a part of this world but has an existence of its own in another dimension.

3. It is a place where one can reunite with his ancestors, tribe or people (Gen. 15:15; 25:8; 35:29; 37:35; 49:33; Num. 20:24, 28; 31:2; Deut. 32:50; 34:5; 2 Sam. 12:23). This cannot refer to one common mass grave where everyone was buried. No such graves ever existed in recorded history. Sheol is the place where the souls of all men go at death. That is why Jacob looked forward to reuniting with Joseph in Sheol. While death meant separation from the living, the Old Testament prophets clearly understood that it also meant reunion with the departed.

4. It seems that Sheol has different sections. There is the contrast between "the lowest part" and "the highest part" of Sheol (Deut. 32:22). This figurative language implies that there are divisions or distinctions within Sheol. Perhaps the Old Testament's emphatic distinction between the righteous and the wicked in this life indicates that this distinction continues on in the afterlife. Thus the wicked are said to be in "the lowest part," while the righteous are in "the higher part" of Sheol. While this is not clearly stated in the Old Testament, there seems to be some kind of distinction within Sheol. Later rabbinic writers clearly taught that Sheol had two sections. The righteous were in bliss in one section while the wicked were in torment in the other.

Third, the condition of those in Sheol is described in the following ways:

1. At death man becomes a *rephaim*, i.e., a "ghost, "shade," or "disembodied spirit" according to Job 26:5; Ps. 88:10; Prov. 2:18; 9:18; 21:16; Isa. 14:9; 26:14, 19. Instead of describing man as passing into nonexistence, the Old Testament states that man becomes a disembodied spirit. The usage of the word *rephaim* irrefutably establishes this truth. Langenscheidt's *Hebrew-English Dictionary to the Old Testament* (p. 324) defines *rephaim* as referring to the "departed spirits, shades." Brown, Driver and Briggs (p. 952) define *rephaim* as "shades, ghosts . . . name of dead in Sheol." Keil and Delitzsch

define *rephaim* as referring to "those who are bodiless in the state after death."[15]

From the meaning of *rephaim*, it is clear that when the body dies, man enters a new kind of existence and experience. He now exists as a spirit creature and experiences what angels and other disincarnate spirits experience. Just as angels are disincarnate energy beings composed only of "mind" or mental energy and are capable of supradimensional activity and such things as thought and speech without the need of a physical body, even so once man dies, he too becomes a disembodied supradimensional energy being and is capable of thought and speech without the need of a body. This is why the dead are described as "spirits" and "ghosts" throughout the Scriptures.

This concept is carried on into the New Testament in such places as Luke 24:37–39. A belief in "ghosts" necessarily entails a belief that man survives the death of the body.

2. Those in Sheol are pictured as conversing with each other and even making moral judgments on the lifestyle of new arrivals (Isa. 14:9–20; 44:23; Ezek. 32:21). They are thus conscious entities while in Sheol.

3. Once in Sheol, all experiences related exclusively to physical life are no longer possible. Those in Sheol do not marry and procreate children because they do not have bodies. Neither do they plan and execute business transactions. Once in Sheol, they cannot attend public worship in the temple and give sacrifices or praise. There are no bodily pleasures such as eating or drinking. Those in Sheol do not have any wisdom or knowledge about what is happening in the land of the living. They are cut off from the living. They have entered a new dimension of reality with its own kind of existence (Ps. 6:5; Eccles. 9:10, etc.).

4. God's judgment upon the wicked does not cease when the wicked die in their sins. Thus some of the spirits in Sheol experience the following:

a. God's anger (Deut. 32:22): According to Moses, the wicked experience the fire of YHWH's anger in the "lowest part of Sheol." This passage would make no sense if the wicked are nonexistent and Sheol is the grave.

b. Distress (Ps. 116:3): The Hebrew word *matzar* refers to the distress that is felt when in the straits of a difficulty.[16] It is found in this sense in Ps. 118:5. Also, the word *chevel*, which is the poetic parallel for *matzar*, means "cords of distress" (2 Sam. 22:6; Ps. 18:6).[17]

c. Writhing in pain (Job 26:5): The Hebrew word *chool* means to twist and turn in pain like a woman giving birth.[18]

It is obvious that nonexistence can hardly experience anger, distress, or pain. Thus, there are hints in the above passages that not everyone experiences blessedness in the afterlife. Beyond these three passages, the Old Testament does not speak of torment in the intermediate state. While it speaks of the "everlasting humiliation and contempt" which awaits the wicked after the resurrection (Dan. 12:2), the Old Testament tells us very little about the intermediate suffering of the wicked in Sheol.

5. In the Old Testament, the righteous as well as the wicked went to Sheol at death (Gen. 37:35). Although this is true, the Old Testament saints did not have a clear understanding of what to expect in Sheol. They were constantly torn by mixed emotions when they contemplated their death. They did not experience the same joy and bold confidence that New Testament saints express (Acts 7:59). While New Testament saints think of death as a "gain" (Phil. 1:21), the Old Testament saints thought of it as "loss."

Given the principle of progressive revelation, Old Testament saints simply did not have all the information which was needed to approach death with peace and joy. Just as the lack of New Testament revelation prevented them from obtaining a clear conscience and full assurance of faith (Heb. 10:1–4), even so they could not approach death with joy. That this is true can be established upon several lines of reasoning.

First, the writer to the book of Hebrews tells us that the Old Testament saints were in bondage to the fear of death and that Satan used this to oppress them.

> Since then the children share in flesh and blood, He Himself likewise also partook of the same, that through death He might render powerless him who had the power of death, that is, the devil; and might deliver those who through fear of death were subject to slavery all their lives. (Heb. 2:14, 15)

Only after the Messiah came and wrested the keys of death and Hades from the Evil One would God's people experience freedom from the fear of death (Rev. 1:18).

The bondage of fear which gripped the Old Testament saints expressed itself in different ways. They had a fear of being separated from their living loved ones. They were afraid of being severed from the joys of life (Ps. 6). They begged to be delivered from death and Sheol because they did not look forward to death (Ps. 13). This is why they spoke of the "sorrows" (KJV) and "terrors" of death (Ps. 18:4; 55:4; 116:3) instead of the triumph in death which New Testament saints express (2 Tim. 4:6–8).

Second, while the overall picture of death was somewhat gloomy in the Old Testament, yet God had begun to reveal to His people that they would be ushered into His joyous presence after death. To be sure, these were only hints of glory, but hints they were. The ascension of Enoch and Elijah to heaven indicated that the righteous could be taken into God's presence (Gen. 5:24, cf. Heb. 11:5; 2 Kings 2:11). The verb which described Enoch's and Elijah's ascension (*laqach*) was later used to describe the passage of the righteous out of Sheol into heaven (Ps. 49:15; cf. 73:24). Asaph expressed the hope that he would go to dwell at the throne of glory at death. Later rabbinic writers consistently spoke of the righteous going to the throne of glory at death.

> Nevertheless I am continually with Thee; Thou hast taken hold of my right hand. With Thy counsel Thou wilt guide me, and afterward *receive me to glory*. Whom have I in heaven but Thee? And besides Thee, I desire nothing on earth. (Ps. 73:23– 25)

The Old Testament saints looked forward to reuniting with their departed loved ones (Gen. 37:35). This must have afforded them some comfort.

Also, the Old Testament believers knew that Sheol was open to God's sight (Job 26:6) and that they would still be in God's presence and protection (Ps. 139:8).

While the patriarchs went in mourning to Sheol, by the time of the Wisdom literature, a more optimistic note was beginning to be sounded. The progress from Gen. 37:35 to Ps. 73:24 indicates a gradual change of attitude toward death which progressive revelation made possible. While Old Testament saints knew that they were going to Sheol at death, there were hints that they might be taken to heaven to be at God's throne after death.

HADES

The second key term in the biblical understanding of death and the afterlife is the Greek word Hades. This word forms a linguistic bridge which takes us from the Old Testament view of death to the New Testament position. The importance of a proper interpretation of this word cannot be overstressed.

In the Septuagint, Hades is found 71 times. It is the Greek equivalent for Sheol 64 times. The other seven times it is found in the Septuagint, it is the translation of other Hebrew words, some of which shed significant light on what Hades meant to the translators of the Septuagint.

In Job 33:22, Hades is the translation of the Hebrew word *memeteim*, or "destroying angels [KJV] . . . the angels who are commissioned by God to slay the man."[19] In this sense it refers to disincarnate spirit creatures.

It is also used in Job 38:17 as the translation for the Hebrew, "the realm of ghosts or shades" (KJV).[20]

It is used for "the shades of the underworld" in Prov. 2:18.[21] This refers to the spirits of the departed in Sheol who are viewed as "the dwellers in the Kingdom of the dead as in Homer and Virgil and like the Latin word Inferi, it stands for the realm of disembodied souls."[22]

Not once is Hades the Greek equivalent of the Hebrew word for grave (*kever*). Not once does it mean nonexistence or unconsciousness. The times it is used for words other than Sheol, it clearly means the world of spirits. There is, therefore, no way to escape the conclusion that the translators of the Septuagint clearly understood that Hades referred to the realm of disembodied souls or spirits; and, we must also emphasize, that the translators of the Septuagint did not obtain this concept from Platonic Greek thought but from the Hebrew concept of Sheol itself.

The Lexicographical Evidence

When we turn to the lexicographical material, we find that the authors of the Septuagint were correct in their usage of Hades as the Greek equivalent for the Hebrew Sheol.

Arndt and Gingrich based their *A Greek-English Lexicon of the New Testament* on the work of W. Bauer, one of the greatest Greek scholars who ever lived. They define Hades as "the underworld . . . the place of the dead" (p. 16). *Thayer's Greek-English Lexicon* (p. 11) states that Hades comes from two words which joined together mean "invisible," or "unseen." Thus it refers to "the common receptacle of disembodied spirits."

The lexicographical material is so unanimous in defining Hades as the world of disembodied souls that the Princeton theologian, A. A. Hodge, stated:

> Modern Hebrew and Greek scholars . . . unite with near unanimity in maintaining that these words (Sheol and Hades) never on a single occasion in the Bible mean either "hell" or "the grave," but always and only the invisible spirit world.[23]

Modern commentators do not hesitate to define Hades as the place of disembodied souls.[24] This is why no Hebrew or Greek scholar defines Hades as "the grave" or the "state of unconsciousness or nonexistence."

The historical context of Hades and comparative studies or parallel words in other languages have so firmly established that Hades refers to the place of disembodied souls that there is no controversy on this point among biblical scholars. The conditional immortalists, whether cultic or neo-orthodox, simply ignore this linguistic and lexicographical material.

Hades and Its Inhabitants

The KJV mistranslated the word Hades in every occurrence just as it did with the word Sheol. It is found ten times in the Greek New Testament. The Greek text underlying the KJV has it an eleventh time in 1 Cor. 15:55, but this is a corrupt reading.

Perhaps the best way to clarify what the New Testament teaches about Hades is to first of all state what Hades does not mean. Once we have cleared away any misconceptions of this word, then we can present its meaning in the New Testament.

First, Hades does not mean death, because the Greek word *thanatos* is the word for death in the New Testament. Also, Hades and death appear together in such passages as Rev. 1:18 where they cannot be viewed as synonyms.

Second, Hades is not the grave, because the Greek word *mneema* is the word for grave in the New Testament. Also, all the arguments which demonstrated that Sheol cannot mean the grave apply equally to Hades seeing that Hades is the equivalent for the Hebrew word Sheol. The New Testament's dependence upon the Septuagint demonstrates this point.

Third, Hades is not "hell," i.e., the place of final punishment for the wicked, because the Greek word Gehenna is the word for "hell" in the New Testament.

Fourth, Hades is not "heaven," i.e., the place where the soul of the righteous goes at death to await the coming resurrection, because the Greek word *ouranos* is the word for heaven in the New Testament.

Fifth, Hades is not the place of eternal bliss for the righteous after the resurrection, because the new heavens and the new earth or the everlasting kingdom refer to this place (Matt. 25:34; Rev. 21:1).

Having clarified what Hades does not mean, we can now state the New Testament meaning of this crucial word.

First, we must once again emphasize the importance of the principle of progressive revelation. While Hades was consistently used in the Greek version of the Old Testament as the Greek equivalent for the Hebrew word Sheol, this does not mean that Hades should be limited to the Old Testament meaning of Sheol. The New Testament picks up where the Old Testament left off by progressively developing the concept of what happens to the soul of man after death. We should expect that the fuller revelation of Christ and the apostles will clarify what was vague in the Old Testament (Heb. 1:1–3).

During the intertestamental period, the Jewish concept of Sheol had progressed to the stage where it was believed that Sheol had two distinct compartments, or sections. One section was a place of torment to which the wicked went while the other was a place of conscious bliss, often called "Abraham's bosom" or "paradise," to which the righteous were carried by angels.[25] The rabbis even discussed how many angels it took to carry the righteous to Abraham's bosom.

The rabbinic understanding of Sheol is the basis for Christ's illustration in Luke 16:19–31. While only the rich man was directly said to be "in Hades" (v. 23), the phrase "Abraham's bosom" to which the angels carried Lazarus (vv. 22, 23) must be interpreted as the section of Hades reserved for the righteous. The dialogue between the rich man and Lazarus is an echo of multiple stories in which such dialogues were described. Thus, initially, the first occurrence of Hades in the New Testament refers to a concept of an afterlife which had evolved beyond the Old Testament concept of Sheol and reflected the progress of understanding which had been accomplished during the period between Malachi and Matthew.

Given the principle of progressive revelation, that Hades would evolve from merely being the equivalent of Sheol into a word which meant more than Sheol is understandable and expected. That Hades would have an intertestamental rabbinic meaning at the beginning of the New Testament and then evolve to mean more than the rabbinic understanding is also expected.

It is on this basis that all attempts to limit New Testament teaching on the afterlife to the gospel materials such as Luke 16 must be rejected as a defective view. This view is built upon the assumption that what Hades meant in the Gospels is what it must mean in the Epistles. This is a failure to observe the principle of the progress of doctrine as well as the principle of progressive revelation as given in the New Testament itself.[26]

We must also point out that when we state that the Old Testament saints and the intertestamental Jews did not have a clear and precise understanding of what happened after death, this does not mean that their experience was not greater than their understanding. To deny that they understood where they were going at death does not mean that they did not get there!

This also leads us to avoid the unnecessary debate on whether or not the story of the rich man and Lazarus in Luke 16 should be viewed as a literal account or as a parable.

Many orthodox writers treat Luke 16 as a literal account.[27] They deny that it is a parable on the grounds that (1) the beggar must have been a real historical character because his name was given; (2) Abraham was a real historical character; and (3) in parables names are not given. Thus many orthodox writers demand that the story of the rich man and Lazarus be viewed as a literal account.

Other writers usually treat Luke 16:19–31 as a parable and end up denying that it teaches anything about death or the afterlife. They usually give interpretations which are quite wild and far-fetched.[28]

The basic problem is both sides assume that if Christ's story is a parable, it is meaningless, and if it is not, it must be a literal account. They both fail to recognize that Christ's teaching was rabbinic in methodology and that rabbinic parables often revolved around real historical characters.

The rabbinic literature before, during, and after the time of Christ is filled with parables which built imaginative stories around real historical characters.[29] There are multiple examples in the Talmud and Midrash of parables in which Abraham had dialogues with people such as Nimrod, with whom he could never have spoken literally.[30] Everyone understood that these parables and dialogues did not literally take place. It was understood that the rabbis used imaginative stories and dialogues as a teaching method. It was understood by all that these dialogues never took place.

Therefore, it does not bother us in the least to say that Christ used a rabbinic story and dialogue in Luke 16:19–31 which was not "true" or "real" in the sense of being literal. It is obvious that Lazarus did not literally sit in Abraham's literal bosom. The rich man did not have literal lips which literal water could quench.

What is important for us to grasp is that Christ used the mental images conjured up by this rabbinic parable to teach that, in the hereafter, the wicked experience torment and the righteous bliss. This is clear from the rabbinic sources from which he drew this parable.

Since the dialogue between the rich man and Abraham was a teaching tool used by the rabbis before Christ, it is obvious that Christ was not trying to teach that we will talk with the wicked in the hereafter. He was merely using the dialogue method to get across the concept that there is no escape from torment, no second chance, and we must believe the Scriptures in *this* life unto salvation.

That the Epistles would further develop what happens to the soul after death and go beyond the gospel material is also expected. The apostles were conscious of the fact that their understanding was clouded during their sojourn with Christ (John 12:16). It was only after Pentecost and the final revelations given to the apostles that they could, at last, speak of death and the afterlife with clarity. It was only after the last pieces of the cosmic puzzle of revelation were given that they could see the whole picture.

Before Christ's ascension, believers as well as unbelievers were said to enter Sheol or Hades. After Christ's resurrection, the New

Testament pictures believers after death as entering heaven to be with Christ (Phil. 1:23), which is far better than Hades. They are present with the Lord (2 Cor. 5:6–8), worshiping with the angelic hosts of heaven (Heb.12:22, 23) at the altar of God (Rev. 6:9–11). Thus believers do not now enter Hades but ascend immediately to the throne of God.

In the New Testament, there is, therefore, a development of understanding which took place after Christ's resurrection. Before Jesus was raised from the dead, the apostles assumed that everyone went to Sheol or Hades. This Hades had two sections, one for the righteous and one for the wicked. But Christ's resurrection changed this picture. Thus Paul uses the language of transition when he speaks of Christ taking the righteous out of Hades and bringing them into heaven (Eph. 4:8, 9).

That Christ went to Hades, i.e., the world beyond death, is clear from Acts 2:31. While in Hades, Peter pictures Christ as proclaiming to "the spirits now in prison" the completion of His atonement (1 Pet. 3:18–22). Whereas "paradise" in the gospel account (Luke 23:43) referred to the section of Hades reserved for the righteous, by the time Paul wrote 2 Cor. 12:2–4, it was assumed that paradise had been taken out of Hades and was now placed in the third heaven.

According to the post-resurrection teaching in the New Testament, the believer now goes to heaven at death to await the coming resurrection and the eternal state. But, what of the wicked? The wicked at death descend into Hades which is a place of temporary torment while they await the coming resurrection and their eternal punishment.

First, it is clear that the souls of the wicked are in torment during the intermediate state in Hades. The Apostle Peter stated this in language which could not be clearer:

> Then the Lord knows how to rescue the godly from temptation, and *to keep the unrighteous under punishment* for the day of judgment. (2 Pet. 2:9)

First, Peter says that the wicked are "kept" unto the day of judgment. This word is in the present, active, infinitive form, which means that the wicked are being held captive continuously. If the wicked merely pass into nonexistence at death, there would be nothing left to be "kept" unto the day of judgment. Obviously, Peter is grammatically picturing the wicked as being guarded like prisoners in a jail until the day of final judgment.

Second, Peter says that the wicked are "being tormented." This word is in the present, passive, participle form and means that the wicked are continuously being tormented as an on-going activity.

If Peter wanted to teach that the wicked receive their full punishment at death by passing into nonexistence, then he would have used the aorist tense. Instead, he uses those Greek tenses which were the only ones available to him in the Greek language to express conscious, continuous torment. The grammar of the text irrefutably establishes that the wicked are in torment while they await their final day of judgment.

When the day of judgment arrives, Hades will be emptied of its inhabitants, and the wicked will stand before God for their final sentence (Rev. 20:13–15). Thus, we conclude that Hades is the temporary intermediate state between death and the resurrection where the wicked are in conscious torment. Hades will be emptied at the resurrection, and then the wicked will be cast into "hell" (Gehenna).

GEHENNA

The third and last crucial term is the word Gehenna. This word is found twelve times in the New Testament and is correctly translated each time by the KJV as "hell." It is a word which describes the ultimate fate of the wicked after the general resurrection and judgment. While Sheol and Hades describe the temporary abode of the dead until the resurrection, Gehenna is the place of future punishment in the eternal state.

The Lexicographical Evidence

The word Gehenna is the Greek equivalent for "the valley of Hinnom" (Josh. 15:8; 18:16; Neh. 11:30). It thus originally referred to the Valley of Hinnom, which was just outside the city of Jerusalem. According to *Thayer's Greek-English Lexicon* (p. 111), it was the place where idolatrous Jews gave human sacrifices to pagan deities (2 Kings 23:10; 2 Chron. 28:3; 33:6). Because of these horrible idolatrous practices, the Valley of Hinnom was hated and considered "unclean" by pious Jews. In Christ's day, this hatred of the Valley of Hinnom caused the valley to become the town dump where all the garbage of Jerusalem could be thrown. Unclean corpses as well as normal garbage were thrown into it. Because garbage was constantly being thrown into the valley, the fires never stopped burning and the worms never stopped eating.

This picture of an unclean garbage dump where the fires and the worms never died out became to the Jewish mind an appropriate description of the ultimate fate of all idol worshipers. Gehenna came to be understood as the final, eternal garbage dump where all idolators would be thrown after the resurrection. The wicked would suffer in Gehenna forever because the fires would never stop burning them and the worms would never stop gnawing them.

Arndt and Gingrich also point out that the Jewish belief, before Christ, placed the last judgment of the wicked in the Valley of Hinnom. They concluded that it means "the place of judgment."[31] *The International Standard Bible Encyclopedia* (Vol. II, p. 1182) states that Gehenna refers to "the place of eternal punishment of the wicked." McClintock and Strong's *Encyclopedia of Biblical, Theological and Ecclesiastical Literature* defines Gehenna as "the place of eternal punishment." Both Coon and Mills define Gehenna as referring to "the place of eternal punishment."[32]

The Intertestamental Literature

The wicked do not descend into Gehenna at death, because it is the final place of punishment for the wicked after the resurrection.[33]

> In that hour the Lord will requite the nations of the world with a great and ceaseless retribution, and hurl them down to the Gehenna, where they will be punished for generation upon generation. (Mid. Gen. 908)

The talmudic literature states that there are two classes of people who descend into Gehenna. The disobedient among Israel descend into Gehenna for "twelve months" in order to be cleansed of their sins in its fire. They then ascend to the throne of glory in paradise where the righteous among Israel had already ascended at death (Bab. Tal. RH64). Idolaters and blasphemers remain in Gehenna "to be punished for all generations" (Bab. Tal. RH65).

The figurative language utilized in the rabbinic description of Gehenna, such as "fire" (Mid. Gen. 214), "worms" (Bab. Tal. Shah 777, 778; The Wisdom of Sirach VII.9), "weeping" (Bab. Tal. ER129), "darkness" (Mid. Gen. 257), "judgment" (Bab. Tal. ER126), etc., are all carried over by the teaching of Christ and the apostles into the New Testament itself. The descriptive language of the Jewish apocalyptic literature, such as "fire and torment" (4th Macc. 12:12, 13), "fire and sulfur" (Enoch LXVII.6), "black recesses of hell" (Sibylline IV, p. 83), etc., are clearly utilized by Peter, Jude and John in their descriptions of the ultimate fate of the wicked after the resurrection.

This intertestamental evidence is so strong and consistent that the great Church historian Phillip Schaff states:

> Everlasting punishment of the wicked was and always will be the orthodox theory. It was held by the Jews at the time of

Christ, with the exception of the Sadducees, who denied the resurrection.[34]

After an extensive research of intertestamental literature, the greatest Christian Talmudic scholar, Alfred Edersheim, a noted Hebrew Christian, concluded that Gehenna was understood in Christ's time to refer to the place of eternal, conscious punishment for the wicked after the resurrection.[35] We have placed his discussion of the rabbinic sources in Appendix I for the benefit of the reader.

Christ and Gehenna

The awful mental image of everlasting torment in the fires of Gehenna was conjured up in the minds of the early disciples by the Master himself. Out of its twelve occurrences in the New Testament, Gehenna is found no less than eleven times on the lips of the Lord Jesus himself.

To think that Christ was ignorant of what Gehenna meant to the common people of His day or to assume that He was mistaken in using the rabbinic descriptions of Gehenna is to do great injustice to Him who was the greatest teacher who ever lived. Indeed, the mere fact that Christ utilized the rabbinic language connected with Gehenna, such as "unquenchable fire" and "never-dying worms," demonstrates beyond all doubt to any reasonable person that He deliberately used the word Gehenna to impress upon His hearers that eternal punishment awaits the wicked after the resurrection. No other conclusion is possible.

The teaching of Christ concerning Gehenna is as follows:

First, Gehenna is the place of judgment (Matt. 23:33). He even used the rabbinic expression, "the judgment of Gehenna" (Bab. Tal. ER126).

Second, Gehenna is always placed at the end of the world after the resurrection (Matt. 5:22; 23:33). This was expounded by John in Rev. 20:1–15. This was also the rabbinic position (Mid. Gen. 159).

Third, Gehenna is the place where the body as well as the soul is punished (Matt. 5:22; 10:28; Mark 9:43–48). The rabbis saw that the resurrection of the wicked was necessary in order for them to receive their full punishment in the body (Mid. Gen. 159; 211n4).

Fourth, Gehenna was the place of conscious torment. When Christ used the phrases "unquenchable fire" and "never-dying worms" (Mark 9:47, 48, author's paraphrase), He was utilizing biblical (Isa. 66:24), apocryphal (Judith XVI:17), and talmudic (Mid. Gen. 214) images which all meant conscious suffering.

The annihilationists have a counter argument at this point. They point out that, literally speaking, while the worms and the fire in a city dump may destroy a dead carcass, it cannot be said that the dead carcass feels any torment. Therefore, they conclude that Christ's language must be interpreted to mean that the wicked will be annihilated, not tormented.

The problem with this interpretation is that it fails to take into account that when Christ spoke of Gehenna in such terms as "worms and fire," He was clearly using rabbinic phraseology. Thus, it is more crucial to discover how these words were understood in rabbinic literature than by pointing to modern city dumps.

The intertestamental literature is clear that the Jews believed that the departed could feel what was happening to their dead body. Indeed, when the worms start gnawing on the body, "the worms are as painful to the dead as a needle in the flesh of the living" (Bab. Tal. Shah. 777, 778).

Since the "gnawing worms" clearly meant conscious torment in rabbinic thought, the annihilationists' argument is invalid due to their ignorance of the meaning of such rabbinic terminology. That Judith XVI:17 also teaches conscious torment is clear.

Fifth, the wicked are cast into Gehenna and will remain there for all eternity (Matt. 5:29, 30). In Gehenna, the wicked are "destroyed" (Matt. 10:28).

That the word "destroyed" (*apollumi*) does not mean "to annihilate" or "to pass into nonexistence" is clear from the rabbinic meaning of the word, the lexicographical significance of the word, and the way the word is used in the New Testament.

Thayer's Greek-English Lexicon defines *apollumi* as "to be delivered up to eternal misery" (p. 36). Since Thayer himself was a Unitarian who did not believe in eternal punishment, his definition could only be the result of his knowledge of the meaning of this Greek word. There is no lexicographical evidence for the annihilationist's position that *apollumi* means "to annihilate" or "to pass into nonexistence."

That this word cannot mean "nonexistence" is clear from the way it is consistently used in the New Testament (Matt. 9:17; Luke 15:4, 6, 8, 9; John 6:12, 27; 2 Cor. 4:9; etc.). Do people pass into nonexistence when they are killed by a sword (Matt. 26:52) or a snake? (1 Cor. 10:9). Do people become nonexistent when they are hungry? (Luke 15:17). Do wineskins pass into nonexistence when they are destroyed by bursting? (Matt. 9:17). Is food annihilated when it spoils? (John 6:27).

In every instance where the word *apollumi* is found in the New Testament, something other than annihilation is being described. Indeed, there isn't a single instance in the New Testament where *apollumi* means annihilation in the strict meaning of the word.

CONCLUSION

Gehenna as a place of final punishment was a clear rabbinic teaching before Christ was ever born. The Midrash, the Babylonian and Jerusalem Talmuds, and apocryphal literature refer to Gehenna hundreds of times. The Midrash alone refers to Gehenna over seventy-five times.

The vivid imagery and striking phraseology found in the intertestamental literature, which described Gehenna as the ultimate place of eternal torment for the wicked, was clearly carried over into the New Testament itself by the teaching of Christ and the apostles.

That the ultimate fate of the wicked will be eternal, conscious torment will be further argued in a later chapter, but we have demonstrated in this chapter that Gehenna is the ultimate fate of all impenitent sinners according to rabbinic and New Testament literature. The concept of Universalism, which sees no one going to Gehenna, or Gehenna ultimately being emptied of all sinners, is an ideal which is absolutely foreign to the intertestamental and New Testament literature. The idea of annihilationism, in which the wicked cease to exist, may indeed be found in some of the intertestamental literature, particularly those works which were influenced by the Sadducees or Stoics. But enough has been given in this chapter to demonstrate that the majority view, that of the common man in the street, was of an eternal, conscious torment of the wicked in Gehenna.

NOTES

1. Keil & Delitzsch, *Commentaries on the Old Testament* (Grand Rapids: Wm. B. Eerdmans Pub. Co., n.d.), Vol. I, p. 338.

2. *Selected Shorter Writings of Benjamin B. Warfield* (ed. J. Meeter; New Jersey: Pres. & Ref. Pub. Co., 1970), pp. 339, 345.

3. See the works of Charles, Fife, Hough, Motzer, Marcarnty, Tromp, etc., for the details.

4. N. Tromp, *Primitive Conceptions of Death and the Nether World in the Old Testament* (Rome: Pontifical Biblical Institute, 1969), p. 6.

5. R. Charles, *A Critical History of the Doctrine of a Future Life* (London: Adam & Charles Block, 1913), pp. 34f.; L. Bailey, *Biblical Perspectives on Death* (Philadelphia: Fortress Press, 1979), pp. 5f.

6. M. Fisher, "Some Contributions of Ethiopic Studies" in *The Law and the Prophets* (New Jersey: Pres. & Ref. Pub. Co., 1974), p. 81.

7. *Essays in Greco-Roman and Related Talmudic Literature* (New York: KTAV Pub. House, 1977), p. 36.

8. Ibid., p. 42.

9. Midrash: Gen. 96, 908; Bab. Tal. Shah 589; 777–779: Enoch 103:7, etc.

10. Midrash: Gen. 409, 516; Num. 733; Ecc. 83,229; Bab. Tal. Shah 777–779; PT Mo'ed Katan 111.5,826, Yebamuth XVI.3,15c, Bereshith Rabba c. 7, Vayyekin Rabba XVIII.1; Kohelith Rabb 1.15, ed., Rom. 6a; Ruth Rabba 111.3,6c, etc.

11. C. Hodge, *Systematic Theology* (London: James Clarke & Co., Ltd., 1960), Vol. III, p. 770; see also: Hough, p. 66; Bailey, p. 75; Bartlett, p. 143, 168; Strong, p. 994; Schaff, Vol. II, pp. 566, 606, 607; Charles, p. 167; Fife, p. 25; Buds, p. 16; Pussey, p. 49, etc.

12. *Essays in Greco-Roman and Related Talmudic Literature*, pp. 43, 44.

13. *Lang's Commentary on the Holy Scriptures*, Vol. I., p. 589.

14. Ibid., p. 588

15. Keil & Delitzsch, ibid., Vol. II on Job, p. 52.

16. Brown, Driver, and Briggs, p. 865.

17. Ibid., p. 286.

18. Ibid., p. 297.

19. Keil & Delitszch, ibid., Job II, p. 228; Lange, ibid., Vol. IV, p. 558.

20. Lange, ibid., p. 604.

21. Keil & Delitzsch, ibid., Prov., p. 83.

22. Lange, ibid., Prov., p. 56.

23. A. Hodge, *Evangelical Theology* (Edinburgh: The Banner of Truth Trust, 1976), pp. 372, 373.

24. See Lange, Robertson, Alford, etc.

25. A. Edersheim, *The Life and Time of Jesus the Messiah* (Grand Rapids: Wm. B. Eerdmans Pub. Co., 1962), Vol. II, pp. 279–281, 791–796. For further sources in rabbinic literature, see: Midrash: Gen. 68; Exo. 48; Lev. 405; 55:80; Ecc. 197. Bab. Tal.: Ber. 173; Shah. 589; ER 129.

26. The Classic work by Bernard, *The Progress of Doctrine in the New Testament*, given at Oxford University, develops this position brilliantly.

27. J. Calvin, *Psychopannychia*, p. 431.

28. For examples of bizarre interpretations see: *Let God Be True* (New York: Watchtower and Tract Society, 1946), p. 78f.; R. Whitelaw, *Hell, the Abode of the Dead* (Virginia: G.A.M. Printers, 1981), pp. 19–28.

29. Midrash: Lev. 407; Eth. Enoch 22; Kohelith Rabba 1.15, d. Rom. 6a; Ruth Rabba 111.3, 6c.

30. Midrash: Gen. 310, 311.

31. Arndt and Gingrich, ibid., p. 152.

32. Coon, *The Doctrine of Future and Endless Punishment Proved*

(Cincinnati: J.F. & V.P. James, 1850), p. 72; *Perspectives on Death* (ed. L. Mills; New York: Abingdon Press, 1969), p. 32.

33. Midrash: Gen. 22N9, 159:T.Shah. XIII.4, 5; etc.

34. P. Schaff, *History of the Christian Church* (Wm. B. Eerdmans Pub. Co., 1973), Vol. II, pp. 606, 607.

35. A. Edersheim, *The Life and Times of Jesus the Messiah* (Wm. B. Eerdmans Pub. Co., 1962), Vol. II, pp. 791–796.

36. *Thayer's Greek-English Lexicon of the New Testament*, p. 64.

Chapter 4

IMMORTALITY, RESURRECTION, AND EVERLASTING LIFE

When someone asks us if we believe in "the immortality of the soul," we respond by asking them to define their words because what they mean by "the immortality of the soul" will determine our answer.

Some are thinking of "essential immortality," which refers to a life having neither beginning nor end. According to the Bible, only God has essential immortality as an attribute of His being (1 Tim. 6:16). Since man begins at conception and does not come from eternity, he does not have essential immortality. Only God is from eternity to eternity (Ps. 90:1, 2).

Other people have in the mind the Greek idea of the preexistence of the soul or the Eastern ideas of transmigration or reincarnation. The Bible is clearly against such ideas. Man does not preexist his conception in the womb, and neither does he go through an endless cycle of rebirths. Since we have already dealt with these subjects in *Reincarnation and Christianity* (Bethany House Pub., 1980), no further comment will be made on these subjects.

Others may be thinking of "natural immortality," which views man as an autonomous and independent immortal being through some kind of innate power. This also is erroneous, because man is always and absolutely dependent upon the Creator for this life as well as for the next life. Man should never be viewed as independent or autonomous. Life in this world and in the next must always be viewed as a gift from God.

Or again, some view death as "normal" and man's existence in an afterlife as "natural." While it is natural for angels to exist as spiritual entities, it is not natural for man to do so. Thus, man's death is not normal but a terrible ripping apart of what was never intended to be separated. The spiritual and physical sides of man are separated by death. And his existence as a spiritual entity alone is unnatural. This is why the resurrection is necessary. Man was created as a physical-spiritual being and must ultimately be reconstituted in the same way. Death is an unnatural event and man's subsequent disembodied state is an unnatural existence which only the resurrection will remedy.

IMMORTAL AND INCORRUPTIBLE

Still others confuse the concept of a conscious afterlife with the biblical terms "immortality" and "incorruptibility." The word "immortality" is found five times in the KJV. The authors of the KJV translated two different Greek words as immortality. They were correct with one word but mistranslated the other.

The first word is *athanasia*. This is a combination of two Greek words which literally mean "no death." This word means "never-ending existence" or "the state of being incapable of death." It is used to describe the resurrection body in 1 Cor. 15:43, 53.

The second word is *aphtharsia*. This is also a combination of two Greek words which literally mean "no corruption." It means "the state of being incapable of corruption, decomposition, or degeneration." It is used to describe God in Rom. 1:23 and the resurrection body in 1 Cor. 15:42, 50, 52–54. The KJV mistranslates it as "immortality" in 1 Tim. 1:17 and 2 Tim. 1:10.

While *athanasia* reveals that the resurrected saints will never experience death, but exist for all eternity, *aphtharsia* reveals that this will not be a mere eternal existence but the fullest life of joy and satisfaction possible, because the resurrected saints cannot experience any degeneration in the functions of body or mind. No corruption will disrupt the bliss of the eternal state.

From our examination of the terms "immortal" and "incorruptible," it is obvious that they describe the attributes of the resurrection body and do not speak of the condition of man's soul after death. As a matter of fact, the phrase "the immortality of the soul" is never found in Scripture, because the biblical authors wish to avoid the pagan connotations such as preexistence or transmigration which such a phrase would imply.

A typical argument is often raised at this point by the annihilationists.[1] Since the Bible does not use the phrase "immortal soul," and the word "immortal" refers only to the resurrection, they argue that the Bible teaches a bodily resurrection but not a conscious afterlife. They thus pit resurrection against a conscious afterlife as if the two were in conflict with each other.

This argument is, first of all, based on the assumption that if a certain theological word or phrase is not found in the Bible, then the concept which that word or phrase represents cannot be found in the Bible. For example, the Jehovah's Witnesses, using the same line of reasoning, argue: "Since the word 'Trinity' is not found in the Bible, therefore the doctrine of the Trinity is not Biblical."

What the Witnesses fail to see is that theological terminology was developed over the centuries in order to capsulize biblical teaching. Thus the concept of God in three persons is not based on the term "Trinity," but the term is based on the biblical concept of God in three persons.

It is on this same basis, therefore, that we are not overly impressed by arguments based on the absence in Scripture of such words as "Trinity" or "immortal soul." All such arguments from silence are obviously invalid.

Second, they falsely assume that the concepts of a conscious afterlife and a bodily resurrection are mutually exclusive. If one is true, the other is false. They thus present us with the dilemma of choosing either the immortality of the soul or the resurrection of the body.[2]

They correctly point out that man was a physical whole at his creation. Man was not created to be an angel or to exist as a spiritual entity. Thus the resurrection of the body is necessary in order to reconstitute man to live once again as he originally did in the paradise of God. Creation explains the need for resurrection. It cannot explain man's existence as a disembodied spirit in a conscious afterlife. Therefore, they conclude the concept of an afterlife is unnecessary and inexplicable when examined from the viewpoint of creation.

The fatal flaw in their argument is their failure to see that while the creation explains the resurrection, the fall of man explains death and the afterlife.

At creation, man was made a living being. He was not created to die but to live. It seems that if Adam and Eve would have resisted the temptation of Satan and continued in their relationship with God, they would have been glorified—i.e., their bodies would have been transformed from mortal to immortal, from corruptible to incorruptible without experiencing death.

This is why the Apostle Paul points out in 1 Cor. 15:49–57, Phil. 3:20, 21 and 1 Thess. 4:15–17 that those living at Christ's return will be changed from mortal to immortal without dying.

The radical nature of the fall is something the annihilationists have consistently overlooked. At the fall, man was separated from God, the world, others, and finally, from his own body. The terribly tragic effects of sin ultimately result in the ripping of man's mind or soul out of his body and his unnatural continuance as a disembodied spirit in a conscious afterlife.

If the annihilationists' argument was valid, they would have to deny the concept and reality of death as well as a conscious afterlife, because neither of them is explicable on the grounds of the creation alone. It is only the radical fall into sin that explains death and the afterlife.

We must conclude that all arguments drawn from the creation and the resurrection are invalid, because death and the afterlife are explicable only on the basis of the radical fall of man into sin.

EVERLASTING LIFE

Another frequent error is the assumption that the phrase "everlasting life" refers to "unending existence after the resurrection." Thus everlasting life is viewed as a quantitative term referring to an eternal or unending existence.

First, the phrase everlasting life, as found in extra-biblical Greek literature, means an endless quality of life which the righteous enjoy now as well as in an afterlife.[3] It refers to the fullness of life, such as joy and peace.

Second, the phrase "everlasting life" in the rabbinic literature refers to an endless quality of life which the righteous receive now as well as in the hereafter.[4] Thus the Hebraic sense, according to F. F. Bruce, referred to "the life of the age to come or the resurrection life" which was the present possession of the righteous.[5]

Third, at the moment of regeneration (new birth), the saints receive "everlasting life" as a present possession (John 3:15, 16, 36; 5:24; 6:47, 54; 10:28; 1 John 5:13, 14, etc.). This must be understood as referring not to an eternal duration or quantity of life but to experiencing an endless and abundant quality of life, i.e., a life of satisfaction and joy.[6] True believers can taste the kind of life that will be theirs after the resurrection. As the hymn writers put it, the saints "pick celestial fruit on Canaan's ground." They experience "everlasting life" now.

Fourth, it was a rabbinic tradition to speak of the wicked as "dead" while they were still existing in this world, and to speak of the righteous as possessing "life" from God.[7] In the New Testament, Jesus and the apostles continued this rabbinic tradition by describing unbelievers as "dead" and believers as receiving "life" at the moment of regeneration (Luke 9:60; John 5:24; Eph. 2:1–5; 1 Tim. 5:6; 1 John 5:12).

It is obvious that "life" does not refer to "existence" any more than "death" refers to "nonexistence." The wicked are "dead" while they yet exist in this world. The saints do not begin to exist when they are regenerated. Thus the "life" which a believer receives at regeneration must be understood as being a quality of life, not just an extention of existence. Indeed, Jesus came to give us "abundant life" (John 10:10). The "life" which we receive at regeneration is not to be a temporary experience. The life which we receive is described as being "eternal."

> And the witness is this, that God has given us eternal life, and this life is in His Son. He who has the Son has the life; he who does not have the Son of God does not have have the life. (1 John 5:11, 12)

A true believer in vital relationship with Christ can never lose or be robbed of his living relationship to the Lord Jesus Christ. The Apostle Paul speaks of the relationship between Christ and the believer as being incapable of being severed even by death itself.

> For I am convinced that neither death, nor life, nor angels, nor principalities, nor things present, nor things to come, nor powers, nor height, nor depth, nor any other created thing, shall be able to separate us from the love of God, which is in Christ Jesus our Lord. (Rom. 8:38, 39)

This biblical promise makes soul sleep or annihilationism impossible. The life which a believer receives at the moment of regeneration is to be viewed as lasting forever. If a believer is in a living relationship to Christ, not even death can sever his communion with the living God.

Fifth, believers are said to enter into the full enjoyment of everlasting life at the resurrection (Matt. 25:46; Mark 10:30; John 6:40, etc.).

A proper interpretation of the phrase "everlasting life" completely undercuts one of the main arguments of the conditional immortalitists. The classic Adventist scholar Leroy Froom argued:[8]

> Premise 1: Everlasting life means endless existence after the resurrection.
> Premise 2: Only those who believe in Jesus receive everlasting life.
> Conclusion: Only believers will exist forever. The wicked will pass into nonexistence.

The mistake is made in the first premise. Froom interprets "everlasting life" in a quantitative sense as referring to unending physical existence after the resurrection, but everlasting life is actually an endless quality of life which is received at regeneration.

Froom also commits the fallacy of four terms (*quaternis terminorum*). The phrase "everlasting life" in the second premise does not have the same meaning that it bears in the first premise. Froom's argument is invalid not only on exegetical grounds but also on logical grounds.

CONCLUSION

While believers experience everlasting life now as a present possession, they look forward to the resurrection when they will at last be immortal and incorruptible in body as well as in soul.

NOTES

1. See: *Let God Be True*, ibid., pp. 59–80; J. Hick, *Life and Death Eternal* (New York: Harper & Row, 1976); L. Froom, *The Conditionalist Faith of Our Fathers*, Vol. I, pp. 319–321.

2. D. Cullman, *Immortality of the Soul or Resurrection of the Dead?* (London: The Epworth Press, 1958).

3. J. Baille, *And the Life Everlasting* (New York: Charles Scribner's Sons, 1933), 244; F. Grant, *Facts and Theories as to a Future State* (New York: Loizeaux, Bros, 1889), p. 176.

4. Ps. Sol. 3:16; Bal. Tal. RH 64, etc.

5. F.F. Bruce, *New Testament History* (New York: Anchor Books, 1972), p. 280.

6. *Dictionary of New Testament Theology*, Vol. III, p. 832.

7. Midrash: Ecc. 229, etc.

8. Froom, ibid., Vol. I, pp. 305, 458, etc.; H. Constable, *The Duration and Nature of Future Punishment*.

Chapter 5

PUNISHMENT: CONSCIOUS AND ETERNAL

Having investigated the biblical understanding of the nature of man, Sheol, Hades, and Gehenna, we will now consider the scriptural teaching on the subject of eternal punishment. There are several guiding principles which should be emphasized at this point.

First, we must beware of allowing our emotions to dictate to God what He can and cannot do. We frequently hear, "Well, if I were God, I would not punish anyone. I would make everyone happy. There would be no pain or suffering in this world or in the next."

The important word is "if," because man is not God and God is not man. Thus the Lord God reminded humanity that:

> "My thoughts are not your thoughts, neither are your ways My ways," declares the Lord. "For as the heavens are higher than the earth, so are My ways higher than your ways, and My thoughts than your thoughts." For who has known the mind of the Lord that he should instruct Him? (Isa. 55:8, 9; 1 Cor. 2:16)

This observation sweeps away all the emotion and *ad hominem* arguments which fill the pages of those who feel that any punishment for sin is too much or that eternal punishment is somehow more horrifying than annihilation. The issue is not what we feel or think, but what God has revealed in His Word.

We wish there was no suffering or pain in this world or in the next. We do not delight in these things. To do so would be a moral sickness. Neither does God delight in punishing sinners, for He said:

> "I have no pleasure in the death of anyone who dies," declares the Lord God. "Therefore, repent and live." (Ezek. 18:23, 32; cf. 33:11)

Just as our emotional aversion to the pain and suffering we see in this life does not alter the fact that it exists, neither does our aversion to any future punishment in the eternal state alter the fact that it will exist.

And let us add that we have an emotional aversion to the annihilationist's position that God punishes people into nonexistence. Some annihilationists present the idea that while they see eternal punishment as emotionally unacceptable, they do not evidently feel any problem with the extinction of sinners.[1]

Lest the Universalists feel justified at this point, let us remind them that we feel a strong moral as well as emotional aversion to their idea that rebel sinners like Hitler do not get the justice they so richly deserve. The idea that there is no ultimate justice or final punishment for sin is repugnant. Therefore, since we all feel a mixture of emotions when we consider sin, suffering, pain, justice and punishment, let us avoid building our theology on the quicksand of human emotions.

Second, because of the emotional nature of the subject, we must strive to be honest and fair in our interpretation of Scripture. To approach the Bible determined to make it say what we want it to say is a disgrace. We should have the attitude of the Apostle Paul who said, "Let God be found true, though every man be found a liar" (Rom. 3:4).

THE NATURE OF DIVINE PUNISHMENT

When the orthodox speak of eternal punishment being administered by the justice of God to rebel sinners, they are referring to an ultimate and irreversible alienation and separation from God, the benefits of His common grace, and the good gifts of God which result in perpetual grief, misery, and remorse.

The Scriptures never give us a metaphysical explanation of the nature of this suffering. Any speculative questions which focus on the nature of the mental and physical aspects of this suffering are never considered by the biblical authors. We must categorically state that such mixed metaphors as "darkness" and "fire" used in Scripture only give us hints as to what the suffering will mean. All we are definitely told is that rebel sinners will suffer the eternal mental and physical consequences of their ultimate and irreversible alienation and separation from the person and gifts of God.

The Work of Christ

It is at this point that the vicarious atonement of Christ is crucial to our understanding of divine punishment.

First, the fact of the atonement reveals the necessity of divine punishment for sin.

Second, Christ took the punishment for sin which His people would have suffered.

Third, the nature of Christ's vicarious punishment will be a good indication of the nature of divine punishment of rebel sinners.

Christ experienced divine punishment by (1) *Alienation and separation from the person and gifts of God*: "My God, My God, why hast Thou forsaken Me?" (Matt. 27:46). (2) *Conscious pain, suffering, and misery from the alienation and suffering*: "Surely our griefs He Himself bore, and our sorrows He carried; yet we ourselves esteemed Him stricken, smitten of God, and afflicted. . . . The Lord was pleased to crush Him, putting Him to grief . . . as a result of the anguish of His soul" (Isa. 53:4–11). "Thus it is written, that the Christ should suffer" (Luke 24:46). "Christ also suffered for you" (1 Pet. 2:21). "Christ has suffered in the flesh" (1 Pet. 4:1). (3) *Death*: "Christ Jesus died for our sins according to the Scriptures" (1 Cor. 15:3).

His death on the cross illustrates the separation of body and soul which takes place when death occurs. Thus, when He died, His body remained intact in the tomb while in His spirit or soul He went to Hades according to Peter in Acts 2:27 and in 1 Pet. 3:18–20. This is echoed in the Apostles' Creed which said that "he descended into hell [Hades]."

We must pause at this point and emphasize that nonexistence was not the punishment inflicted on the body and soul of Christ. If the annihilationists were right, then Christ should have disintegrated on the cross and would have ceased to exist in body and soul. However, Christ's body was not annihilated but intact in the tomb while His soul was conscious in Hades.

Since the annihilationists believe that the body and soul of sinners pass into nonexistence either at death or the resurrection and that this is the nature of divine judgment, how do they explain the existence of Christ's body in the tomb?

The Jehovah's Witnesses state that Christ's body probably dissolved into gases and ceased to exist. In order for Christ's punishment to parallel the total destruction of body and soul which will happen to sinners, they feel that Christ must be totally destroyed in body and soul. Thus, they go on to deny the bodily resurrection of Jesus Christ. They state that Jesus was raised as a spirit creature.[2]

The Witnesses fail to realize that the Apostle Peter interpreted Ps. 16:10, 11 as a divine guarantee that the body of Christ would never suffer harm in any way while His soul was in Hades (Acts 2:25–28). The biblical evidence for Christ's bodily resurrection is so overwhelming that only a totally biased mind could possibly deny it.

What can be said of the Adventists and neo-Adventists who also claim that Christ's death meant total annihilation? Fudge's claim that "Jesus' death involved total destruction"[3] is an example of this kind of thinking. How they ignore the existence of Christ's body in the tomb while His soul was in Hades and pretend that Christ was "totally destroyed" stretches the imagination. If they are consistent, they will have to end up denying the bodily resurrection of Christ as do the Jehovah's Witnesses.

Another annihilationist argument is often brought forth at this point: "Since Christ's punishment was not eternal but had an end, then the punishment of sinners will not be eternal, but have an end as well."

First, the annihilationists forget that they have a problem here as well. If Christ's punishment was only temporary and He was restored to life, then they would have to conclude on the basis of the way they were arguing that the punishment of sinners will only be temporary and will end as they are restored to life. Obviously, Christ experienced neither eternal torment nor eternal nonexistence, because He was resurrected.

Second, both problems are solved by the implications of Christ's divine nature, which is eternal, and the infinite value of Christ's sacrifice. Thus the author to the Hebrews argues from the deity of Christ (Heb. 1:1–13) and the sufficiency of His once-for-all suffering (Heb. 9:25–28) as the basis for the perfection of the atonement.

There is no way to escape the fact that Christ did not experience total annihilation in body and soul on the cross. What He did experience was suffering as a result of moral alienation from God. This is the ultimate fate awaiting rebel sinners.

THE NECESSITY OF DIVINE JUDGMENT

Is judgment really necessary? Cannot God simply forgive and forget our sins? Isn't God too good to condemn man and isn't man too good to be condemned?

Questions such as these are frequently asked. The main point is whether or not God must punish sin. Much of "pop" Universalism assumes that divine judgment is not necessary and that God's loving character excludes any idea of His punishing sin.

We are convinced that the Scriptures clearly teach that God's character necessitates divine punishment and that He cannot simply pass over our sins and remain God at the same time.

If you were asked "Can God do anything?", how would you answer? It would seem that the only pious answer is that God can do anything. Yet upon closer examination, it is clear that God cannot do everything, for He cannot do anything which contradicts His nature or character. All things are possible for God as long as they do not contradict His character or nature, "for He cannot deny Himself" (2 Tim. 2:13).

This leads us to consider whether the character of God demands a divine punishment for sin.

The Justice and Righteousness of God

God's justice and righteousness are both attributes of His moral character. Because God is just and righteous, His works are described as being just and righteous. We should not make the mistake of thinking that God's justice is only a description of His works and not reflective of His being. God is just and therefore He acts justly.

God's justice and righteousness are consistently joined together in Scripture as being descriptive of God's very being and character. Moses declared that God is just and right (Deut. 32:4). The psalmist declared, "Righteousness and justice are the foundation of Thy throne" (Ps. 89:14). Zeph. 3:5 states that "the Lord is righteous within her. He will do no injustice." The Apostle John tells us to confess our sins to God, "for He is faithful and righteous" (1 John 1:9).

Because God is just and righteous, He will never do anything which would contradict these attributes. This is the underlying assumption behind Abraham's famous statement: "Shall not the Judge of all the earth deal justly?" (Gen. 18:25). The Apostle Paul asks the same type of question in Rom. 9:14: "Is there unrighteousness with God?" (KJV), or, "There is no injustice with God, is there?" The judge of all the earth cannot do anything unless it is in conformity to His own righteousness. It is blasphemy to attribute injustice to God. His ways are always just and right.

The Scriptures also teach us that God cannot simply forgive sinners and let their sins go unpunished; God's justice is displayed by the vindication of His righteousness in the punishment of sin. All human government recognizes the importance and the necessity of judging criminal elements for the sake of protecting their society and furthering the peace and well-being of those in it. If this is so among earthly governments, how much more in the heavenly kingdom! Again, how much respect in the eyes of its subjects would an earthly government command if that government gratuitously loosed criminally destructive elements into that society? None! This surely is one of the reasons God said to Moses, "I will not acquit the guilty" (Ex. 23:7); or again, "He will by no means leave the guilty unpunished" (Ex. 34:7). Does not the psalmist state: "For Thou art not a God who takes pleasure in wickedness; no evil dwells with Thee. The boastful shall not stand before Thine eyes; Thou dost hate all who do iniquity. Thou dost destroy those who speak falsehood; the Lord abhors the man of bloodshed and deceit"? (Ps. 5:4–6). This same principle is found in Rom. 2:5, 6: "But because of your stubbornness and unrepentant heart you are storing up wrath for yourself in the day of wrath and revelation of the righteous judgment of God, who will render to every man according to his deeds."

The justice and righteousness of God demand that sin be punished. Either the sinner himself must be punished or a suitable substitute must be found who will be able to bear the full punishment of sin.

The Holiness of God

The holiness of God has central place in the Old Testament concept of the character of God. YHWH is distinguished from the pagan gods on the basis of His holiness, for "who is like Thee among the gods, O Lord? Who is like Thee, majestic in holiness?" (Ex. 15:11). God's veracity is based upon His holiness, because God swore, "Once I have sworn by My holiness; I will not lie to David" (Ps. 89:35). Thus the Law (Ex. 15:11), the Writings (Ps. 89:35), and the Prophets (Amos 4:2) all point to the centrality of God's holiness.

In the New Testament, the seraphim's cry of "Holy, Holy, Holy, is the Lord of Hosts" (Isa. 6:3) is seen as trinitarian in form, for Holy is the Father (John 17:11), Holy is the Son (Acts 3:14), and Holy is the Spirit (Matt. 1:18). Blessed God three in One!

Because God is holy, His "eyes are too pure to approve [look upon] evil, and Thou canst not look on wickedness with favor" (Hab. 1:13). Or again in Ps. 5:4–6, we find: "For Thou art not a God who takes pleasure in wickedness; no evil dwells with Thee. The boastful shall not stand before Thine eyes; Thou dost hate all who do iniquity. Thou dost destroy those who speak falsehood; the Lord abhors the man of bloodshed and deceit."

Man was created to bear God's image, and thus it is not surprising that man was created with original holiness. But man fell into sin and lost that holiness. When God looked upon man after the fall, instead of holiness, He "saw that the wickedness of man was great on the earth, and that every intent of the thoughts of his heart was only evil continually" (Gen. 6:5).

God's holiness demands judgment against sin, and thus we find that the history of redemption is filled with awesome displays of God's holy anger. We could examine man's expulsion from the garden, the flood, the tower of Babel, the judgments on Egypt and on the Jews in the wilderness, the destruction of the Canaanites, the Assyrian and Babylonian captivities, etc. All of these judgments arose because God is holy and man unholy.

God's Hatred of Sin

Moses warned the people that God would judge them if they disobeyed His commandments, because "our God is a consuming fire" (Deut. 4:24, 27). The people were assured that the wicked Canaanites would be punished, because "your God . . . is crossing over before you as a consuming fire" (Deut. 9:3). The writer of the book of Hebrews warns that apostasy results in God's judgment, because "our God is a consuming fire" (Heb. 12:29).

Because of God's moral character, He hates sin and is provoked by it to consume it in judgment. Simply to dismiss divine punishment for sin is impossible, because "He cannot deny Himself" (2 Tim. 2:13).

The Law of God

In the Old Testament the nature and function of the law of God revealed to Israel the necessity of a satisfactory atonement for sin because it also revealed the necessity of God's punishment of sin. When we turn to the Old Testament Scriptures, we find that the Old Testament law placed either promise or penalty, and blessing or cursing, before the people.

> "See, I am setting before you today a blessing and a curse: the blessing, if you listen to the commandments of the Lord your God, which I am commanding you today; and the curse, if you do not listen to the commandments of the Lord your God, but turn aside from the way which I am commanding you today, by following other gods which you have not known." (Deut. 11:26–28)

> "See, I have set before you today life and prosperity, and death and adversity; in that I command you today to love the Lord your God, to walk in His ways and to keep His commandments and His statutes and His judgments, that you may live and multiply, and that the Lord your God may bless you in the land where you are entering to possess it. But if your heart turns away and you will not obey, but are drawn away and worship other gods and serve them, I declare to you today that you shall surely perish. You shall not prolong your days in the land where you are crossing the Jordan to enter and possess it." (Deut. 30:15–18)

The promise of the Law is the reward which was gained through absolute obedience. In order to gain this blessing, our obedience must be (1) personal: "See, I am setting before you today a blessing and a curse" (Deut. 11:26); (2) perfect: "And now, Israel, what does the Lord your God require from you, but to fear the Lord your God, to walk in all His ways and love Him, and to serve the Lord your

God with all your heart and with all your soul?" (Deut. 10:12); (3) perpetual: "Oh that they had such a heart in them, that they would fear Me, and keep all My commandments always, that it may be well with them and with their sons forever!" (Deut. 5:29).

The only obedience acceptable before God was that of total obedience.

> For whoever keeps the whole law and yet stumbles in one point, he has become guilty of all. (James 2:10)

The penalty of the Law was the reward of the curse of God, obtained through disobedience. Was it not the Apostle Paul who said: "For as many as are of the works of the Law are under a curse; for it is written, 'Cursed is every one who does not abide by all things written in the book of the law, to perform them' "? (Gal. 3:10). Do we not find God giving explicit warnings of cursings for disobedience in Deut. 27:15–26; 28:15–68?

The curse of God for man's disobedience is death in contrast to God's blessing of life. In the garden, did not God warn Adam and Eve that disobedience would lead to death? (Gen. 2:17). Did not Moses sternly warn the people: "You shall surely perish" if they disobeyed God's law? (Deut. 30:18). Does not the New Testament teach that disobedience leads to death? (Rom. 6:23; James 1:15).

The execution of the promise or penalty of the Law rests upon God's covenantal faithfulness.

> "Know therefore that the Lord your God, He is God, the faithful God, who keeps His covenant and His lovingkindness to a thousandth generation with those who love Him and keep His commandments; but repays those who hate Him to their faces, to destroy them." (Deut. 7:9, 10)

God could not merely sweep aside the requirement of His law. Why not? Because His character is unchanging (Mal. 3:6) and man is still God's image-bearer (James 3:9).

Therefore, the law of God as given through Moses showed us:

1. A perfect, personal and perpetual obedience must be executed by the person or his substitute in order to gain the reward of eternal life and thus satisfy the just demands of God's law.

2. The punishment of God must be endured either by the person or by his substitute in order to satisfy fully the just penalty of the curse of God for disobedience.

When we come to the New Testament, the Apostle Paul in such places as Galatians 3 shows that Jesus Christ had to suffer the full punishment of the Law in order to redeem His people. The necessity of the atonement is the final answer to the question of whether or not God must punish sin.

DIVINE PUNISHMENT IN THIS LIFE

One clue as to the nature of God's ultimate and eternal punishment is found in the fact that God punishes rebel sinners in this life as well as in the next. The nature of God's punishment upon sinners in the past and the terminology which is employed to speak of it is very important.

The annihilationists claim that this issue is where their position is demonstrated beyond refutation. Leroy Froom in *The Conditionalist Faith of Our Fathers* (vol. 1, pp. 106–109) presents a list of 70 words which he says "must mean annihilation." He claims that "no loop holes are left" (p. 107). Ever since his presentation, annihilationists have simply repeated his lists and his claims.[4]

What we must do is check to see if Froom's list of 70 words holds up under close scrutiny. Must Froom's words mean "annihilation unto nonexistence"?

First, many of the words do not mean nonexistence or annihilation, even in the English language. For example, Froom claimed that the word "tear" means "to annihilate." Yet it is obvious that tearing some paper or cloth into smaller pieces hardly means that the paper or cloth went into nonexistence. The same can be said for such words as "break," "cast off," etc.

Second, there are words on the list which cannot mean nonexistence. For example, Froom includes the word "scatter." Yet, who would say that when the people of Israel were "scattered" among the nations, they went into nonexistence or were annihilated?

Third, he literalizes dozens of figures of speech to mean annihilation. For example, he refers to ice or candles "melting" as proving annihilationism. Besides the illegitimate literalization, Froom fails to realize that neither the water nor the wax cease to exist; they simply take on different forms. Many of the words on his list are nothing more than figures of speech.

Fourth, Froom's list is now reduced to a few key words, such as "destroy," "perish," and "consume." Now, we must point out that Froom simply asserts that these words mean annihilation. Neither Froom nor those who follow him offer any lexicographical evidence or exegetical material. But starting from their unfounded assumption that these words mean annihilation, whenever these words appear in Scripture, intertestamental writings or patristic literature, they always claim that the authors were conditional immortalitists. They assume that any piece of literature which uses these words automatically teaches conditionalism.

In this way, Froom and others can put forth dozens of passages from biblical and extra-biblical literature as supporting their position. The problem is their beginning assumption that these key words mean annihilation is erroneous. Once this is established, the foundational assumption which runs throughout most of their arguments is overturned. Let us examine some of these key words which they assume mean annihilation.

1. *"Destroy"* or *"destruction."* Various forms of the words "destroy" or "destruction" appear 495 times in the KJV. They represent approximately 50 different Hebrew words and 12 different Greek words. None of them have the lexicographical meaning of "annihilation" or "to cause something to pass into nonexistence"; and an exegetical examination of the texts where these words are found reveals they cannot be arbitrarily defined as annihilation.

For example, in the Old Testament, the word *ahvad* is the word which is usually translated as "destroy." In Num. 21:29, the people of Chemosh were "undone" ("destroyed" in NIV). In the context, the meaning of *ahvad* is that the people were conquered and sold into slavery. They were not annihilated, but enslaved. In 1 Sam. 9:3, 20, Saul's asses were *ahvad*, i.e., lost. These asses were not annihilated, but lost. In Ps. 31:12, an *ahvad* vessel is merely broken, not annihilated. In Hab. 1:15, the word *Gah rar* means to catch something in a net, not to annihilate it. *Dah chah* in Isa. 53:10 is translated, "It pleased the Lord to bruise him." Here it refers to Christ's sufferings, not to nonexistence. In Hos. 4:6, God's people are "destroyed" for lack of knowledge. In the context, this cannot mean that they were nonexistent. The same can be pointed out in the case of *hoom* (Ps. 55:2) and *ghah ram* (Josh. 6:8; Mic. 4:13).

In Jer. 23:1, 2, we have a classic example of the usage of the words "destroy" and "scatter." In this text, it is obvious that these words cannot mean annihilation.

> "Woe to the shepherds who are destroying and scattering the sheep of My pasture!" declares the Lord. Therefore thus says the Lord God of Israel concerning the shepherds who are tending My people: "You have scattered My flock and driven them away, and have not attended to them; behold, I am about to attend to you for the evil of your deeds," declares the Lord.

In the Greek, *apollumi* is used to describe ruined wineskins, lost sheep, and spoiled food (Matt. 9:17; 15:24; John 6:27). *Apolia* in Mark 14:4 refers to wasted perfume. *Diapthero* refers to moth-eaten cloth in Luke 12:33; *kathairesis* to the pulling down of a fortress (2 Cor. 10:4); *kataluo* refers to lodging for the night (Luke 9:12); *katargeo* to a fig tree which "encumbered the ground" (Luke 13:7); *luo* refers to putting off one's shoes (Acts 7:33); *portheo* refers to persecuting the church in Gal. 1:13; *phthiro* refers to defiling the temple of God in 1 Cor. 3:17.

The assumption that the words "destroy" and "destruction" automatically mean annihilation is not good English, much less good Hebrew or Greek. We can think of someone being "destroyed" or "wiped out" in an emotional sense without implying that the person has ceased to exist.

2. *"Perish"* or *"perished."* In various forms the word "perish" appears 152 times in the KJV.

In the Old Testament, there are 11 Hebrew words which are translated as "perish." The main word *ahvad* is the same word which is frequently translated as "destroy." We have already seen that it is erroneous to assume that *ahvad* means annihilation. *Sha mad* is found in Jer. 48:42 where Moab is said to be destroyed in the sense of the people being enslaved, not annihilated. *Shah ghath* is used of ruined girdles and vessels in Jer. 13:7; 18:4; *kah rath* is used of cutting a covenant or cutting timber to build the temple in Gen. 15:18; 1 Kings 5:6; *gah vag, nah phal,* and *gah var* are used to describe a miserable emotional state (Ps. 42:7; 55:4; 88:15, 16).

In the New Testament, there are ten different Greek words which are translated "perish." Some of these words such as *apollumi* were also translated as destroy and do not mean annihilation. *Apothneesko* is used in John 12:24 to describe the grain of wheat which when planted "dies" and then sprouts. Obviously, it cannot mean annihilation. *Aphanizo* refers to things which moths and rust can "corrupt" (Matt. 6:19, 20). *Kataphthiro* is used to describe "corrupt" minds in 2 Tim. 3:8 (KJV).

Even in English we speak of fruit as "perishable" in the sense that it can spoil. Burned out light bulbs have "perished." In neither case is annihilation intended.

3. *"Consume"* or *"consumed."* Forms of these words appear in the KJV 162 times. In the Old Testament, 20 different Hebrew words are translated as "consume." The usual word, *ah chal,* is also used in Ps. 78:45 where the psalmist says that the flies "devoured" or consumed the Egyptians. The psalmist surely meant that the flies tormented them, not annihilated them. Jeremiah used another word, *bah lah,* in Lam. 3:4, saying that his flesh and skin were "made old," or consumed, i.e., he was consumed with grief, not annihilated. *Kah lah* is used in Ezek. 13:13 where hailstones "consumed" a wall, i.e., knocked it down, not annihilated it. *Dah gach* is the normal word for putting out a fire. When we "put out a candle," we do not annihilate the candle.

In the New Testament, three Greek words are translated "consume." The main verb *analisko* is used in Gal. 5:15 to describe the Christians as "consuming" one another, i.e., fighting and tormenting each other, not annihilating each other.

Even in English we speak of people being consumed with "grief, greed, or lust," yet we do not mean that the person has ceased to exist.

We have demonstrated that the annihilationists are in error when they arbitrarily assume and then assert that such words as "perish" necessarily mean annihilation. Once this point is granted, one is no longer impressed by such works as Froom where hundreds of quotes from biblical and extra-biblical literature are given to prove conditionalism simply upon the erroneous assumption that the mere presence of such words in the text means that the authors believed in annihilationism.

The Judgment of God

While the conditional immortalists assume that God's judgment means a passing into nonexistence, the Scripture speaks of God afflicting people with mental and physical suffering as his punishment for sin.

On the day that man sinned in the Garden of Eden, he "died," i.e., he was separated and alienated from the person and gifts of God. This alienation led to conscious fear, anxiety, guilt, and remorse (Gen. 3:7, 10).

God's first punishment for sin not only included mental suffering and a guilty conscience, but also physical suffering, as they would have to wear clothing against the cold, obtain food by the sweat of their brow, and experience pain in childbirth (Gen. 3:16–24). Divine punishment for Adam and Eve did not mean annihilation, but mental and physical suffering.

Throughout redemptive history, man's sin has led to a separation and alienation from the person and gifts of God (Isa. 59:1–10). This alienation has provoked God to afflict sinners with suffering. These afflictions are not, however, retributive or sadistic; rather they are remedial (Ps. 119:67, 75). For example: (1) God vexes people, i.e., causes them mental fear, terror, grief, confusion, and bitterness (Deut. 28:20; 2 Chron. 15:6; Job 27:2; Ps. 2:5; 6:3, etc.). (2) God afflicts people, i.e., causes them internal and external adversities and griefs (Ruth 1:21; Ps. 88:7; 90:15; 119:67, 71, 75; Nah. 1:12, etc.). The divine punishment which fell upon Christ was "affliction" and not annihilation according to Isa. 53:4, 7. (3) God troubles people (Deut. 31:17; 1 Sam. 16:15; Job 27:13–17. (4) God punishes people with great suffering such as the plagues of Egypt (Ex. 7–12), or by consuming them, or causing them failure and grief at whatever they do (Lev. 26:36–42; 31:17).

One need only look around himself to see all the pain and suffering which results from man's sin and God's punishment of this sin. To pretend that such suffering does not exist or that it is not ultimately related to man's sin and God's judgment is impossible. And we must hasten to add that any objection based on a supposed conflict between the character of God and eternal suffering is doomed to failure, because there is no conflict between God's character and suffering in this present life. As a matter of fact, the Scriptures indicate that God begins the process of punishing sinners with sufferings in this life, and He continues to punish them in the intermediate state (2 Pet. 2:9) and warns of eternal punishment in the final state (Matt. 25:46).

BIBLICAL TERMINOLOGY

That divine punishment awaits rebel sinners is something which is so clear in Scripture that no honest exegesis can avoid it. The issue which divides the orthodox from the annihilationists is the duration of this punishment. The orthodox believe that it is eternal, while the annihilationists think it once-for-all passing into nonexistence. The debate has centered on whether or not such biblical words as *olam* imply that eternal punishment awaits sinners. Thus we must first define such words as *olam* in order to see what they mean.

Old Testament Terms

While there are eleven Hebrew words which were translated as "forever," "everlasting," "eternal," "eternity," etc., in the KJV, only *olam* is used specifically of the final judgment of the wicked. Such words as *nehtzagh* refer to perpetual things in this present life. It is even used of "perpetual pain" (Jer. 15:18). The wicked "perish forever" at death, i.e., they leave this present world never to return to normal physical life. That they will be resurrected and further punished is not logically in conflict with the idea that the wicked leave this life never to return. The word *ad* is used of the eternity of God in Ex. 15:18. It is used in Ps. 21:4 of an extended lifetime in this world. Also Asaph prayed that his enemies would be "ashamed and dismayed forever" (*ad*—Ps. 83:17). He was probably thinking of seeing this happen to them in their lifetime and not in some future punishment.

We must remark at this point that the annihilationists have the habit of misapplying texts. They consistently put forth dozens of passages which actually pertain to the fate of the wicked in this life as if these passages were speaking of the final punishment of sinners after the resurrection.[6] This habit confuses the issue and ignores the "this world" context of these passages.

Since *olam* is the key word in the Old Testament which is used to speak of the final state of the righteous and the wicked, we will limit our investigation to it.

The word *olam* is found 420 times in the Hebrew Bible. Brown, Driver and Briggs define it as meaning (1) antiquity, i.e., the distant past, (2) a long duration in the present, (3) indefinite unending future of everlastingness, eternity.[7] Langenscheidt defines *olam* as: "time immemorial, time past, eternity, distant future, duration, everlasting time, life time; pl. ages, endless times" (p. 243). Girdlestone summarizes *olam's* meaning in *Synonyms of the Old Testament* (p. 317):

> Eternity is endlessness; and this idea is only qualified by the nature of the objects to which it is applied, or by the direct word of God. When applied to things physical, it is used in accordance with the revealed truth that the heavens and earth shall pass away, and it is limited by this truth. When applied to God, it is used in harmony with the truth that He is essentially and absolutely existent, and that as He is the *Causa Causarum* and without beginning, so in the very nature of things it must be held that no cause can ever put an end to His existence. When the word is applied to man's future destiny after the resurrection, we naturally give it the sense of endlessness without limitation.

THE EXEGETICAL CONSIDERATIONS

The word "everlasting" (*olam*) is a word which describes a contrast between things. It is a contrastive word in that whenever something is called everlasting, we must ask, "Everlasting as contrasted to what?"

Olam is used to speak of the past, the present and the future. When speaking of the past, whenever God is said to be "from everlasting" (Ps. 90:2), this is in contrast to the present world, which had a beginning. God is thus "beginningless," or "eternal," as contrasted to this world. When "everlasting" is used of things which existed before one or more generations of man, they are called "everlasting" in the sense that they are "old" or "ancient" as contrasted to a present generation (Ezek. 36:2).

When *olam* is used of things which to the biblical authors were present realities which would transcend the life span of their own generation, they were called "everlasting." Thus while generations of man come and go, the mountains still remain. They are therefore called everlasting in Hab. 3:6 (KJV). The Mosaic administration was called everlasting because it transcended generations (Ex. 12:17). God is the God of Israel "forever" in the sense that He is the God of perpetual generations (Ps. 48:14). In this sense, *olam* simply means "perpetual throughout generations," not "eternal" in the sense of beginninglessness or endlessness. This is why the word for "generation" (*dor*) is also used to indicate time in Hebrew Scriptures. We can speak of abiding things as "everlasting" in contrast to the brief time span of a generation.

Olam is also used of the future. When it is used of God's future, He is described as being "to everlasting," i.e., endless as contrasted to this present world which shall have an end (Ps. 90:2). Thus in Ps. 102 the beginning and end of the world is contrasted to the endlessness or eternity of God (vv. 12, 25–28).

In this way, the final order of things after the resurrection is called "everlasting" in contrast to the present order (Dan. 12:2). While the present order would have a definite end and will cease to exist one day, the final order of things will be "everlasting," i.e., endless. While time is an aspect of the present order, it will not be part of the final or eternal state.

The Old Testament concept of *olam* avoids the static Greek idea of eternity, because the Scriptures never speak of *olam* as existing in and by itself. It is always used to contrast one thing to another. What is germaine for us to consider is that whenever the final order is described as "everlasting," it clearly means "endless" in contrast to the temporal nature of the present order. Since time no longer exists, whenever *olam* refers to the final state, it cannot mean a longer or shorter time, for time as we know it has ceased.

This understanding removes one of the arguments used by the annihilationists. They have argued that "everlasting punishment" does not mean everlasting punishment because the word "everlasting" is used of mountains in Hab. 3:6 (KJV). Therefore they argue that the punishment will only be temporary and not eternal.

What the annihilationists fail to realize is that they are ignoring the relative contexts of *olam*. When it is used to speak of such things as mountains, it has reference to things which exist throughout different generations in this present world. When *olam* is used of the final order of things, it always means endlessness in the fullest sense. The respective context for *olam* should not be ignored.

Let us examine Dan. 12:1–3, which is the only clear passage in the Old Testament which speaks of the final state of both the righteous and the wicked.

> "Now at that time, Michael, the great prince who stands guard over the sons of your people, will arise. And there will be a time of distress such as never occurred since there was a nation until that time; and at that time your people, everyone who is found written in the book, will be rescued. And many of those who sleep in the dust of the ground will awake, these to everlasting life, but others to disgrace and everlasting contempt. And those who have insight will shine brightly like the brightness of the expanse of heaven, and those who lead the many to righ-

teousness, like the stars forever and ever." (Dan. 12:1-3)

In Daniel's vision of the end times, he describes the rise and fall of the Antichrist (11:40–45), who is called the "king of the South." He will appear at the end of the present order of things and will bring about "a time of distress such as never occurred since there was a nation" (12:1). That Daniel is describing the Antichrist and not Antiochus Epiphanes is clear from the fact that this is how Christ himself interpreted this passage in Matt. 24:22.[8]

During this time of distress, Satan will seek to destroy the church by launching a worldwide persecution (cf. Rev. 13:7, 8). Because of the magnitude of Satan's persecution against the church, Michael the archangel will arise to protect the people of God from occultic forces (Dan. 12:1). That the "Michael" referred to in Dan. 12:1 is the archangel and not Christ is clear from Dan. 10:13 and Rev. 12:7.

Many evangelical scholars believe that the end of the tribulation period, God's elect, i.e., those written in the book of life, will be rescued (Dan. 12:1; cf. Rev. 13:8). This naturally gave rise to the question, "What about those who died during this time and were not alive at the time of deliverance?"

Daniel now jumps ahead to the final order of things in order to answer the question of the fate of the righteous dead. But instead of limiting his answer to the fate of the righteous, he also includes the fate of the wicked.

In opposition to the numerically "few" who will survive the last holocaust (Matt. 24:22), "many," numerically speaking, will be raised. Although prophetic opinion varies among many evangelical Christians, all believe that the word "sleep" as a metaphor is used to describe the bodies which await a "waking up" at the resurrection. Not once in all of Scripture is the word "raised" or "resurrection" used of the soul or spirit. It always strictly refers to the resurrection of the body.

The "waking up," or resurrection, which Daniel has in mind, is one which has two classes of people involved. In this sense it is a general resurrection and not limited to the righteous dead alone. The righteous are raised unto the reward of "everlasting life" (Dan. 12:2). This is the first and only time the phrase "everlasting life" appears in the Old Testament. Subsequent usage in rabbinic and New Testament literature interprets this phrase in a qualitative sense as referring to participating in the well-being or life of God, such as fullness of joy and self-fulfillment. It does not simply mean "eternal existence," because the wicked are devoid of God's "life" while they exist in this world.[9]

The distinction between well-being and existence should not be ignored. For example, a mentally ill patient with immense physical problems may "exist," but he or she is not experiencing "well-being." In the same way, only the elect will experience "eternal well-being."

The saints are said by Daniel to experience the future joys of the final state "forever." What does *olam* mean when it refers to the final order of things? It always means "unendingness," or "eternal," as a contrast to the temporal character of the present order. Thus the saints will experience fullness of life, or well-being, throughout all eternity with no threat of it ever ending.

Daniel then describes others as being resurrected to receive "disgrace and everlasting contempt." The nature and duration of the fate of the wicked is now the crucial issue before us. What did Daniel mean when he said "disgrace and contempt" await the wicked after the resurrection?

The first word, *gherpah*, is usually translated as "shame" (KJV) or "disgrace." This word is found 90 times in the Hebrew Bible and is translated in the KJV as "reproach" 45 times, "shame" 3 times, and "rebuke" 2 times.

In nearly every instance where *gherpah* is used, it describes the mental suffering and grief which someone feels when experiencing shame, disgrace, or the taunts and rebukes of others. For example, the word is used to describe (1) barrenness of the womb (Gen. 30:23), (2) widowhood (Isa. 54:4), (3) uncircumcision (Gen. 34:14), (4) injuries from enemies (1 Sam. 11:2, etc.).

Because *gherpah* almost without exception refers to grief and disgrace, it is used in connection with other emotive words such as "great distress" (Neh. 1:3), "broken heart" (Ps. 69:20) and "shame" (Isa. 30:5).

The adjective *olam* modifies *gherpah* two times: "And he smote his enemies in their hind ends (unto) everlasting shame" (Lit. Heb., Ps. 78:66). "And I will bring to you everlasting shame and ever-lasting disgrace which will not be forgotten" (Lit. Heb., Jer. 23:40).

In Psalm 78, Asaph recites the history of Israel "to tell to the generations to come the praises of the Lord, and His strength and His wondrous works that He has done" (v. 4).

After describing why God gave His people over to national defeat, Asaph then speaks of the days of Samuel, Saul and David when the Philistines were driven back (vv. 54–66).

In 1 Sam. 5:6—6:18, God sends an infection of "emerods," probably hemorrhoids, to cause the Philistines discomfort as well as shame. God also sends a plague of mice among them. These judgments of God cause them "perpetual shame" or "embarrass-ment." In this context, *olam* refers to temporal disgrace and does not describe the final state of the wicked after the resurrection.

In Jer. 23:40, Jeremiah rebukes the lying prophets and priests of his day. He pronounces God's judgment upon them and describes it in the most fearful terms:

> "Therefore behold, I shall surely forget you and cast you away from My presence, along with the city which I gave to you and your fathers. And I will put an everlasting reproach [shame] on you and an everlasting humiliation [disgrace] which will not be forgotten." (Jer. 23:39, 40)

While there is nothing in the context which speaks of the resurrection or the final state, these words do seem to hint that these false prophets will suffer "endless" shame and disgrace.

While it is clear that they will suffer these things "perpetually" throughout their lifetime, the words seem too strong to be exhausted in this manner. Even so, we must conclude that this passage does not clearly speak of the final state of the wicked—although it may hint at this.

The second word, *deraown*, is found only twice in the Hebrew Bible (Isa. 66:24; Dan. 12:2). In both places it has an eschatological context, i.e., it deals with the final order of things.

In Isa. 66:22, the ushering in of "the new heavens and the new earth" signals the beginning of the final order. While the final state of the righteous is described in verses 22, 23, the fate of the wicked is described in verses 24:

> "Then they shall go forth and look on the corpses of the men who have transgressed against Me. For their worm shall not die, and their fire shall not be quenched; and they shall be an abhorrence to all mankind." (Isa. 66:24)

In verse 24, two metaphors are used to describe the wicked. In one scene, the righteous visit the battlefield where the corpses of rebel sinners are viewed with contempt:

> "They shall go forth and look on the corpses of the men who have transgressed [Lit. Heb. rebelled] against me."

Then the scene changes and the wicked are not only tormented by the contempt of the righteous but "their worm shall not die and their fire shall not be quenched." As we have already seen, the Hebraic idiom of undying worms and unquenchable fire referred to the eternal, conscious pain and suffering which the wicked experience in Gehenna. The climax of God's judgment is reached when Isaiah says that "they shall be an object of abhorrence to all mankind." While the word *olam* is not used in Isa. 66:24 to describe how long the wicked will be an object of abhorrence, the context clearly implies this because the final order of things is endless in duration and this is the specific context.

From what has already been seen from our investigation of the words "shame" and "contempt," it is obvious that "shame" refers to the inner turmoil of the wicked as they feel the "contempt" of the righteous. The shame and contempt are personally felt by the wicked.

For how long will the wicked feel shame and be an object of contempt? Daniel used the word *olam* twice in verse two. Once it refers to the endless well-being of the righteous and once to the endless shame and contempt of the wicked.

First, the word "shame" is used in its plural form to denote the fullness of the intensity of suffering which the wicked will experience.[10]

Second, the word *olam* can grammatically be viewed as modifying both "shame" and "contempt."

Third, as in Isaiah 66, the context concerns the final unending order of things.

Fourth, there is no way to escape the obvious grammatical contrast between the unending well-being of the righteous and the unending shame and contempt of the wicked. To limit the suffering of the wicked without limiting the bliss of the righteous is grammatically impossible.

Fifth, in verse three, Daniel continues his description of the final state of the righteous by saying that they will be like bright stars "forever [*olam*] and ever [*ad*]." Once again Daniel has described "unendingness" or "eternity." At no point can the word *olam* be viewed as meaning anything other than "eternally" or "unending."

In conclusion, Dan. 12:1–3 clearly speaks of the final destiny of the righteous and the wicked after their resurrection. That this resurrection will involve all the dead is clear from the interpretation that Christ himself gave in John 5:28, 29. Both destinies are said to be "unending" or "eternal."

Several points can be established upon our exegesis of Dan. 12:1–3.

First, the Universalists are in error when they say that the Scriptures never speak of the punishment of the wicked as "eternal." In this passage the shame and contempt of the wicked is "unending for all eternity."

Second, the annihilationists such as the Jehovah's Witnesses are in error when they claim that the wicked cease to exist at death and are never resurrected.

Third, the annihilationists such as the Adventists are in error when they claim that the Bible never speaks of the wicked experiencing "unending" or "eternal" torment after their resurrection.

We close this discussion of Dan. 12:1–3 with the concluding remarks of the famous commentator C. F. Keil:

The salvation of the people, which the end shall bring in, consists accordingly in the consummation of the people of God by the resurrection of the dead and the judgment dividing the pious from the godless, according to which the pious shall be raised to eternal life, and the godless shall be given up to everlasting shame and contempt.[11]

THE RABBINIC LITERATURE

The rabbinic literature encompasses all the noninspired writings which were produced by the Jews before or during the 400 years between the Old and New Testaments. In this sense the Apocrypha, the Apocalyptic, the Pseudepigrapha, the Babylonian and Jerusalem Talmud, the Midrash and Mishna can all be classified, for convenience' sake, as rabbinic writings.

Since conditional immortalitists operate on the false assumption that such words as "perish" or "destroy" automatically mean annihilation, they rush through the rabbinic literature and seize upon any text where such words appear. In this way some annihilationists can present a number of texts which supposedly teach their position.[12]

The Adventist Froom admits the presence of the doctrine of intermediate and eternal punishment for the wicked in the rabbinic literature but sweeps it aside as "pagan" incursions.[13] His chart on page 650 in *The Conditional Faith of Our Fathers*, Vol. 1, lists eight books for annihilationism and seven books for eternal punishment in the rabbinic literature.[14]

The books which Froom admits teaches eternal punishment are: *Second Maccabees, Book of Jubilees, Wisdom of Solomon, Fourth Maccabees, Philo,* and *Josephus.* Froom then claims that *Tobit, Sirach, Sibyllin Oracles, Enoch, Baruch, Second Esdras* and the *Dead Sea Scrolls* clearly teach that the wicked pass into nonexistence after the resurrection.

Because of the importance of this historical point, we have reproduced in Appendix I the statement of the greatest Hebrew Christian rabbinic scholar that the church ever had, Dr. Alfred Edersheim.

The Apocrypha

The series of books which we call the Apocrypha were definitely written before or during the intertestamental period and reflect what the Jews believed during that time. We do not consider them inspired or part of Scripture but look upon them solely in terms of their historical value.

For the most part, the authors of the Apocrypha simply utilized biblical terms such as "perish" or "destroy" when they described the fate of the wicked. Since these words do not mean annihilation in Scripture, the rather simplistic approach of Froom, Fudge and others who put forth passages which speak of the wicked "perishing" as absolute proof that this literature teaches conditionalism cannot be viewed as having any merit whatsoever. Also, the annihilationists put forth passages which describe the death of the wicked in this life as if these passages describe the final judgment. In this way the annihilationists assemble a multitude of texts which in reality are either taken out of context or based on the false assumption that such words as "perish" automatically and necessarily always mean annihilation.

JUDITH

The book of Judith was probably written around 150–125 B.C. The book celebrates the heroic victories of Judith over the enemies of Israel.

In Chapter 16, she takes up a song of victory much like Miriam did in Exodus 15. At the close of her song she exclaims:

> "Woe to the nations that rise up against my Kindred! The Lord Almighty will take vengeance on them in the day of judgment, in putting fire and worms in their flesh; and they shall feel them, and weep forever." (16:17)

Several things can be clearly seen in this text.

First, the final state of the wicked after the day of judgment is clearly described.

Second, the reference to "worms" and "fire" is clearly taken from Isa. 66:24.

Third, the "worms" and "fire" do not annihilate the wicked. Instead, they torment the wicked. Other rabbinic literature also interprets Isa. 66:24 as referring to torment.

Fourth, the wicked will be tormented "forever." This must be interpreted in the Hebraic sense of "endlessness," or "eternity." Thus the eternal punishment of the wicked is here clearly taught.

The Adventist Froom and other annihilationists are forced to admit that eternal punishment is clearly taught in Judith 14, but they merely dismiss this as pagan influence and downplay its importance.[15]

SECOND MACCABEES

There are four Maccabean books which were written around 110 B.C. In Chapter 6, Eleazar is martyred. Before his death, he said that he would not renounce his faith because no one "can escape the hands of the Almighty, alive or dead" (6:36). Here he clearly states that the judgment of God cannot be avoided by death. The dead are here viewed as conscious and capable of experiencing God's punishment.

After Eleazar's death, the king orders a mother and her seven sons to eat pork. When they refuse, they are tortured (7:1).

At their death, the sons speak clearly of the resurrection of the righteous to everlasting life [7:9, 11]. The king is warned, "Thou shalt have no resurrection to [everlasting] life" (7:14).

The reference is clearly to Dan. 12:2 in that the king will be resurrected to everlasting shame and contempt and not to everlasting life. He is again warned, "Abide awhile, and behold his great glory, how he will torment you and your seed" (7:17). Here the fifth brother warns the king of future torment. The sixth brother boldly tells the king, "But think thou not, that takest in hand to strive against God, that thou shalt escape unpunished" (7:19). The king shall not escape torment by peacefully slipping into nonexistence. Eternal torment awaits him. The last son dies warning the king: "Thou . . . shall not escape the hands of God. . . . Thou . . . shalt receive just punishment for thy pride. . . . Thou by torments and plagues mayest confess that he alone is God" (7:35–37). The king is told that under divine torments, he will have to acknowledge the true God.

The annihilationists attempt to dismiss this passage as unacceptable. These martyrs clearly warned the king that he faced torment for his sins. Nowhere did they warn him that he would simply cease to exist as God's punishment. As we shall see later, the rest of the Maccabean books clearly interpret this passage as a reference to eternal, conscious torment.

ECCLESIASTICUS

This book was probably written around 195–171 B.C. It is also called Sirach.

In 7:16, 17, we read:

> Number not thyself among the multitude of sinners, but remember that wrath will not tarry long. Humble thy soul greatly: for the vengeance of the ungodly is fire and worms.

The motivation which the writer urges as to why his readers should not join with sinners is that the ungodly will suffer the punishment of "fire and worms." This is clearly a reference to Isa. 66:24 and must be linked to Judith 16:17 as teaching eternal torment. There is nothing in the context to indicate that it means annihilation.

WISDOM OF SOLOMON

There is still some confusion as to when this book was written. The best guess places it between 50–30 B.C.

In Chapter 1, the author warns against joining with sinners. Then in Chapter 2 he explains that the ungodly sin because they think that man does not have an immortal soul and at death he simply ceases to exist. Since they think there is no further torment awaiting the wicked, they can do as they please.

> For the ungodly said, reasoning with themselves, but not aright, "Our life is short and tedious, and in death there is no remedy—neither was there any man known to have returned from the grave. . . . We shall be hereafter as though we had never been: for the breath in our nostrils is as smoke . . . which being extinguished, our body shall be turned to ashes, and our spirit shall vanish as the soft air. . . . Our life shall pass away as the trace of a cloud and shall be dispersed as a mist. . . . Our time is a very shadow that passeth away; and after our end there is no returning. . . . Come on therefore, let us enjoy the good things that are present . . . costly wine and ointments . . . voluptuousness . . . joyfulness in every place: for this is our portion and our lot is this. . . . Let us oppress . . . not spare . . . nor reverence. . . . Let us lie in wait for the righteous; because . . . he is clearly contrary to our doings; he upbraideth us with our offending the law and objecteth to our infamy the transgressings of our education." (2:1–12)

Froom and other annihilationists take portions of the above material out of context and present it as if it is the opinion of the author and of the righteous.[16] They fail to inform their readers that it is the ungodly who say, "We shall be hereafter as though we have never been."

The author of *The Wisdom of Solomon* plainly states that the ungodly did not speak "aright." This is another solid example of the basic unreliability of Froom's historical research and argumentation.

The author of *The Wisdom of Solomon* answers the annihilationists of his day by arguing that the image of God in man is his immortality (2:23). After death the souls of the righteous are with God where no torments can offend them (3:1). The righteous dead condemn the ungodly (4:16).

God will "rend" the ungodly and "cast them headlong" into Hades. They will become "speechless" and "utterly laid waste." Thus, the author concludes, the ungodly will "be in sorrow . . . they shall come with fear: and their own iniquities shall convince them to their face" (4:19, 20).

Let the reader here note the usage of the favorite terms which the annihilationists arbitrarily assume mean nonexistence: "rend," "cast down," "laid waste," etc. Let the reader note that the author goes on to describe the wicked as experiencing conscious sorrow and fear in the next life. Even Froom admits that this is what the passage is saying.[17] Surely this is yet another proof that such terms do not automatically mean annihilation.

The Pseudepigrapha

These books are generally thought to have been written around 200–100 B.C. Since they have been quoted in support of Universalism, annihilationism and eternal punishment, obviously the literature must have statements which can be read in a number of ways. The most we are prepared to do is to review those statements which express the idea of eternal punishment. This should silence those who claim that the orthodox position was never held by those who wrote the pseudepigrapha.

FOURTH MACCABEES

According to this book, while the righteous ascend to conscious bliss at death (10:15; 13:17; 17:18; 18:23), the wicked descend to conscious torment (9:8, 32; 10:11, 15; 12:19; 13:15; 18:5, 22).

In Chapter 9, the authors retell the story of the death of the mother and her seven sons, which was previously given in II Macc. 7. That the boys warned the king of eternal torment will now be established beyond all doubt. Note the words which these brave martyrs used.

> "But you, for the wicked and despotic slaughter of us, shalt, from the Divine vengeance, endure torture by fire." (9:8)
> "But thou, for thy impiety and blood-shedding, shalt endure indissoluable torment." (10:11)
> "The eternal punishment of the tyrant." (10:15)
> "Divine vengeance is reserving for you, eternal fire and torments, which will cling to you for all time." (12:12)
> "The danger of eternal torment laid up for those who transgress the commandment of God." (13:15)

These statements are so clear that Universalists and annihilationists make no reference to them whatsoever in their writings.

BOOK OF JUBILEES

It is thought that this book was written around 135 B.C. Froom admits that this book teaches the orthodox position.[18] At death, the soul, or spirit, leaves the body (23:29–31). The wicked "shall depart into eternal execration: so that their condemnation may be always renewed in hate and in execration and in wrath and in torment and in indignation and in plagues and in disease forever" (36:9–11).

Despite these texts and Froom's concession, some annihilationists like Fudge still claim that the Book of Jubilees teaches that the wicked will simply cease to exist.[19]

4TH ESDRAS

This work, which is sometimes called 4th Ezra, was written around 200–100 B.C. It describes the fate of the wicked in the following passages:

> And then shall a lake of torment appear, and over against it the place of refreshment; the oven of Gehenna shall be manifest, and over it the Paradise of delight. (7:32–35)

In this passage, there is an obvious contrast between the conscious torment of the wicked in Gehenna and the conscious bliss of the righteous in paradise. The author goes on to say:

> A lake of torment shall appear . . . the oven of Gehenna. . . . There fire and torments . . . there souls . . . shall wander about henceforth in torments, ever grieving and sad. (7:36)

That the author speaks of eternal, conscious torment in the above passage cannot be doubted.

THE BOOKS OF ENOCH

These books and fragments of books appear in several ancient languages, such as Ethiopian and Slavonic. They were probably written by 50 B.C.

The Book of Enoch states that upon the wicked "great judgment shall be for all generations of the world. Woe to you, for you shall have no peace" (103:8). Thus the wicked are warned of "eternal judgment" (104:6) where their "souls are punished and bound there forever" (121:22).

I Enoch, or the Ethiopian Enoch, graphically depicts the souls of the righteous and the wicked as being conscious in bliss or torment after death (chs. 22, 27, 67, 108). Froom labels these graphic descriptions of the torment of the wicked as "a forerunner of Dante's *Divine Comedy.*"[20]

II Enoch, or the Slavonic Enoch, clearly teaches eternal torment. The wicked are tormented in "murky fire" (10:1–6). They experience pain and limitless judgment (40:12, 13; 63:4). They are described as experiencing heat and cold at the same time (10:1–6). Froom admits that II Enoch describes eternal torment.[21]

II BARUCH

When this book was written is not altogether clear. The best guess is the first century A.D.

II Baruch clearly teaches eternal torment. When the day of judgment arrives, the wicked "shall know that their torment has come" (30:4). Thus the wicked do not cease to exist but, rather, depart to torment (44:12–15; 51:5, 6; 59:2; 64:7–10; 83:8). Their eternal fate will be in "the dwelling . . . of fire" (44:13–15). In 36:12, we read:

[The wicked] now recline in anguish and rest in torment till the last time come; in which they shall come again and be tormented yet more.

How Froom can ignore these passages and claim that this book teaches that the wicked simply cease to exist on the day of judgment mystifies us.[22] The feeble attempt of Fudge to say that the anguish and torment which the wicked endure in the fires of Gehenna are unconscious is absurd.[23] The words "anguish" and "torment" can apply only to conscious beings. Nonexistence can hardly feel anguish or torment.

THE SIBYLLINE ORACLES

This book probably dates from the second century B.C.

According to the author, the disembodied souls of the wicked which are in torment in Sheol reflect on their sin and God's judgment (4:43, 44). When the day of judgment comes, the wicked will be consigned "to murky *tartarus* and the black recesses of hell" (4:83). While the righteous "shall live again on earth," the wicked descend into *tartarus* or hell forever (4:76–90).

We must point out that *tartarus* always meant the place of eternal, conscious torment in Greek literature and that it is impossible to glibly say that it means the grave or nonexistence. Arndt and Gingrich comment (p. 813):

Tartarus, thought of by the Greeks as a subterranean place lower than Hades where divine punishment was meted out, was so regarded in Jewish apocalyptic as well. (En. 20:2; Philo, Exs. 152; Jos. C. Ap. 2:240; Sib. Or. 2, 302; 4, 186).

Let the reader here note that Arndt and Gingrich interpret the reference to *tartarus* in *The Sibylline Oracles* as a reference to the place of eternal, conscious torment.

THE PSALMS OF SOLOMON

This first century B.C. work probably came from Hasidic Jews. In 3:11 we read that "the perdition of the sinners shall be forever."

They shall "perish forever" (15:12, 15). Their tongues will be on fire (12:5).

The mere presence of the word "perish" does not imply annihilation as the conditionalists attempt to state. The context of these passages clearly contrasts the eternal bliss of the righteous to the eternal misery of the wicked. Only the righteous receive the reward of eternal well-being or everlasting life (3:12–16). The wicked in contrast will receive eternal misery.

THE ASSUMPTION OF MOSES

The date of authorship is not known for sure. It may have been written around 200–100 B.C.

The only passage which speaks of the fate of the wicked describes them as the object of the contempt of the righteous.

"You shall look from on high and shalt see thy enemies in Ge[henna] and thou shalt recognize them and rejoice." (10:7, 10)

That "Ge" is an abbreviation for Gehenna is no longer questioned. In this passage, the wicked have not passed into nonexistence. They still remain in Gehenna and can be recognized and scorned by the righteous.

THE ASCENSION OF ISAIAH

This document must be dated in the second or first century B.C. In 1:3 we read that "eternal judgments and the torments of Gehenna" await the wicked. Once again, torment, not nonexistence, is the fate of the wicked.

Philo and Josephus

That Philo (LI,5; XVIII,12; XXXVIII.4) and Josephus (Wars II, pp. 154–166) clearly taught that the soul survived death and that eternal punishment awaits the wicked is not denied. Josephus states that this was the belief of the Pharisees and Essenes. Only the Sadducees, who were the materialists of that age, denied those doctrines.

The Talmudic Literature

The Babylonian Talmud reflects Jewish beliefs before Christ and was the main vehicle for keeping alive the faith of scattered Israel. It describes Gehenna as a place of fire (Ger. 357) and of weeping (ER 129). There the wicked shall be "punished for all generations" (RH 65). God's "everlasting anger . . . imprisons [them] forever" (Ber 173). While in Gehenna, they shall not be consumed (Shab. 762, 763).

The Midrash

The wicked shall be "punished for generations upon generations" in "the ceaseless retribution of the wicked" (Gen. 908). They can "never escape" (Num. 726). While in Gehenna, they are not annihilated (Exo. 449).

> In that hour the Lord will requite the nations of the world with a great and ceaseless retribution, and hurl them down to Gehenna where they will be punished for generation upon generation. (Gen. 908)

The translators of the Midrash comment:

> [The wicked] will be resurrected and their bodies continue to exist so as to receive punishment. (Gen. 211 n 4)

Chief Rabbi Weil pointed out:

> The Talmud and the other traditional monuments do not fail to proclaim the eternity of sufferings and of rewards in the Halacha no less than in the Agada. . . . The Mishna brings before its tribunal certain individuals and certain generations devoting some . . . to endless suffering. (Shah. CII, Mishna 2, 3)

In Rosh Hashana we find that the wicked "go down to Gehenna and are punished there to all generations" (17:1). "Sons of Gehenna are those who forever abide in Gehenna" (17a).

Borrowing from Isa. 33:14, the Targums speak of Gehenna as the place of "everlasting burnings." Thus Shurer in *The History of the Jewish People in the Age of Jesus Christ* (p. 545) states that the Jews clearly taught that the damnation of the wicked was eternal. Leon Morris in *The New Bible Commentary* (p. 302) points out that such rabbinic expressions as "2nd death" clearly taught eternal punishment.

In Bab. Tal. Shah. XIII. 4,5 we read that "Gehenna is shut in their faces and they are judged there for generations of generations." Also, in De Rationes, Ch. XIII, the rabbi said:

> We do not fear him who appears to be able to kill the body;
> for Abraham, Isaac and Jacob receive those who die for the law;
> but greater danger of eternal torment is the allotment of the soul.

Other passages could be called upon.[24] But enough has been given to establish that it was the general belief of the Jews that eternal punishment awaited the wicked. The attempt of the annihilationists to seize upon any passage where words such as "perish" are found is doomed to failure. Since these words in Scripture do not mean "to cause something to pass into nonexistence," their attempt to use any literature which uses such words in support of annihilationism is invalid and must be deemed the result of faulty research.

AION AND AIONIOS

Just as *olam* is the Hebrew word which expresses the idea of eternity or endlessness when applied to the final order of things after the resurrection, even so *aion* and *aionios* are the two Greek words which were used in the Septuagint to translate *olam*.

The Septuagint

The word *aion* is found in the Septuagint 308 times. Except for about 20 cases, where it is used to translate such words as *ad*, it is always used as the Greek equivalent of *olam*.

Aionios is used 92 times in the Septuagint and is the equivalent of *olam* except in six cases.

With both words, the various shades of meaning of *olam* are maintained by the translators of the Septuagint. These words are used to speak of the endless quality of the final order of things (Dan. 12:1–3).

The importance of this point should not be overlooked. As Sasse pointed out in *The Dictionary of New Testament Theology* (pp. 200, 201):

> These [words] contain nothing peculiar to the N.T. From the time of the LXX they formed part of the common usage of Hellenistic Judaism. . . . Hence it may be seen that the usage of the N.T. is distinguished from that of the LXX only by an intensification of the tendency already displayed in the LXX to replace the simple formula by more complicated.

We also read in Girdlestone's *Synonyms of the Old Testament* (p. 317):

> These Greek phrases, therefore, when they appear in the N.T., must be interpreted in accordance with the usage of the word *olam*.

McClintock and Strong state (Vol. III, p. 314) in their encyclopedia:

> The Greek term Aion remarkably corresponds to the Hebrew Olam in nearly all these sense, and is its usual rendering in the Sept.

In the later Jewish apocalyptic literature, the contrast between the temporary present age and the endless or eternal age to come was greatly intensified. This dichotomy, dualism or contrast between the present order and the final order is summarized in Strack and Billerbeck in *Kommentar Zum Neuen Testament Aus Talmud und Midrasch* in Vol. IV, 799ff. For example, in Slav. Enoch we find "this *aion*" (66:7) is contrasted to the "endless *aion*" (50:2; 66:6a). While the present order will end, the final order means "endless eternity" (65:3ff.). The same idea is found in Syriac Baruch and especially in 4th Ezra.

The attempt by some Universalists and annihilationists to deny that "endlessness," or "eternity," is an essential part of the meaning of *aion* when it refers to the final order of things[25] cannot stand up to close scrutiny.[26]

To say that *aion* only means "pertaining to the coming age" is not enough. It has been pointed out by many scholars that when *aion* refers to the final order, it means "pertaining to the *endless* age to come."[27]

The New Testament

The word *aion* in its various forms is found 108 times in the Greek New Testament. It is translated in the KJV as follows:

World: 41 times
Forever: 26 times
Forever and ever: 23 times
Never: 7 times
For evermore: 3 times
Ages: 2 times
Eternal: 2 times
Worlds: 2 times
Without end: 1 time
Course: 1 time

The word *aionios* is found 70 times in the New Testament and is translated in the KJV as "eternal" 41 times, "everlasting" 25 times, "world" 3 times, "forever" 1 time.

It is obvious that *aion* and *aionios* follow *olam* in having a wide range of meaning.

THE LEXICOGRAPHICAL MATERIAL

Arndt and Gingrich (pp. 26, 27) define *aion* as referring to (1) eternity past which has no beginning, (2) a segment of time as in either a present or past age, (3) the world in a spatial sense, and (4) the coming age which has no end or eternity future. Thayer (pp.

18, 19) defines *aion* as: (1) forever, eternity, (2) ancient times, (3) the world, (4) this present order of things (usually viewed as evil), (5) the final order of things. *The Dictionary of New Testament Theology* (vol. 3, p. 826) points out that "when it is directed to the on-going future, *aion* can take the meaning of eternity." Jeremias in Kittel's *Theological Dictionary of the New Testament* (vol. 1, p. 147) states that "in respect of the duration of this sojourn [in the age to come], there can be no doubt that it was originally thought to be everlasting."

The lexicons define *aionios* as meaning basically the same as *aion*.[28]

THE EXEGETICAL EVIDENCE

First, both *aion* (1 Tim. 1:17) and *aionios* (Rom. 16:26) are used to speak of God's absolute eternity. All the members of the Trinity are described as "eternal" in the sense of being beginningless and endless (1 Tim. 1:17; Heb. 9:14; 13:8).

Second, both *aion* (John 9:32) and *aionios* (Titus 1:2) are used to encompass all of time since creation. The "world" is thus viewed in a temporal sense as well as in a spacial sense.

Third, both *aion* (Matt. 21:19; John 8:35) and *aionios* (Luke 16:9; Philemon 15) describe a long, indefinite period of time.

Fourth, both *aion* (Col. 1:26) and *aionios* (Rom. 16:25) describe past ages or generations.

Fifth, *aion* is used to speak of this present evil age or world system (Rom. 12:2; Gal. 1:4; Eph. 2:2).

Sixth, *aion* is used to describe the present order of things which will end when Christ returns (see Matt. 12:32; 13:29, 40, 49; 24:3, etc.).

Seventh, both *aion* (Matt. 12:32; Luke 18:30; Eph. 1:21; 2 Tim. 4:10; Titus 2:2) and *aionios* (2 Cor. 4:17, 18) are used in context where the present temporal order is contrasted to the final order in that the final order is endless in duration.

Eighth, both *aion* and *aionios* are used to describe actions which begin in this present age and continue on into the eternal state without interruption or end. These activities are thus endless in duration in the fullest sense of the word.

In doxological contexts, God is to receive endless glory and praise throughout this present age and into the age to come without end. Both *aion* (1 Tim. 1:17; 2 Pet. 3:18) and *aionios* (1 Tim. 6:16) are used in this sense.

Christ's kingdom (Luke 1:17, *aion*) and resurrection life (Rev. 1:18, *aion*) are said to be "forever," i.e., endless in duration. That this is what "forever" means in the context is clear from Luke 1:33

which states that Christ's kingdom is "forever" in the sense that it "shall have no end." The final state is thus designated as endless in duration, in contrast to the temporal order which will have an end.

Both *aion* (John 10:28) and *aionios* (John 3:36; 5:24; 6:47, 54; 1 John 5:11–13) are used to describe the kind of life which is received at regeneration. This quality of life is the possession of believers now and in the age to come without end or interruption. This is why Christ could say that those who possess eternal life shall never die (John 6:51, 58; 8:51, 52; 11:26).

The indwelling of the Holy Spirit and the possession of the truth are both "eternal," i.e., endless in duration (John 14:6; 2 John 2). Whereas Christ's earthly presence was temporal and had an "end," the Holy Spirit's indwelling was not temporal but would be "forever," i.e., endless in duration.

The writer of Hebrews dealt with the problem of apostasy. People who had been professing Christians were now turning back to Judaism because of persecution and trials. In order to deal with this problem, he demonstrates the superiority of Christianity over Judaism by contrasting the temporal character of Judaism to the permanent and endless character of Christianity.

While the Old Testament priests only had a temporal office and ministry, which at their death passed on to someone else, Christ's priesthood was "forever," i.e., endless in duration in that (1) He would never die, (2) He would remain as God's high priest forever, and (3) He would never pass on His priesthood to anyone else (Heb. 5:6; 6:20; 7:17, 21, 24, 28).

Because Christ's priesthood is endless and permanent, His work of salvation and redemption is viewed as being "eternal," i.e., endless in duration (Heb. 5:9; 9:12). Whereas the redemptive work of Old Testament priests was defective and superseded by Christ's work, there is nothing which will supersede the work of Christ. His priestly work is perfect in nature and endless in duration.

It is in this sense that the author refers to "the eternal covenant" in Heb. 13:20. The superiority of the new covenant over the old covenant is established on the basis of the contrast between the temporal nature of the old covenant, which had an end, and the permanent nature of the new covenant, which shall have no end. There is no "third" covenant in God's plan. The new covenant is God's final and only method of dealing with man.

This insight provides a solid answer to those cultists who put forth new covenants and revelations which supposedly superseded the work, covenant, and revelation of Christ as given in the New Testament. The author of Hebrews clearly bases the superiority of the new covenant on the finality and permanence of its revelation

(1:1, 2) and the endless nature of the person and work of its mediator. The attempt of the Mormons, Moonies, Adventists, etc., to add their modern revelations to the new covenant revelation of the New Testament is here clearly condemned.

We must pause at this point and deal with annihilationists like Froom who attempt to argue that *aion* and *aionios* only mean "endless in result and not process."[29]

Froom refers to Heb. 6:2 and 9:12 as proving his case. Other annihilationists have adopted Froom's position as their foundational argument.[30]

In Heb. 6:2, the author of Hebrews refers to "eternal judgment" as one of the elementary teachings of Christianity. The contrast is between a temporary verdict or sentence in which there is still hope of a reversal and an endless or permanent verdict which is irreversible.

On the day of judgment, when a rebel sinner receives the final divine verdict or sentence, it is an endless one. There is no second chance. The fires of Gehenna will not purge sinners of their evil and then cause a new verdict to be rendered. The verdict is on the books for all eternity. It is endlessly binding and in force.

We fail to see how the annihilationists are correct in their attempt to make "judgment" into a verb, i.e., a word of action. It is a noun, not a verb. Yet, this is exactly how annihilationists argue. They begin their argument by defining "judgment" as "a word of action." They ridicule the idea of an eternal act or process of judging. They then state that the results of judging are eternal but not the process.[31]

What these annihilationists fail to recognize is that the word "judgment" is in its noun form which means that an endlessly binding verdict is being described. Also, the endlessness of this verdict is part of the superiority of the new covenant.

The annihilationists also refer to Heb. 9:12, "eternal redemption." Once again they erroneously define "redemption" as a verb and not as a noun. The author of Hebrews is contrasting the defective temporal ceremonial redemption of the old covenant (9:1–10) to the perfect, permanent redemption of the new covenant (9:11–28). Whereas some of the people "redeemed" under Moses ultimately perished through unbelief (Heb. 3:16–19), those who believe in Christ remain redeemed forever. While old covenant redemption was temporal and had an end (10:1–4), new covenant redemption is endless in duration (9:12).

We must thus conclude that such passages as Heb. 5:9 and 9:12 refer to the permanent and irreversible salvation which Christ accomplished for the believer through His atoning work. The word "everlasting" refers to its permanence (Heb. 9:25, 26).

We must also point out that the annihilationists are in error when they put forth these and other like passages as if they were describing the final order of things after the resurrection. They attempt to connect "eternal redemption" with "eternal punishment" in order to argue that the punishment of the eternal state will be endless in result and not in process.

Their fundamental error is the same as when they argue from "everlasting mountains" to prove that "eternal punishment" is not eternal. They have taken *aion* and *aionios* out of their respective biblical and temporal contexts and connected passages which contextually referred to different ages.

When discussing passages where *aion* and *aionios* describe the final state after the resurrection, it is illegitimate, hermeneutically speaking, to bring up passages which deal with things in this present age.

What is clear from the usage of *aion* and *aionios* in the book of Hebrews is that "endlessness in duration" is an essential part of new covenant salvation and judgment. It is an essential element of the superiority and perfection of Christ's atonement.

Ninth, both *aion* and *aionios* are used to speak of the final order of things after the resurrection.

AION:
Eternal life in the age to come (Mark 10:30)
Eternal life in the age to come (Luke 18:30)
No marriage in the age to come (Luke 20:35)
The ages to come (Eph. 2:7)
Powers of the age to come (Heb. 6:5)
Black darkness forever (2 Pet. 2:17)
Black darkness forever (Jude 13)
The smoke of their torment goes up forever and ever; and they
    have no rest day and night (Rev. 14:10, 11)
Her smoke rises up forever and ever (Rev. 19:3)
Tormented day and night forever and ever (Rev. 20:10)
They shall reign forever and ever (Rev. 22:5)

AIONIOS:
Eternal fire (Matt. 18:8)
Eternal fire (Matt. 25:41)
Eternal punishment, eternal life (Matt. 25:46)
Eternal sin (Mark 3:29)
Eternal life in the age to come (Luke 18:30)
Eternal destruction (2 Thess. 1:9)
Eternal judgment (Heb. 6:2)
Eternal kingdom (2 Pet. 1:11)

First of all, *aion* and *aionios* are used in context where the temporal character of this present age is contrasted to the endless character of the final order.

In Mark 3:29, the blasphemy of the Holy Spirit is called an "eternal sin" because it will always be eternally viewed by God as a sin, and no forgiveness is possible in this present age or in the final state to come:

> It shall not be forgiven him, either in this age, or in the age to come. (Matt. 12:32)

Once again the annihilationists pretend that the word "sin" in Mark 3:29 is a verb.[32] The word "sin" is actually in its noun form and is not a word of action. Christ is simply saying that God will look upon this sin as unforgivable for all time and eternity.

We must also point out that *aionios* is here used to speak of God's judgment which begins in this age and is carried on into the age to come without interruption, end or hope of reversal.

The Universalist at this point has a terrible dilemma. Christ clearly states that those people who commit the sin of blasphemy of the Holy Spirit will never be forgiven. Once they enter into Gehenna, they will not be cleansed of evil and forgiven. This passage is absolutely clear that there is a class of persons for whom divine forgiveness is an eternal impossibility.

Secondly, both *aion* (Mark 10:30; Luke 18:30) and *aionios* (Matt. 25:46; Luke 18:30) are used to speak of the saints' entrance into the full possession and enjoyment of divine life in the age to come. This is in contrast to the pain, sorrow, persecution and trials which they experienced while in this life (Rev. 21:4).

The phraseology which is employed by the biblical authors to speak of the eternal duration or process of the fullness of life which the saints will enjoy in the final order becomes crucial at this point.

The saints are to receive "eternal life": *aion* (Mark 10:30; Luke 18:30) and *aionios* (Matt. 25:46; Luke 18:30). Did the authors of the New Testament mean that the results of life would be eternal while the saints themselves passed into nonexistence? Or did they mean that the believers would enjoy life as an endless process or state of well-being?

The saints not only enjoy the fullness of divine life forever as a state of well-being or process but they also "shall reign forever and ever" (*eis tous aionas ton aionon*) (Rev. 22:5).

Did John mean that the results of their reign would be endless while they themselves passed into nonexistence? Or did he mean that they would be involved in the process of reigning for all eternity? Was the duration of their reign endless?

The emphatic language employed by John in Rev. 22:5 can only be interpreted as referring to an eternity of process or duration.

When he used the wording "unto the ages of ages," he used the plural form of *aion,* which in the Greek is the most emphatic way to express the absolute eternity of duration or process. Their kingdom will last forever (2 Pet. 1:11).

We must also point out that the book of Revelation as well as 2 Peter and Jude clearly depends upon Jewish apocalyptic literature from which much of their imagery, phraseology and language is derived. The plural usage of *aion* in "unto the ages of the ages" meant eternity of process or duration in this literature. Just the plural form itself speaks of absolute eternity of duration in such places as Eph. 2:7, "the ages to come."

When the biblical authors wished to speak of an eternity of process or duration, they used those words and phrases which in contemporary language expressed that idea.

Thirdly, both *aion* (Rev. 20:10) and *aionios* (Matt. 25:41, 46) are used to describe the final condition of Satan and the demonic host after the resurrection.

Before we begin our investigation of those passages which speak of the final state of Satan and the demonic host, there is one consideration which should be raised at this point. The New Testament clearly teaches that there are certain angels who are now in conscious torment awaiting the day of judgment. There is no concept of soul sleep for those angels who are now in hell.

2 Peter 2:4

> For if God did not spare angels when they sinned, but cast them into hell and committed them to pits of darkness reserved for judgment. . . .

First, when Peter stated that some angels were cast into hell, he used a form of the word *tartarus,* which in Greek literature always meant the place of deepest conscious torment or hell in the netherworld. It never meant nonexistence and it never meant the grave. Second, God committed them to "pits of darkness." This Jewish apocalyptic phrase referred to the place of mental anguish and terror in the underworld.

Third, they are "reserved" in the black pits of *tartarus* until the day of judgment. The word "reserved" is in the present passive participle tense, which means that they are continually kept or reserved unto judgment. It is thus gramatically impossible to avoid the clear teaching in this passage that these angels are in conscious torment in the black pit of *tartarus* until the day of judgment.

Jude 6

> And angels who did not keep their own domain, but abandoned their proper abode, He has kept in eternal bonds under

136

darkness for the judgment of the great day.

The interdependence of 2 Peter and Jude and their mutual reliance on Jewish apocalyptic literature is clearly illustrated by a comparison of 2 Pet. 2:4 and Jude 6.

The angels which did not keep to their own domain are "kept" or guarded "in eternal bonds." The word translated "eternal" is *aidios*, which is a word that is found only in Rom. 1:20 where it refers to God's eternal power. According to the lexicons, it was used in Greek and rabbinic literature as a word for absolute eternity.[36]

These angels are in eternal bonds or chains "under darkness." The word *zophos* refers to "the darkness of the nether regions" (OD.20,356) and these regions themselves (Lil.15,191; 21,56; OD.ii,57)."[37] Neither Peter nor Jude taught that the angels passed into nonexistence when they were cast into the blackness of hell. This class of angels entered into conscious torment at their fall, and will remain in that condition for all eternity.

There is not a single text in the New Testament which speaks of a final salvation for Satan or his angels. Christ's redemption is clearly limited to human beings in Heb. 2:14–17. Thus the Universalists' attempt to see an ultimate salvation for the demonic host cannot stand up to a grammatical exegesis of 2 Pet. 2:4; Jude 6; Matt. 25:41, 46; Rev. 20:10.

The New Testament is clear in its teaching that some of the angels are in conscious torment now and that they will be joined by all the demonic host on the day of judgment.

Now we come to consider the final state of Satan and the demonic host.

Matthew 25:41, 46

> **"Then He will also say to those on His left, 'Depart from Me, accursed ones, into the eternal fire which has been prepared for the devil and his angels. . . .' And these will go away into eternal punishment, but the righteous into eternal life."**

In a passage which is filled with rabbinic imagery and vocabulary,[33] Christ speaks of the coming of the Son of Man at the end of this age to separate the sheep from the goats (vv. 31–46).

In verse 41, Christ uses the rabbinic metaphor of "eternal fire" to speak of the ultimate fate of Satan and his angels. It was already an established teaching that Satan and the demonic host would suffer eternal punishment. Those rabbis who believed this used such words as "eternal fire" as a metaphor for eternal punishment. This is why in verse 46, Christ drops the metaphor of "eternal fire" and speaks instead of the reality of "eternal punishment." That "eternal fire" and "eternal punishment" mean the same thing is obvious, as both are put forth as the destination of wicked angels and men.

In Hebraic usage, when *aion* or *aionios* were used to speak of the final order of things, they always meant an eternity of duration or endlessness. In this passage, Christ clearly equates the metaphor of "eternal fire" with "eternal or unending punishment" as the final state of Satan and his angels after the resurrection.

It is to be noted that Christ explicitly stated that eternal fire and eternal punishment are viewed in this passage as being the ultimate fate of both rebel angels and rebel sinners.

Revelation 20:10

> And the devil who deceived them was thrown into the lake of fire and brimstone, where the beast and the false prophet are also; and they will be tormented day and night forever and ever.

The Antichrist and the false prophet were thrown alive into a lake of sulfuric fire in Rev. 19:20:

> And the beast was seized, and with him the false prophet who performed the signs in his presence, by which he deceived those who had received the mark of the beast and those who worshiped his image; these two were thrown alive into the lake of fire which burns with brimstone.

After "one thousand years" the devil himself is cast down into the fiery lake where the false prophet and Antichrist were still suffering (Rev. 20:10). That the false prophet and Antichrist still existed in the lake of fire after a "thousand years" of torment is a grammatical necessity because John goes on to say, "They [i.e., the devil, the false prophet and the Antichrist] will be tormented." If they had passed into nonexistence, then John would have said "he" and not "they."

Speaking of all three, John says, "They shall be tormented day and night forever and ever."

First, notice that John uses the word "tormented," which is a word of action and not just result. This is the same word used in II Macc. 7:13 where the seven brothers were tortured with excruciating pain. It is also used in Rev. 11:10 to speak of the mental torment of the wicked caused by the rebukes of righteous prophets. It is used throughout the Gospel accounts to speak of the torment that demons themselves caused in their victims. In this passage, the word is used in the third person plural future indicative passive tense to speak of a process or activity of torture.

Second, notice that the expression "day and night" is used to indicate ceaseless torment. The phrase "day and night" is used elsewhere by John to describe the ceaseless worship of God (Rev. 4:8; 7:15), and the ceaseless accusations of Satan (12:10).

Third, in order to emphasize unending ceaseless torment, John adds "forever and ever" (*eis tous aionas ton aionon*). This phrase modifies "day and night" by indicating that their torment will not cease for all eternity.[34]

John uses the phrase "forever and ever" in 1:6, 4:9, 5:13, etc., to speak of the endless worship of God. In 4:10, 10:6, etc., it refers to the endless life of God. In 11:15, it refers to the endless kingdom of Christ; and in 22:5, it speaks of the endless reign of the saints in the final state.

What is exegetically crucial is to discover what *eis tous aionas ton aionon* meant in every instance other than where the fate of wicked angels and men is described.

In every instance where "forever and ever" was used in some other context other than the final fate of wicked angels or men, it always, without exception, meant absolute endlessness, or eternity.[35]

Hermeneutically, this means that we must begin with the assumption that *eis tous aionas ton aionon* will mean absolute endlessness when applied to the fate of angels and men. To begin with, the assumption that it doesn't matter what these words meant in every other occurrence and to arbitrarily assert that they only meant "a long time" is exegetically and hermeneutically impossible.

Once we begin with the sound hermeneutical principle that words should be understood in terms of how they are used elsewhere in Scripture, the fate of Satan and his angels, according to Rev. 20:10, is that they will suffer eternal, ceaseless, conscious torment. No other honest interpretation is possible.

Fourth, both *aion* (2 Pet. 2:17; Jude 13; Rev. 4:11; 19:3) and *aionios* (Matt. 18:8; 25–46; Mark 3:29; 2 Thess. 1:9; Heb. 6:2; Jude 7) are used to describe the final state of the wicked after the resurrection.

Perhaps the best way to approach these passages is to examine them book by book.

2 PETER

We have already seen that in 2 Pet. 2:4, there is a class of angels who have already been cast into the black pit of hell and are now under conscious torment while they await the judgment day. This has been repeatedly pointed out by most commentators.[38] After the judgment, future torment awaits all the demonic host (Matt. 8:29; Luke 8:31).

In 2 Pet. 2:9, the condition of the ungodly between death and resurrection is described in virtually the same terms as Peter used in verse 4 to describe the condition of the angels in *tartarus*.

The ungodly are kept for the day of judgment while being consciously tormented. The punishment is not future but a present experience of the ungodly while they await their final sentence.

This has been pointed out, by such commentators as Alford, A. T. Robertson, and Vincent, as the only grammatical interpretation possible. The classic Lutheran commentator, R. H. Lenski, states that the ungodly are held

> for Judgment day while they are being punished. [*Terein*] markedly repeats the [*Teroumenos*] used in v. 4 and refers to keeping them in hell as the added participle shows: "while being punished" ("under punishment," R.V.; not final; "to be punished" A.V.).[39]

Peter is obviously drawing a parallel between the torment of angels and the torment of sinners as they await the day of judgment.

Aion and *aionios* describe the final state in 2 Peter in 1:11, where Peter speaks of the saints' entrance into "the eternal kingdom of our Lord and Savior Jesus Christ."

That *aionios* here means that Christ's kingdom will endure forever, i.e., it will have no end, is obvious. Endless duration is clearly what *aionios* means in 2 Pet. 1:11.

In 2 Pet. 3:18, *aion* is used in a doxological sense to describe the unceasing glory which shall ascend to God for all eternity. Again, it is an eternal process which is being described.

Having already mentioned the murky darkness of *tartarus* in 2:4, Peter in 2:17 speaks of the unrighteous as sharing in the same fate as the angels. Thus he speaks of "the darkness" which had already been mentioned in 2:4.[40]

> These are springs without water, and mists driven by a storm, for whom the black darkness has been reserved.

The KJV has *aion*, "forever," in the text, but the textual grounds for that reading is weak and it was probably inserted from Jude 13.[41]

What is important for us to note is that the wicked will be cast into "the murky netherworld of deep darkness."[42] They are pictured as dwelling in murky *tartarus* where their lot is torment.

JUDE

Jude describes the intermediate and future suffering of the angels in verse 6:

> And angels who did not keep their own domain, but aban-

doned their proper abode, He has kept in eternal bonds under darkness for the judgment of the great day.

The phrase "under darkness" denotes that the gloom is oppressing or tormenting these angels.[43] Their bonds are eternal in duration. There is no hope of their escaping or being released.

The question naturally arises as to why Jude and Peter both discuss the intermediate and future punishment of angels. The angels are introduced as an illustration of why and how the ungodly will be punished. Thus Jude speaks of the condemnation of false prophets in verse 4 and then illustrates their fate by referring to examples of divine judgment such as the generation of Moses that perished in the wilderness (v. 5), the punishment of angels (v. 6), Sodom and Gomorrah (vv. 7, 8), and Cain and Balaam (v. 11).

It is in this sense that the sulfuric fire which destroyed Sodom and Gomorrah and the cities around them is a type or sign of the future fiery punishment which awaits the wicked. Since the future punishment had been described as torment by "eternal fire" in Jewish apocalyptic literature, Jude speaks of "eternal fire."[44]

The annihilationists have traditionally stated that this text says that these cities were destroyed by "the punishment of eternal fire" in order to prove (sic) that aion only means "unending in result and not in process."[45] Since the fire which destroyed these cities is now extinguished, it cannot literally be "eternal fire." Thus, the annihilationists with glee have always pointed to this passage that "eternal fire" need not be eternal.

The problem with their interpretation is that the Greek text does not say the cities suffered "the punishment of eternal fire." Lenski comments:

> These cities lie before [the eyes] as a *deigma*, "indication or sign" . . . , that points like a finger to "eternal fire." The participle states how they lie before men's eyes to this day, namely "in undergoing justice" (*dike*). Our versions and others combine in the wrong way. The Cities of the Plain are not "suffering the punishment of eternal fire." What lies before us at the Dead Sea is "a *sign* of eternal fire." Fire and brimstone made the place what it is, a sign, indeed, of the eternal fire of hell, a warning for all time. So writes Jude.[46]

The Greek in verse 7 literally says, "a sign of fire eternal." Lenski's comment is thus confirmed by the Greek grammar of the text itself. The annihilationists are grammatically incorrect when they make "eternal fire" modify *diken* (punishment) instead of *deigma* (sign).

Beck translates verse 7 as:

> Just like Sodom and Gomorrah and the towns around them,

who for sexual sins and unnatural vice have suffered punishment
and lie before us as a warning of everlasting fire.

Weymouth and Moffatt also view "eternal fire" as modifying
deigma and not *diken*: "an example of eternal fire" (Weymouth); "a
warning of the everlasting fire" (Moffatt).

This passage emphasizes the absolute necessity of a grammatical exegesis of Scripture in the original text. The annihilationists
depend solely upon the authorized version, and because of this
they are led astray in a proper interpretation of this passage.

Jude 12, 13

**These men are those who are hidden reefs in your love feasts
when they feast with you without fear, caring for themselves;
clouds without water, carried along by winds; autumn trees
without fruit, doubly dead, uprooted; wild waves of the sea,
casting up their own shame like foam; wandering stars, for whom
the black darkness has been reserved forever.**

Jude continues his description of the character and destiny of
the ungodly. They are "wandering stars," possibly comets or shoot-
ing stars, "for whom the murky netherworld [*zophos*] of deep darkness unto or into eternity has been kept" (Lit. Gk.).

Modern translators have rendered the verse to indicate that
the fate of the wicked will be eternal in duration.[47] "For whom the
nether gloom of darkness has been reserved eternally" (Moffatt).
"For whom dark gloom is reserved forever" (Beck). "For whom the
nether gloom of darkness has been reserved forever" (RSV).

Jude speaks of "the murky netherworld of deep darkness"
because he had already mentioned the place in verse 6. Both Jude
and Peter taught that evil angels and rebel sinners would be tormented together in the same place in the same way for the same
length of duration.

Just as there are angels which are now in conscious torment in
the netherworld (2 Pet. 2:4; Jude 6), even so the ungodly join them
in the netherworld in the intermediate state between death and
resurrection (2 Pet. 2:9).

Just as eternal torment awaits the rebel angels (2 Pet. 2:4; Jude
6), even so eternal torment awaits rebel sinners (2 Pet. 2:17; Jude
13).

Jude 21

**Keep yourselves in the love of God, waiting anxiously for
the mercy of our Lord Jesus Christ to eternal life.**

Jude here speaks of the future fullness of life which the saints will possess when Christ returns. It is clear that *aionios* here refers to an endless quality of life which the saints will experience forever. It does not mean endless in result but in duration. This is in contrast to the wicked who will be in gloomy darkness forever (v. 13).

Jude 25

To the only God our Savior, through Jesus Christ our Lord, be glory, majesty, dominion and authority, before all time and now and forever. Amen.

In their doxological context, the plural form of *aion* (ages) can only mean absolute eternity. God will receive glory not only in this age which will have an end but also in the infinite number of ages to come in the final state. There is no way to limit *aion* to result, as opposed to process. The process of glorifying God is an eternal one.

Given the usage of *aionios* in verse 21, *aion* in verse 25, and *aidios* in verse 6, the only possible exegetical interpretation of *aion* in verse 13 would state that eternal torment awaits the ungodly in the blackness of hell.

REVELATION

Revelation 14:10, 11

He also will drink of the wine of the wrath of God, which is mixed in full strength in the cup of His anger; and he will be tormented with fire and brimstone in the presence of the holy angels and in the presence of the Lamb. And the smoke of their torment goes up forever and ever; and they have no rest day and night, those who worship the beast and his image, and whoever receives the mark of his name.

In this passage, the Apostle John uses those words which in the Greek language were the only ones available to him which could express the idea of eternal, conscious torment. He could not have expressed this idea by any clearer vocabulary. If we take these words in their natural meaning, we will agree with the German commentator, Joseph Meyer, who said:

Everyone who in any way resigns himself to the beast, incurs that eternal torment.[48]

First, the word "torment," as we have already seen, clearly refers to painful torture.[49] There is no way to make *basanizw* mean annihilation. No conditional immortalitist even tries to do this, because the meaning of this Greek word is too obvious.

In verse 10, the ungodly "will be tormented with fire and brimstone [sulfuric fire]." This is clearly the terminology for eternal torment used in Jewish apocalyptic literature.[50] And we emphasize that "sulfuric fire" in this text does not annihilate the wicked but torments them. This reveals at once the falsity of the annihilationists' argument that "fire and brimstone" always refer to burning something into nonexistence.

Second, the wicked "will be tormented by sulfuric fire in the presence of the holy angels and in the presence of the Lamb." This scene echoes passages in the apocalyptic literature, such as Enoch 27:2, 3; 48:9, etc. Joseph Meyer points out:

> They suffer this their pain before the eyes of the holy angels, and of the Lamb . . . on this account, to render it the more bitter.[51]

Third, having described the nature and context of the punishment inflicted upon the wicked, John now speaks of its duration. The words and phrases he uses are so strong and emphatic that such commentators as A. T. Robertson, Alford, Lenski, Lange, Hendriksen, Swete, Hengstenberg, etc., point out that eternal torment is the only grammatical interpretation possible.

Since the metaphor of sulfuric fire is used to express the idea of eternal torment,[52] in verse 11, John uses the metaphor of eternally arising smoke to build the mental image of the eternal process of torment. He uses the same metaphor in 19:3, where the "smoke," i.e., torment, goes on "forever and ever."

Since the torment is "forever and ever" and the metaphor of fire is used to symbolize it, then the smoke from this fire is said to ascend "forever and ever." The eternity of the literal torment is symbolized by the metaphor of eternally ascending smoke in 14:11 and 19:3.

The annihilationists try to view the fire and smoke as literal. As soon as the fire and smoke consumes the wicked, the smoke ceases. Thus they ignore the fact that the fire and smoke in 14:11 and 19:3 are merely metaphors for eternal punishment. The metaphors of fire and smoke are both called "eternal" because the punishment which they symbolize is eternal in duration. It would make no grammatical sense whatsoever to use such metaphors if the punishment is not endless in duration.

Also, their assumption that the fire and the smoke are literal leads them to ridicule the idea of eternal fire and smoke as if the orthodox position required such literalization. But these are clearly figures of speech which symbolize the reality of conscious torment.

John uses two phrases to describe the duration of the torment. First, he says that it will endure "forever and ever." Lenski strongly points out that the phrase "for the eons of the eons" clearly means eternal torment.[53]

> The strongest expression for our "forever" is *eis tous aionan ton aionon*, "for the eons of eons"; many eons, each of vast duration, are multiplied by many more, which we imitate by "forever and ever." Human language is able to use only temporal terms to express what is altogether beyond time and timeless. The Greek takes its greatest terms for time, the eon, pluralizes this, and then multiplies it by its own plural, even using articles which make these eons the definite ones.[54]

Since the phrase "forever and ever" elsewhere always means absolute eternity, there is no honest way to escape this meaning in Rev. 14:11 and 19:3.

Second, John goes on to amplify and magnify the "forever and ever" duration of time by saying that the wicked will not have any periods of rest in which they will be unconscious of torment. "They have no rest [from torment] day or night."

When we experience pain in this life, we sometimes can rest or escape from it during the times we fall asleep in the day or night. But John here clearly states that the wicked will never slip into peaceful sleep and escape conscious torment. This is why John used the exact words which he previously used to describe the ceaseless and sleepless worship of God by the four beasts.

> And the four living creatures, each one of them having six wings, are full of eyes around and within; and day and night they do not cease to say, "Holy, holy, holy, is the Lord God, the Almighty, who was and who is and who is to come." (4:8)

The annihilationists have never come to grips with John's clear statement that the wicked will never slip into peaceful nonexistence of sleep but will experience conscious torment forever. Since they question that *aionios* means "endless," let them here note "no rest day or night," which explains the meaning of *aionios*. That it means ceaseless in duration is obvious.

By every rule of hermeneutics and exegesis, the only legitimate interpretation of Rev. 14:10, 11 is the one that clearly sees eternal, conscious torment awaiting the wicked.

MATTHEW

In this gospel, Christ speaks of the final state of the wicked, using *aionios* to describe its duration in three passages.

Matthew 18:8, 9

"And if your hand or your foot causes you to stumble, cut it off and throw it from you; it is better for you to enter life

crippled or lame, than having two hands or two feet, to be cast into the eternal fire. And if your eye causes you to stumble, pluck it out, and throw it from you. It is better for you to enter life with one eye, than having two eyes, to be cast into the hell of fire."

Several things should be noted in this text.

First, nothing is so important in this life that it makes going to hell worthwhile. The rabbinic expression "hand or foot" referred to those things which are so important to people that they are willing to chance hell in order to possess them.

Second, notice that the wicked will be thrown or "cast" (ballw) into Gehenna. In this context it carries the same meaning as apolluo which means "to deliver up to eternal misery" (Thayer's Greek-English Lexicon, p. 64).

Third, the same warning was previously given in Matt. 5:29, 30, although slightly different wording was used. Both passages will be considered together.

Fourth, the phrase "enter into life," which is the opposite of "being cast into hell," refers to the resurrection life. Christ here contrasts the unending quality of life which the saints will fully possess after the judgment, to the eternal torment of Gehenna.

Fifth, the following chart sets before us a comparison of 5:29, 30 and 18:8, 9.

5:29–30:	"whole body"	"cast"	"into hell [Gehenna]"
18:8:	"two hands and feet"	"cast"	"into eternal fire"
18:9:	"two eyes"	"cast"	"into the hell [Gehenna] of fire"

The expression "whole body" (lit. all of the body) means the entire body with no hands, feet or eyes missing. This echoes Christ's statement in Matt. 10:28 when He speaks of the body as well as the soul being cast into hell. Note the necessity of the resurrection of the wicked. Each must have a body which can be cast into hell. Watchtower annihilationists have never adequately wrestled with the implications of this text as to the resurrection of the wicked.

Since in Matt. 5:22, Christ has already spoken of the fire of Gehenna, in 5:28, 29, He merely speaks of Gehenna. Note that in 5:22, the Greek is emphatic—"the fire of the Gehenna."

> The addition of the adjective by means of a second article makes it emphatic.[55]

The place called Gehenna is often connected with fire which was used as a metaphor to speak of the condition of those in it— namely, that those in Gehenna were in torment. Thus "the fire of the Gehenna" referred not to some temporal fire but to "the eternal fire" which would torment the wicked in Gehenna forever.[56]

The fire which torments the wicked in Gehenna is *"the* eternal fire" (18:8). The Greek emphasizes the word "eternal" by placing a definite article before it. In this first usage of *aionios* in the New Testament, A. T. Robertson comments:

> The word [aionios] means ageless, without beginning or end as of God (Rom. 16:26), without beginning as in Rom. 16:25, without end as here and often. The effort to make it mean "aeonian" fire will make it mean "aeonian" life also. If the punishment is limited, *ipso facto*, the life is shortened.[57]

The place of final punishment is Gehenna. The condition of those in it is torment symbolized by fire. The duration of their torment is eternal. Thus the New Testament speaks of the "the eternal fire of the Gehenna."

Whenever "Gehenna," "fire," "eternal fire," or "fire of Gehenna" are used in the New Testament, they have reference to the eternal torment of the wicked in hell.

First, note the use of "fire" in the New Testament to signify future torment and the adjectives which are used with it:

"Unquenchable fire" (Matt. 3:12)

"The hell [Gehenna] of fire" (Matt. 5:22)

"The furnace of fire; in that place there shall be wailing and gnashing of teeth" (Matt. 13:42, 50)

"The eternal fire" (Matt. 18:8)

"The hell [Gehenna] of fire" (Matt. 18:9)

"Eternal fire" (Matt. 25:41)

"The unquenchable fire" (Mark 9:43)

"The fire is not quenched" (Mark 9:48)

"Unquenchable fire" (Luke 3:17)

"Flaming fire" (2 Thess. 1:7)

"Eternal fire" (Jude 7)

"Tormented with fire and brimstone" (Rev. 14:10)

"Thrown alive into the lake of fire burning with brimstone" (Rev. 19:20)

"Thrown into the lake of fire and brimstone" (Rev. 20:10, 14, 15)

"The lake that burns with fire and brimstone" (Rev. 21:8)

It is clear from the above passages that the fire connected with Gehenna is:

1. Eternal (Matt. 18:8; 25:41; Jude 7).
2. Unquenchable, i.e., it will never die out or be put out (Matt. 3:12; Mark 9:43, 48; Luke 3:17). The word *asbestos* used in Matt. 3:12 and Mark 9:43 was used in Greek literature to refer to an eternal fire which would never be extinguished.[58]

In Mark 9:48, the Greek uses the word *sbemmumi*, which means that the fire cannot be put out.[59]

3. Signifies torment and not annihilation. The rabbinic picture used by Christ of people "weeping and gnashing their teeth" in the excruciating pain caused by the fires of Gehenna cannot be ignored or downplayed (Matt. 13:42, 50). In Rev. 14:10, 11, we are explicitly told that they will be tormented by sulfuric fire . . . for all eternity . . . without rest day or night. The words of the Apostle could not be clearer or plainer. The text says "tormented," not annihilated.

Matthew 25:41, 46

"Then He will also say to those on His left, 'Depart from Me, accursed ones, into the eternal fire which has been prepared for the devil and his angels. . . .' And these will go away into eternal punishment, but the righteous into eternal life."

In this sober scene of the final judgment, Christ says in verse 41 that the wicked will be sent to dwell in "the eternal fire." The Greek has "the fire, the eternal one," which emphasizes that it is the eternal fire of Gehenna and not some other fire. Their fate is contrasted to the righteous who are sent to dwell in "the eternal kingdom" (v. 34; cf. 2 Pet. 1:11).

In verse 46, the scene reaches its climax with the righteous and the wicked going to their respective eternal destinies.

"And these will go away into eternal punishment, but the righteous into eternal life."

In this verse, the contrast between the righteous going into "eternal life" and the wicked going into "eternal punishment" is based on the contrast between "life" and "punishment."

The contrast centers on where they are going and what they will experience when they get there. Thus the righteous go into the eternal kingdom, where they will experience endless fullness of life, while the wicked go to Gehenna (symbolized here by "eternal fire"), where they will suffer endless punishment. As Alford pointed out:

Observe the same epithet is used for *kolasis* and *zoe*—which are here contraries—for the *zoe* here spoken of is not bare existence, which would have annihilation for its opposite; but blessedness and reward, to which punishment and misery are antagonistic terms. . . . Those who set this coincidence aside, and interpret each portion by itself, without connection with the rest, are clearly wrong.[60]

Joseph Meyer warns:

The absolute idea of eternity, in regard to the punishment of hell . . . is not to be gotten rid of either by a popular taming down of the force of Aionios . . . by appealing to the figurative character of the term fire . . . or the supposed incompatibility between the idea of eternity and such a thing as evil and its punishment. . . . But [the meaning of Aionios] is to be regarded as exegetically established in the present passage by the opposed Zoe aionios, which denotes the everlasting Messianic life.[61]

The classic commentators are unanimous on the fact that an honest exegesis of Matt. 25:31–46 will reveal that if *aionios* means "endless fullness of life" for the righteous, then it must mean "endless punishment" for the wicked.[62] Lenski comments:

Regarding Aionios as meaning "eternal" little needs to be said. Those who would reduce the fire of hell to a shorter or a longer period of time must then similarly reduce the joys of heaven. But Aionios was spoken of by the king after time has already ceased, and after all angels and men have entered on their final fixed and unchanged fate and, therefore, cannot be understood in this limited sense. And if this Greek adjective does not mean "eternal," which Greek adjective does have that meaning? Or did the Greek world, including the Jewish (Jesus spoke Aramaic) world, have no words for eternity or eternal? . . . Here Aionios plainly refers to both punishment and life, so that it is impossible to give the word two different meanings. This settles the question: hell is as eternal as heaven; heaven no more than hell.[63]

Lenski's insight into the fact that the context of verse 46 is the final order when time as we know it is over is well taken. How can *aionios* only mean "a short time" or "a long time" in this context when there isn't any time at all? We must also add that when *olam* is used in this context, it always means eternity (Dan. 12:2, 3).

The observation that verse 46 is in the context of the eternal timeless state reveals the absurdity of the annihilationists and Universalists who attempt to weaken the force of *aionios* by referring to "everlasting hills." The phrase "everlasting hills" is in the context of the time framework of this age. It is thus illegitimate to correlate these two uses of the word *olam, aion,* or *aionios.* The context must be observed.

We close our discussion of this text with a comment by John Broadus, whose classic commentary on Matthew is still unequaled.

It will at once be granted, by any unprejudiced and docile mind, that the punishment of the wicked will last as long as the life of the righteous; it is to a great degree improbable that the Great Teacher would have used an expression so inevitably suggesting a great doctrine he did not mean to teach.[64]

Broadus' subsequent treatment in his commentary of this passage has never been answered by annihilationists or Universalists because Matt. 25:46 is so obvious in meaning that the average Christian has no problem whatsoever in seeing that eternal punishment is clearly taught in this text.

2 Thessalonians 1:8, 9

Dealing out retribution to those who do not know God and to those who do not obey the gospel of our Lord Jesus. And these will pay the penalty of eternal destruction, away from the presence of the Lord and from the glory of His power.

In his opening remarks to the saints at Thessalonica, Paul comforts them with the knowledge that those who are persecuting them will be recompensed by God when Christ returns.

> Therefore, we ourselves speak proudly of you among the churches of God for your perseverance and faith in the midst of all your persecutions and afflictions which you endure. This is a plain indication of God's righteous judgment so that you may be considered worthy of the kingdom of God, for which indeed you are suffering. For after all it is only just for God to repay with affliction those who afflict you, and to give relief to you who are afflicted and to us as well when the Lord Jesus shall be revealed from heaven with His mighty angels in flaming fire. (vv. 4–7)

When Jesus comes, He will take vengeance on the wicked by tormenting them just as they had tormented the saints.

While in Matt. 25:41, 46, the "eternal punishment" of the wicked was symbolized by the metaphor of "eternal fire," in 2 Thess. 1:8, 9, the punishment of the wicked is symbolized by the metaphor of "flaming fire." Once again fire is used to symbolize future torment.

In verse 9, having stated that the wicked will suffer punishment, Paul then describes the nature of this coming punishment as "eternal destruction."

First, the Greek word *olethros*, according to Thayer's *Greek-English Lexicon* (p. 443), means "the loss of a life of blessedness after death, future misery."

The word *olethros* is translated "ruin" in 1 Tim. 6:9 to describe the lost and wretched spiritual condition of someone who lusts after riches. Then in verse 10, Paul amplifies their "ruination" by saying that they have "wandered away from the faith and pierced themselves with many a pang." In this passage, it is clear that *olethros* does not mean annihilation but "ruination" or "spiritual misery or wretchedness."

In this light, it is not surprising to discover that *olethron aionion* in 2 Thess. 1:9 is translated as "eternal ruin" or "everlasting ruin" by Goodspeed, Wuest, New English Bible, Twentieth Century New Testament, etc. The wicked face "ruination," not annihilation.

Second, the word *aionion* refers to the final judgment after time is no more. Therefore it can only have the meaning of endlessness, or eternity.

Summary

Having examined the usage of *aion* and *aionios* in the New Testament, it is clear that it follows *olam* in meaning absolute endlessness, or eternity, when it refers to the final state. Since the final state or eternity begins when time ends, the attempt to interpret these words as a "longer or shorter period of time" is impossible, because "time" no longer exists. Also, these words are modified by such phrases as "which shall have no end," and "no rest day or night," which can only refer to an endless and ceaseless activity or state of being. Rebel men and angels face ultimate and irreversible eternal torment as the punishment for their rebellion against the God who made them.

GENERAL TEXTS

In addition to the passages where *aion* and *aionios* are used to describe the future endless, conscious punishment of the wicked, there are a multitude of general texts which teach the same thing.

Matthew 7:13, 14

> "Enter by the narrow gate, for the gate is wide, and the way is broad that leads to destruction, and many are those who enter by it. For the gate is small, and the way is narrow that leads to life, and few are those who find it."

First, Christ plainly here states that only "the few" will be saved while "the many" will be lost. The Universalists have always had difficulty with this passage because it employs the language of finality. There is no room in this passage for the ultimate salvation of the many.

Second, notice again how "life" is not mere existence but a quality of well-being. Only "the few" will enjoy this life, which is elsewhere called "eternal life."

Notice that the fate of the wicked is designated as *apoleia*, which, according to Thayer (p. 71), means "the loss of eternal life, eternal misery, perdition, the lot of those excluded from the kingdom of God."

It is translated as "perdition" (KJV) in such passages as Phil.

1:28; 1 Tim. 6:9; Heb. 10:39; 2 Pet. 3:7; Rev. 17:8.

In Matt. 7:13, it is translated as "ruin" by Weymouth and "perdition" by Knox and the New English Bible. That it does not mean nonexistence is clear from its usage in Mark 14:4 where "wasted" oil is mentioned and in 1 Tim. 6:9 where the wicked who lust after great wealth drown in spiritual misery and wretchedness.

Apoleia is also used in the rabbinic expression "a son of perdition" (KJV) in John 17:12 and 2 Thess. 2:3. In the former it refers to Judas and in the latter to the Antichrist.

The phrase "son of perdition" did not mean "son of nonexistence" but, according to A. T. Robertson, this Hebraic expression meant "the son marked by final loss, not annihilation, but meeting one's destiny."[65] Or, as Thayer defined it, "a man doomed to eternal misery."[66]

With this Hebraic understanding in mind, such commentators as Hendriksen point out that *apoleia* does not mean annihilation, but everlasting perdition.[67] Indeed, as Lenski points out:

> In the New Testament this negative term refers to the state after death and the complete loss of the true heavenly life (*zoe*), (C.-K. 789). The term never means annihilation, neither does any synonymous term nor any description of what it represents.[68]

Matthew 7:21–23

> **"Not everyone who says to Me, 'Lord, Lord,' will enter the kingdom of heaven; but he who does the will of My Father who is in heaven. Many will say to Me on that day, 'Lord, Lord, did we not prophesy in Your name, and in Your name cast out demons, and in Your name perform many miracles?' And then I will declare to them, 'I never knew you; depart from Me, you who practice lawlessness.' "**

Christ describes the punishment of the wicked in terms of exclusion from His kingdom. The "second death" is that final irreversible separation from the presence of God. This is spoken of elsewhere in such places as Matt. 25:41, 46 and 2 Thess. 1:9.

While this exclusion is "from" the presence of Christ, it is also said to be "unto" conscious torment in the blackness of Gehenna.

> "And I say to you, that many shall come from east and west, and recline at the table with Abraham, and Isaac, and Jacob, in the kingdom of heaven; but the sons of the kingdom shall be cast out into the outer darkness; in that place there shall be weeping and gnashing of teeth." (Matt. 8:11, 12)

The phrase "the outer darkness" was a rabbinic expression which referred to Gehenna where the wicked would be "weeping and gnashing their teeth" because of their pain and torment.[69] The definite article is used to refer to "the outer darkness," i.e., Gehenna.

Notice that the rabbinic phrase "weeping and gnashing of teeth" cannot be interpreted in any other way than to say that the lost will suffer excruciating pain and torment. This passage cannot be reduced to annihilation.

Matthew 22:11–14

"But when the king came in to look over the dinner guests, he saw there a man not dressed in wedding clothes, and he said to him, 'Friend, how did you come in here without wedding clothes?' And he was speechless. Then the king said to the servants, 'Bind him hand and foot, and cast him into the outer darkness; in that place there shall be weeping and gnashing of teeth.' For many are called, but few are chosen."

In this rabbinic parable, Christ refers to eternal, conscious torment in terms of binding them and throwing them into the "ultimate darkness where there will be the wailing and the gnashing of teeth" (Lit. Gk.).

Once again Gehenna is spoken of as designated by the definite article before "darkness." Both "wailing" and "gnashing" have definite articles (as in 8:12) to emphasize that the torment experienced in Gehenna cannot be compared to the sufferings in this life.

Matthew 10:28; Luke 12:4, 5

"And do not fear those who kill the body, but are unable to kill the soul; but rather fear Him who is able to destroy both soul and body in hell. . . . And I say to you, My friends, do not be afraid of those who kill the body, and after that have no more that they can do. But I will warn you whom to fear: fear the One who after He has killed has authority to cast into hell; yes, I tell you, fear Him!"

First, despite all the attempts of the annihilationists to reduce the soul to the physical life of the body, Christ here plainly says that while we can kill or cut off the physical life of a body, we cannot kill or harm the soul, i.e., the immaterial transcendent self, mind or ego. He employs the body/soul dichotomy which is found throughout the Scriptures.

We pause to point out that the biblical dichotomy is different from the classic Platonic view. As we shall point out in our chapter on annihilationism, the common ploy of bringing up arguments against a Platonic dichotomy have no effect on Christ's scriptural dichotomy. To equate the two is erroneous.

Second, while man cannot harm the soul when he kills the body, God can "destroy" both body and soul in Gehenna.

The conditional immortalitists assume that the word "destroy" means to annihilate. In addition to this being an erroneous understanding of the Greek word *apollumi*, as we have already demonstrated, the Gospel parallel of this passage in Luke 12:4, 5 uses the word *ballw* (cast) as the synonym for *apollumi* (destroy).

"Cast into hell [Gehenna]" (Luke 12:5).

"Destroy . . . in hell [Gehenna]" (Matt. 10:28).

The wicked are "cast" or "destroyed," i.e., delivered up unto eternal misery (Lit. Gk.), in Gehenna in the sense of being delivered up to eternal torment. The use of *ballw* as the synonym for *apollumi* makes annihilation an impossible interpretation.

Matthew 11:21–24

> "Woe to you, Chorazin! Woe to you, Bethsaida! For if the miracles had occurred in Tyre and Sidon which occurred in you, they would have repented long ago in sackcloth and ashes. Nevertheless I say to you, it shall be more tolerable for Tyre and Sidon in the day of judgment, than for you. And you, Capernaum, will not be exalted to heaven, will you? You shall descend to Hades, for if the miracles had occurred in Sodom which occurred in you, it would have remained to this day. Nevertheless I say to you that it shall be more tolerable for the land of Sodom in the day of judgment, than for you."

In this passage, Christ reveals that there will be degrees of punishment in hell. While all sinners in hell will be perfectly miserable, they will not be equally miserable.

In determining the degree of punishment in hell, our Lord takes into account the words (Matt. 12:26, 37) and works (Matt. 16:27; Rev. 20:11–15; 22:12) of sinners.

Disobedience and unbelief due to ignorance do not deliver one from punishment, for ignorance of the Law is no excuse (Lev. 5:17). But sins done in ignorance will not receive as much punishment as sins done consciously in violation of known law.

> "And that slave who knew his master's will and did not get ready or act in accord with his will, shall receive many lashes, but the one who did not know it, and committed deeds worthy of a flogging, will receive but few. And from everyone who had been given much shall much be required; and to whom they entrusted much, of him they will ask all the more." (Luke 12:47, 48)
>
> "Truly I say to you it will be more tolerable for the land of

Sodom and Gomorrah in the day of judgment, than for that city."
(Matt. 10:15)

The writer to the Hebrews speaks of some people receiving more punishment than others.

> How much severer punishment do you think he will deserve who has trampled under foot the Son of God, and has regarded as unclean the blood of the covenant by which he was sanctified, and has insulted the Spirit of grace? (Heb. 10:29)

The sin of the Pharisees was made greater by their contact with Christ (John 15:22).

While the fact of judgment is determined by what we are, i.e., our nature, the degree of punishment is determined on the basis of true knowledge we have received and the quality of life that we live (Rom. 2:3–6).

It is obvious that annihilation admits of no degrees. Someone cannot be "more" or "less" unconscious or nonexistent. Indeed, annihilation levels out the punishment by having all sinners pass into nonexistence.

The scriptural teaching of degrees of punishment is a solid argument for eternal, conscious torment. According to Christ, some sinners will receive greater torment than others.

Since there will be degrees of punishment, God's justice will be revealed. If annihilation were true, then God's justice would be imperiled, for He could not take into account the life of a sinner in determining the degree of punishment that is due, but all sinners would simply pass into the same judgment of nonexistence.

Matthew 23:15

> **"Woe to you, scribes and Pharisees, hypocrites, because you travel about on sea and land to make one proselyte; and when he becomes one, you make him twice as much a son of hell as yourselves."**

In this passage Christ delivers one of the most scathing attacks on the Pharisees anywhere recorded in Scripture. In His attack, Christ used the rabbinic phrase "a son of Gehenna" to refer to their converts.

According to A. T. Robertson, the phrase "son of hell" means "one fitted for and so destined for Gehenna."[70] It is synonymous with the "son of perdition" (John 17:12).

Let the Universalists here note that Christ himself speaks of a class of men who are destined to dwell in Gehenna. There is no ray of hope for such. The phrase is used of Satan and men as they share a common fate.

John 3:36

> "He who believes in the Son has eternal life; but he who
> does not obey the Son shall not see life, but the wrath of God
> abides on him."

First notice that both "life" and "everlasting life" do not mean
mere existence but a quality of life which the righteous receive at
regeneration and will fully enjoy after the resurrection.

Second, the wicked will not experience divine life in this world
or in the next. Instead of fullness of life, the wicked will experience
the wrath of God in this world and in the next.

When John said that the wrath of God "abides" on the wicked,
he used the word *meno* in the present indicative tense to state that
the wrath of God was continually abiding on the wicked as an on-
going process.[71]

Since "the wrath of God," which presently abides on the
wicked, obviously does not mean annihilation, we are warranted
to assume that its future administration will not mean annihilation
either. The passage speaks of the wrath of God abiding upon rebel
sinners forever.

John 5:27–29

> "And He gave Him authority to execute judgment, because
> He is the Son of Man. Do not marvel at this; for an hour is
> coming, in which all who are in the tombs shall hear His voice,
> and shall come forth; those who did the good deeds, to a res-
> urrection of life, those who committed the evil deeds to a res-
> urrection of judgment."

First, as in Dan. 12:2, the wicked are bodily resurrected unto
judgment. The annihilationists, such as the Jehovah's Witnesses,
who deny any future resurrection for the wicked are here clearly
condemned.

Second, there is a class of people who will suffer eternal punishment after the resurrection.

Since the resurrection is the beginning of the eternal state, the
judgment to which the wicked are committed is final and irreversible. There is no hope for those who rise in the second resurrection
to experience the second death of final and ultimate separation from
God.

> Blessed and holy is the one who has a part in the first res-
> urrection; over these the second death has no power, but they
> will be priests of God and of Christ and will reign with Him for
> a thousand years. . . . And death and Hades were thrown into
> the lake of fire. This is the second death, the lake of fire. And if

anyone's name was not found written in the book of life, he was thrown into the lake of fire. (Rev. 20:6, 14, 15)

Summary

As one reads the New Testament, it is impossible to escape the sobering fact that divine judgment will be ultimately satisfied by the final and irreversible punishment of sinners who have transgressed the laws of God and refused the mercies of God.

We may not like the idea of ultimate justice. We may even try to avoid thinking about it. But its reality is based on the historicity of Christ's bodily resurrection from the dead.

> "Therefore having overlooked the times of ignorance, God is now declaring to men that all everywhere should repent, because He has fixed a day in which He will judge the world in righteousness through a Man whom He has appointed, having furnished proof to all men by raising Him from the dead." (Acts 17:30, 31)

We must always remember that there is nothing more valuable than the salvation of one's immortal soul.

> "For what will a man be profited, if he gains the whole world, and forfeits his soul? Or what will a man give in exchange for his soul? For the Son of Man is going to come in the glory of His Father with His angels; and will then recompense every man according to his deeds." (Matt. 16:26, 27)

Christ's statement in Matt. 26:24 that it was better for Judas that he should have never been born makes no sense whatsoever if Universalism or annihilationism were true.

If Judas, with all men, ultimately experiences everlasting life, then it would be better to be born to bliss than to remain in nothingness. But if eternal, conscious torment is the fate of the wicked, then it would have been better not to be born.

If annihilationism is true, then Judas and all the wicked who came out of nothingness at conception will simply return to the nothingness from which they came, either at death (the Watchtower) or at the final judgment (S.D.A.).

Either way, the wicked enjoyed their evil ways while alive and will never consciously suffer for their sins.

In 1 Cor. 15:32, Paul said, "If the dead are not raised, let us eat and drink, for tomorrow we die."

If annihilationism is true, then the wicked should practice the gross ethics of hedonism. A lifetime of being a self-conscious ego who experiences the joys of life is intrinsically better than nonexistence. After all, a wicked life is still better than no life at all. But if eternal, conscious torment awaits the wicked, then it would have been better to have never been born.

One consideration which should not be overlooked is that unbelievers who have given themselves over to a path of wickedness always defend their evil ways by adopting either Universalism or annihilationism.

Some say, "All roads lead to God. It doesn't matter how we live or what we believe because we will all make it to heaven in the end. God is a good old chap and would never hurt anyone. Everyone will be happy in the end."

Others claim, "It doesn't matter how we live because when we die, that's it. We are no different from dogs or cats that die. So, since we will die like animals, let us live like them. Eat, drink, and be merry, do anything our hearts desire. We only have 'now' and there is no 'tomorrow.' "

Religious Universalists and annihilationists have never been able to explain why hedonism is not the most obvious and logical way of life if their position is true.

On the other hand, the wicked do not try to defend their evil ways by referring to eternal punishment. Hedonism never appeals to the orthodox hell as a reason for giving oneself over to pleasure. As a matter of fact, the wicked hate the doctrine of hell. They ridicule it just as much as the religious Universalists and annihilationists do. For example, the atheist David Mills, in his *Overcoming Religion*, ridicules the concept of hell from the beginning to the end of his book as the main reason for rejecting all religion.

The fury and intensity of the world's hatred of the doctrine of eternal punishment strongly suggests that it must be the true biblical position. The fact that Universalism and annihilationism are distinctive doctrines of non-Christian cults is yet another indication of the ultimate source from which those doctrines come.

Universalism and annihilationism are ideas which sinners use to comfort themselves in their evil ways and to silence their conscience. A doctrine which gives comfort and encouragement to sinners to continue on in their evil ways cannot be of God.

THE NEW TESTAMENT APOCRYPHA

Just as the Old Testament generated a number of uninspired books which we label apocryphal, it is no surprise that the introduction of the New Testament would likewise produce a host of apocryphal writings.

During the first three centuries of the church, there were numerous works "discovered" which claimed to be "lost" writings of Christ or one of the apostles. These spurious works are generally divided into two main families: the Catholic (i.e. orthodox) and the Gnostic (i.e. the heretical).

Just as the Old Testament Apocrypha was examined in terms of its historical worth as an indication of what the Jews believed, the New Testament Apocrypha does reveal what ideas were current in the early church. We are particularly interested in what the biblical or orthodox Christians believed. Since both the Universalists and annihilationists claim that they were the orthodox view in the early church, a study of the New Testament is essential to our historical opinion.

The most recent edition of the New Testament apocryphal books and fragments is Edgar Hennecke's *New Testament Apocrypha*, Vols. I & II, published by the Westminster Press, Phila., 1963. All verse references are keyed to Hennecke's edition.

As has already been noted, some Universalists and annihilationists claim that the orthodox doctrine of intermediate and eternal, conscious torment was not present in the theology of the early church. That such grandiose claims are erroneous will be demonstrated by an examination of the New Testament Apocrypha and, later, of the writings of the Apostolic Fathers. That the orthodox doctrine was the dominant and historic view of the early church will also become clear.

I Epistula Apostolarum

This account of a dialogue between Christ and the apostles dates from the early part of the second century. It has been found in Coptic, Ethiopic and Latin translations. It was a strong antignostic polemic which emphasized that Christ's physical body was real and that "our Lord and Savior Jesus Christ is God"(3).

That fate of the heretical Cerinthus and Simon is described as "judment and . . . eternal perdition"(7). Another manuscript adds "destruction" in addition to "judgment." "Destruction" clearly did not mean annihilation, because the apostles later ask:

> O Lord, is it really in store for the flesh to be judged [together] with the soul and the spirit, and will [one of these] [Copt. really] rest in heaven and the other [Copt. however] be punished eternally while it is [still] alive? (22).

After Christ answers in the affirmative, He goes on to state that there is going to be a bodily resurrection of all men (24). The wicked will be delivered "to eternal punishment"(26). This punishment consists of "ruin" and "punishment of great pain"(27). or "ruin by . . . eternal punishment (29).

Let the reader note that the words "destruction" and "ruin"

do not mean annihilation unto nonexistence. Christ goes on to state that "the lost will be lost eternally. They will be tormented alive and will be scourged in their flesh and in their soul"(39). Another manuscript states that they shall be "eternally ruined, being punished by fire in the flesh and spirit"(39).

The dialogue concludes with the sober warning that the wicked will be eternally punished"(50).

II Epistula Petri

The apostolic pseudepigrapha includes an epistle supposedly written by the Apostle Peter to James the apostle. It was written at least by A.D. 200.

Peter begins by stating: "If I am false to my word, I shall be accursed living and dead and suffer eternal punishment" (4:3).

He goes on to warn: "If anyone, after that he has made such a vow, does not adhere to it, then will he rightly suffer eternal punishment" (5:3).

In Peter's description of a righteous prophet, he points out that such a man "frequently calls attention to the eternal fire of punishment" (H.III.26:6).

In his conclusion, the wicked face eternal "perdition" (H.XI.32:3).

The Acts of John

During the second and third century, various accounts were written which claimed to describe the life and deeds of the apostles other than Paul whose history had been chronicled in *Acts* by Luke. These apocryphal acts gained some measure of popularity as they satisfied natural curiosity which wanted to know what happened to the other apostles.

In the *Acts of John*, the Apostle John warns the Ephesians that a greedy and selfish man will not succeed because "when he departs from his body [at death] and is burning in the fire, begging for mercy, he shall find no one to pity him (35).

Murderers, sorcerers, swindlers, thieves, sodomites, etc., "shall come to unquenchable fire and utter darkness and the pit of torment and eternal doom . . . eternal misery and torment"(36).

The Acts of Peter

This apocryphal manuscript was probably written by A.D. 180.

Peter warns Rufina that, "If you do not repent while you are still in the body, the consuming fire and the outer darkness shall receive you forever" (1:2).

Both the fire and the darkness are "forever" and denote "everlasting punishment" (5:15) and "the punishment of unquenchable fire" (8:28). The word "consume" is obviously used in a figurative sense.

New Testament Apocalyptic Works

From the first century to the beginning of the Middle Ages, the eschatological hopes and fears of the Christian Church were expressed not only in its liturgy, hymnody and homily but also in the writing of apocalyptic literature in which the coming of Christ, the judgment and the eternal state of the righteous and the wicked were graphically described. That the early apocalyptic writings of the church used the language and format of Jewish apocalyptic literature is no surprise, given the influence such writings had on the authors of the New Testament and the early church fathers.

The Ascension of Isaiah

This apocalyptic work was written in the first century A.D. and manifests both a Jewish and Christian element. In it, King Hezekiah relates how God revealed to him in a dream "the eternal judgments and the punishments of hell" (1:3). Belial and his hosts will be cast into Gehenna (4:14). Once Paradise is recreated on the earth, "it will be as if they [the wicked] had not been created" because "the Beloved will cause a fire to go forth from himself, and it will consume the impious" (9:18).

That the word "consume" is used in a figurative sense is clear from the fact that hell is described elsewhere as "the realm of the [wicked] dead" (10:8–10). If the dead had been annihilated in hell, it could hardly be said they dwell there.

The Apocalypse of Peter

This work was written in the early part of the second century (A.D. 135) and presents one of the most horrifying descriptions of the eternal, conscious torment which awaits the wicked that can be found in any literature.

Peter declares that the wicked "will stand in the depths of the darkness that passes not away, and their punishment is the fire, and angels bring forward their sins and prepare for them a place wherein they shall be punished for ever" (6).

The text goes on to speak of "everlasting torture" (7), "tormented without rest, as they feel their pains" (7), "eternal judgment" (7), etc.

Hell is itself divided into sections where certain sinners are singled out for special torment. Thus abortionists and those who practiced infanticide are singled out for special torment (8). Those who persecuted the righteous (9), those who deceived others (9), those who charged compound interest on loans (10), etc., all receive "the judgment of unceasing torture" (9).

The wicked are reminded that there is no second chance, no chance for repentance in hell, and that forgiveness is impossible (13). Any concept of Universalism is ruled out completely.

Christian Sibyllines

Copying the Jewish Sibyllines, this apocryphal work appeared around A.D. 200. This work is particularly instructive because it has been called into service by the annihilationists to prove their position. They point out that the wicked "perish" (250), "waste away" (305), and are "utterly destroyed" (100). Yet, a closer look reveals that the author understood those words in their biblical and figurative sense of eternal ruination, rather than non-being.

The angels "shall punish [the wicked] fearfully with flaming whips" (285). The wicked will be thrown into Gehenna where "many torments would be laid upon them" (286).

> Burning in a mighty fire. They gnash with their teeth. All wasting away with violent and consuming thirst, and shall call death fair, and it shall flee from them. Neither death nor night shall give them rest anymore. Many an appeal, but in vain, shall they make to God who rules on high, and then will He openly turn away His face from them. (305)

No repentance will be accepted (306). Nothing but eternal, conscious torment awaits them because there is "no end set to the punishment" (P.S.65, p. 743).

The Apocalypse of Paul

This second century work is very similar to the Apocalypse of Peter. The eternal torment of the wicked is described with horrifying mental images. Paul asks to see the fate of sinners and saints (13). The intermediate suffering of the wicked is described in terms of:

> Let Him send him into outer darkness where there is wailing and gnashing of teeth, and let him remain there until the great day of Judgment. (16)

Once the wicked are bodily resurrected and judged, they are cast into the place of punishment (31). Once again, individual groups of sinners are singled out for special torment: unsaved church members, hypocritical elders, deacons, and church workers, magicians, fornicators, adulterers, oppressors of widows and orphans, sodomites, abortionists, infanticidists, etc., are all tortured according to their deeds. Their doom is eternal and there is no hope for them.

Summary

While other material can be adduced from such later works as *The Pseudo-Titus Epistle*, and *The Pseudo-Clementines*, enough has been given to demonstrate beyond reasonable doubt that the doctrinal position of the early church was not that of Universalism or annihilationism. The New Testament Apocrypha clearly teaches that the wicked face eternal, conscious torment after the judgment. That this is also what the apostolic fathers believed will now be demonstrated.

Patristic Material

In answer to Farrar's *Eternal Hope*, which was published in 1879, Dr. Pusey wrote *What of Faith as to Everlasting Punishment* in 1880 as an exposition of the rabbinic and patristic literature on the subject of eternal punishment. Farrar's work has been cited by the Universalists ever since, while Pusey's has remained one of the standard orthodox works.

The classic annihilationist's work is *The Conditionalist Faith of Our Fathers*, by the Seventh-Day Adventist scholar, Leroy Froom. Most annihilationists depend entirely on Froom's work. This is evidenced in such works as *The Fire That Consumes*, produced by Verdict Publications.

All three positions can find material in early Christian literature. The Universalists have Origen, the annihilationists have Arnobius, and the orthodox have Tertullian.

We must begin by pointing out that it is difficult to discern the exact theology of someone from a few books, pages or sentences which have come down to us nearly 2,000 years after his death. But what concerns us is that Universalists and annihilationists dogmatically state no one in the early church expressed the idea of eternal punishment.[72]

In order to settle the record once again, it is necessary to point out those places in early Christian literature where the doctrine of eternal, conscious torment is taught. We will limit ourselves to *Early Christian Fathers*, which is Volume 1 of the Library of Christian Classics published by Westminster Press. Other references are given in Appendix II.

This volume is representative of the literature from the first two centuries of the church, and since Universalists and annihilationists admit that the orthodox position is found in later writings, there is no reason to go beyond the first two centuries.

Let the reader examine the following material and conclude from it if the orthodox position was expressed by early church fathers. They should also keep in mind that church historians, such as Phillip Schaff, who studied early Christian literature during their entire lifetime, concluded that the orthodox position was clearly believed in and taught by early Christians.

The Resurrection of the Wicked

Polycarp to the Philippians

"Whoever perverts the sayings of the Lord to suit his own lusts and says that there is neither resurrection nor judgment—such a one is the first born of Satan" (7:1).

Clement's Second Letter

"Moreover, let none of you say that this flesh will not be judged or rise again" (9:1).

First Apology of Justin

"In the same way unbelief prevails about the resurrection of the dead because you have never seen an instance of it."[19]

Justin goes on to speak of the resurrection of the wicked who are thrown into Gehenna as well as the righteous who rise to everlasting life.

Irenaeus' Against Heresies

"Christ Jesus our Lord, and his coming from the heavens in the glory of the Father to restore all things, to raise up all flesh, that is, the whole human race . . . that he may execute righteous judgment on all" (10:1).

It is clear from these representative texts that the wicked will be resurrected to be judged. The Watchtower's contention that the wicked are annihilated at death and are never resurrected is foreign to the theology of the early Christian Church.

Eternal, Conscious Torment

In his treatment of early Christian literature, Froom devotes several hundred pages in *The Conditionalist Faith of Our Fathers* to demonstrate that all the church fathers taught annihilationism. While his treatment seems, on the surface, to be quite impressive, once a closer look is taken, it becomes obvious that his work is basically unreliable because it is founded on faulty assumptions.

The most basic faulty assumption made by Froom and other annihilationists is that "eternal life" means "eternal physical existence or immortality." Thus whenever Froom found a text where a church father said that the saints would receive "eternal life" at the resurrection, Froom placed that father on the side of the conditionalists.

As we have already demonstrated, "eternal life" refers to the eternal well-being which the saints receive at regeneration and fully experience in the eternal state. Since "ill-being" is the opposite of "well-being" and not "non-being," the opposite of "eternal well-being or life" is "eternal ill-being or misery."

In this light, Froom's massive work must be deemed historically unreliable as well as exegetically erroneous.

Let the reader examine the following passages from *Early Christian Fathers* and come to his own conclusion.

Ignatius' Letter to the Ephesians

"Make no mistake, my brother: adulterers will not inherit God's Kingdom. If, then, those who act carnally suffer death, how much more shall those who by wicked teaching corrupt God's faith for which Jesus Christ was crucified. Such a vile creature will go to the unquenchable fire along with anyone who listens to him" (16:1, 2).

Ignatius' Letter to the Philadelphians

"Make no mistake, my brothers, if anyone joins a schismatic he will not inherit God's kingdom" (1:3).

Ignatius' Letter to the Smyrnaeans

"Let no one be misled: heavenly beings, the splendor of angels, and principalities, visible and invisible, if they fail to believe in Christ's blood, they too are doomed" (6:1).

In the context, Ignatius is saying that the angels will suffer the same fate as sinners.

The Martyrdom of St. Polycarp

"And giving themselves over to the grace of Christ they despised the tortures of this world, purchasing for themselves in the space of one hour the life eternal. To them the fire of their inhuman tortures was cold; for they set before their eyes escape from the fire that is everlasting and never quenched" (2:3).

"But Polycarp said: The fire you threaten burns but an hour and is quenched after a little; for you do not know the fire of the coming judgment and everlasting punishment that is laid up for the impious" (11:2).

Polycarp's contrast between temporary punishment by a fire which burns out in a little while and eternal punishment in unquenchable fire is obvious. There is no way to read annihilation into the above passage.

Clement's Second Letter

"Yes, if we do the will of Christ, we shall find rest, but if not, nothing will save us from eternal punishment, if we fail to heed his commands" (6:6, 7).

"For the Lord said, I am coming to gather together all people, clans and tongues. This refers to the day of his appearing, when he will come to redeem us, each according to his deeds. And unbelievers will see his glory . . . and their worms will not die and their fire will not be quenched, and they will be a spectacle to all flesh. He refers to that day of judgment when men will see those who were ungodly among us and who perverted the commands of Jesus Christ . . . being punished with dreadful torments and undying fire" (17:4–7).

In the above passages, the wicked face future torment by undying fire according to Clement. There is no way to reduce Clement's statement to Universalism or annihilationism.

Letter to Diognetus

"Once you fear the real death kept for those who are condemned to the eternal fire which will punish those that are handed over to it. Then you will admire those who for righteousness sake endure the transitory fire, and will call them happy, when you learn about that other fire" (10:7, 8).

The contrast between "eternal fire" and "transitory fire" is obviously based on the assumption of eternal punishment.

First Apology of Justin

"Plato similarly said that Rhadamonthus and Minos would punish the wicked who came before them. We say that this is what will happen, but at the hands of Christ—and to the same bodies, reunited with their souls, and destined for eternal punishment, not for a five hundred-year period only, as he said" (8).

"Everyone goes to eternal punishment or salvation in accordance with the character of his actions. If all men knew this, nobody would choose vice even for a little time, knowing that he was on the way to eternal punishment by fire; every man would follow the self-restrained and orderly path of virtue, so as to receive the good things that come from God and avoid his punishments" (12).

Notice the word "eternal" modifies both punishment and salvation at the same time. To shorten one is to shorten the other.

"Then there will be weeping and gnashing of teeth . . . the wicked will be sent into eternal fire" (16).

"We believe, or rather are firmly convinced, that every man will suffer in eternal fire in accordance with the quality of his actions. . . . Look at the death of the former emperors, how they died the common death of all; and if this were a departure into unconsciousness, that would be a piece of luck for the wicked. But since consciousness continues for all who have lived, and eternal punishment awaits, do not fail to believe to be convinced and believe that these things are true . . . souls are still conscious after death. . . . Gehenna is the place where those who live unrighteously will be punished. . . . The souls of the unrighteous will be punished after death, still remaining in conscious existence. . . . Those who live unjustly and do not reform will be punished in eternal fire . . . to be punished for endless ages" (vv. 17–20, 21, 28).

"If you respond to these words with hostility . . . [it] will lead to eternal punishment through fire for you" (v. 45).

"For the prophets foretold two comings of Christ. . . . The second . . . he will raise the bodies of all men who have ever lived . . . [and] send those of the wicked, eternally conscious, into eternal fire with the evil demons. . . . The wicked will be punished, still conscious. . . . Their worms shall not rest, and their fire shall not be extinguished. And then they will repent when it will no longer do them any good" (v. 52).

In the above passages, the doctrine of eternal torment could not be expressed more clearly.

Athenagoras' Plea

"Were we convinced that this life is the only one, then we might be suspected of sinning, by being enslaved to flesh and blood and becoming subject to gain and lust. . . We are convinced that when we depart this present life we shall live another . . . close to God and with God . . . or else, if we fall along with the rest, we shall enter on a worse life and one in flames. For God did not make us like sheep and oxen, a bywork to perish and be done away with. In the light of this it is not likely that we should be purposefully wicked, and deliver ourselves up to the Great Judge to be punished. . . . On the contrary, those who deny they will have to give account of the present life, be it wicked or good, who reject the resurrection and who count on the soul's perishing along with the body, and, so to speak, flickering out, are likely to stop at no outrage. But those who are convinced that God will look into everything and that the body with the soul in its unreasonable lusts and passions will be punished along with it, they have no good reason to commit even the slightest sin" (vv. 31, 36).

Irenaeus' Against Heresies

"The judge . . . will send into eternal fire those who alter the truth, and despise his Father and his coming" (2:4).

Summary

From these representative texts, it is obvious that there were early church fathers who taught the doctrine of eternal, conscious torment. The attempts of some Universalists and annihilationists to ignore the above passages and to state dogmatically that the idea of eternal punishment is foreign to the literature of the early Christian Church is erroneous. We must also point out that the early fathers emphasized degrees of punishment. Obviously, someone who believes in degrees of torment cannot believe in annihilation. While there were others who believed in annihilation, such as Arnobius, or who believed in Universalism, such as Origen, let us set the record straight once again that the orthodox position is representative in the literature of the early Christian fathers. For other references, consult Pusey's classic work.

CONCLUSION

Having examined both the Old and New Testaments, we must conclude the Scriptures clearly teach that the wicked will experience eternal, conscious torment after the resurrection.

Because God is eternal and sees all of time before Him as a present vision, there is no "past" or "future" with God. Thus the sins of the wicked are forever in God's sight, and He judicially punishes them forever. An eternal God requires eternal justice.

On the other hand, Christ's work judicially removes the sins of believers from being counted against them. Thus it is said that God "forgets" their sins, i.e., no longer judicially holds these sins against them (Heb. 8:12; Rom. 4:6–8).

The contrast is clear that while God judicially "forgets" the sins of His people, He judicially will never forget for all eternity the sins of the wicked. Thus their torment is forever.

We have further demonstrated that both sinners and fallen angels, during the intermediate state, suffer conscious torment. As we shall see in the chapter on annihilationism, the doctrine of soul sleep is foreign to the New Testament, just as it is foreign to the Old Testament.

We have also demonstrated that the ultimate fate of rebel sinners and rebel angels will be the same. They both go to the same place to experience the same kind of punishment for the same duration. When man decided to follow Satan, he did not know that he would have to follow him into the murky darkness of hell.

The Christian cannot but be moved by the clarity of the New Testament concerning the doctrine of eternal punishment. To realize the worth and importance of sinners is to recognize the need of evangelizing them. Universalism and annihilationism have never launched great missionary enterprises. It is the vision of seeing men and women brought to the saving knowledge of Jesus Christ and their escaping from everlasting punishment that produced the greatest missionaries that the Christian Church has ever owned.

Therefore, let the orthodox reveal their zeal and their love for the souls of men by boldly proclaiming the gospel of their Lord and Savior, Jesus Christ.

NOTES

1. Fudge, pp. 20f.
2. *Studies in the Scriptures,* Vol. II, p. 124.
3. Fudge, p. 228.
4. Ibid., p. 232.
5. Ibid., p. 88.
6. Ibid., pp. 91f.
7. Brown, Driver and Briggs, pp. 761, 762.
8. See: Lange, Leupold, Young, Keil, etc., for other arguments which refute the idea that Antiochus is being referred to by Daniel.
9. Keil & Delitzsch, *Commentary on Daniel,* p. 483.
10. H. Leupold, *Exposition of Daniel* (Grand Rapids: Baker Book House, 1969), p. 531; E.J. Young, *The Prophecy of Daniel* (Grand Rapids: Wm. B. Eerdmans Pub. Co., 1970), p. 256.
11. Keil & Delitzsch, p. 484.
12. Fudge, pp. 125–154.
13. Froom, I, pp. 632f.

14. Froom, I, pp. 665, 666; Fudge, pp. 128, 129.
15. Froom, I, p. 655.
16. Froom, I, p. 676; Fudge, p. 131.
17. Froom, I, p. 679.
18. Ibid., pp. 671, 672.
19. Fudge, p. 147.
20. Froom, I, p. 684.
21. Ibid., p. 286.
22. Ibid., pp. 687–692.
23. Fudge, p. 152
24. Test. Zeb.10; Ash. 7:5; Reub. 5:5; 1 Q 54:12, 13; Josephus B.J. 118, 14, etc.
25. See: Andrews, Farrar, Brunner, Hick, Marchant, etc.
26. *Lange's Commentary on Ecclesiastes,* pp. 44–51, has a good discussion on this point.
27. F.F. Bruce, *Answers to Questions* (Grand Rapids: Zondervan Pub. Co., 1972), pp. 61–63, 202, 203; A. Hodge, *Evangelical Theology* (Edinburgh: Banner of Truth Trust, 1979), p. 391; Fiffe, p. 236; Shedd, pp. 84, 85; Pusey, pp. 38f.; Walker, p. 20.
28. Arndt and Gingrich, pp. 27, 28; Thayer, pp. 20, 21.
29. Froom, I, pp. 441f.
30. Fudge, p. 44.
31. Ibid., p. 44.
32. Ibid., p. 46.
33. Apoc. Bar. XXIX.XXX,CF., IV E6d.7:29, 30, etc.
34. R. Lenski, *St. John's Revelation* (Minnesota: Augsburg Pub. House, 1965), pp. 589–599.
35. See: Gal. 1:5; Eph. 3:21; Phil. 4:20; 1 Tim. 1:17; 2 Tim. 4:18; Heb. 13:21; 2 Pet. 4:11; 5:11; Rev. 1:6, 18; 4:9, 10; 5:13, 14; 7:12; 10:6, 11; 15:7; 22:5.
36. Arndt and Gingrich, p. 21; Thayer, p. 14.
37. Arndt and Gingrich, p. 340.
38. Calvin, Lange, Bede, Wordsworth, Lenski, etc.
39. R. Lenski. *Interpretation of Second Peter* (Minnesota: Augsburg Pub. House, 1963), p. 316.
40. Vincent, et al.
41. Ellicott, Vincent, et al.
42. See our comment on Zophas in connection with Jude 6.
43. H. Alford, *The Greek Testament* (Chicago: Moody Press, 1968), Vol. IV, p. 533.
44. Lenski, ibid.
45. Froom, I, p. 441.
46. Lenski, *Interpretation of Jude* (Minnesota: Augsburg Pub. House, 1963), p. 625.
47. See also Williams, etc.

48. J. Meyer, *Meyer's Commentary on the New Testament* (The Alpha Greek Library, 1980), Vol. XI, p. 398.

49. Thayer, p. 96; Vincent, Vol. I, p. 32.

50. *Expositor's Greek Testament*, Vol. V, pp. 438, 439.

51. Meyer, ibid., p. 398.

52. See: Matt. 25:41; cf. v. 46, etc.

53. Lenski, ibid., p. 438.

54. Ibid., p. 48.

55. Lenski, *The Interpretation of St. Matthew's Gospel* (Minnesota: Augsburg Pub. House, 1963), p. 690.

56. J. Broadus, *Commentary on Matthew* (Philadelphia: America Baptist Pub., 1886, p. 104.

57. A.T. Robertson, *Word Pictures in the New Testament* (Nashville: Broadmen Press, 1930), Vol. I, p. 147.

58. Arndt and Gingrich, p. 114; Thayer, p. 79.

59. Arndt and Gingrich, p. 752; Thayer, p. 572.

60. Alford, Vol. I, p. 257.

61. Meyer, Vol. I, p. 447.

62. See: Meyer, Alford, Hendriksen, Wordsworth, Augustine, Robertson, etc.

63. Lenski, pp. 996, 997, 1001.

64. Broadus, pp. 512–515.

65. Robertson, Vol. V, p. 278.

66. Thayer, p. 71.

67. Hendriksen, *Matthew*, p. 370.

68. Lenski, p. 297.

69. *Expositor's Greek Testament*, Vol. I, p. 140; Broadus, p. 180; Lenski, p. 332; et al.

70. Robertson, p. 182.

71. F. Godet., *Commentary on the Gospel of John* (Grand Rapids: Zondervan Pub. Co., 1963), Vol. I, p. 414; Alford, Vol. I, p. 725.

72. Froom, I, pp. 801f.

PART II

DEFENSE

Chapter 6

THE PRESENT SITUATION

Does man survive the experience we call death or is he snuffed out like a candle? Does the mind or consciousness of man pass through the death of the body and enter a parallel universe or another dimension? What happens to the essence of man at death? Can we contact the departed in the beyond by psychic means? Can disincarnate minds intrude into our experience and invade our dimension? What do we know about the other side of death?

Questions such as these are now being asked by many people. Indeed, at the present time the subjects of death and the afterlife are a fad on most college and university campuses. Packed audiences in almost every major city have been presented with startling "new" evidence which touches on the classical subject of the immortality of the soul. Instead of using the word "soul" the words "mind," "ego," "self," "consciousness," "I-ness," etc., are used. Thus, while the terms are changed, the subject is still the immortality of the soul.

The present popularity of the subject of death and the afterlife is extremely important to all of us, because the death rate is still one per person. Each of us at the appointed time will face the Grim Reaper. Thus the validity or invalidity of the evidence for the existence of conscious life after death should be important. And in order to set the context for the present popularity of the subject, a brief modern history of the idea of the immortality of the soul will help us see what forces have contributed to its present popularity.

During the Middle Ages, the subject of death and the afterlife were all-consuming in Western society. The fear of death and what may happen afterward had a paralyzing grip on society as a whole. Dante's *Inferno* is but the tip of an iceberg of plays, books, art works, etc., which graphically depicted the agonies of the damned and the felicity of the righteous. People were expected to pay off the fines of those incarcerated in purgatory. Thus the living had to make enough money to support the dead as well as the living! This depressing view of the afterlife had developed over a period of a thousand years and represented a blend of pagan concepts, superstitions, wild speculations, and a minimum of biblical truth.

The Protestant Reformation started to a great degree as a reaction against the medieval view of death and the afterlife. The Reformers eventually threw out virtually all the medieval views as unscriptural and unreasonable. No longer would people have to pay money to get their departed relatives out of purgatory and into heaven. Dante's view of hell, in which the devils tortured people, was rejected as foolish and not in accordance with the teaching of the Bible. Since the Reformers desired to keep as close to the Scriptures as possible, this bridled their speculations and disspelled their superstitions.

Once the Reformation had secured freedom of thought, the secular humanists began to develop philosophic systems which were hostile to all forms of Christianity. Yet, even given the anti-Christian bias of the classic European philosophers from Descartes to Hegel, the doctrine of the immortality of the soul remained a part of Western thought.

The only serious attack on the afterlife was made by the English philosopher David Hume.[1] His belief that "all knowledge comes through the five senses of man" required him to question the immortality of the soul. While he himself was reserved in manner, and even attended church as all good Englishman did in those days, those who followed his philosophy fostered aggressive forms of empiricism and skepticism. They attacked the concepts of miracles and the immortality of the soul in particular. The skeptics declared such concepts "foolish" and the empiricists ridiculed them as "nonsense."

A decline in the popularity of the concept of an afterlife began slowly in the 17th century and reached its climax in the mid-18th century.[2] In England, atheistic groups and "hell-fire clubs" sprang up. In America, Thomas Paine wrote *The Age of Reason*, which was a vicious attack on supernaturalism and Christianity. In France, the revolutionaries were busy promoting atheistic views. Even though Paine and Voltaire professed to believe in the doctrine of the immortality of the soul, the doctrine was in serious trouble because their followers relentlessly attacked the concept of an afterlife.

After the initial enthusiasm and excitement for empiricism and skepticism had died down, people began to see the self-refuting character of these philosophies.

David Hume's empiricism was self-refuting because his foundational concept, "All knowledge comes through the senses," did not itself come through the senses but was a metaphysical assumption. If he was right, his system was wrong. If he was wrong, then he was wrong. Either way, empiricism could not stand up once its own foundational principle was turned upon itself. Later, the Vienna School of Logical Positivism would try to restate Hume's empiricism by saying, "In order for a statement to have any meaning, it must be capable of empirical verification. Anything not capable of verification is meaningless." It too proved to be self-refuting, because their verification principle was itself incapable of empirical verification.

Skepticism has likewise always labored under the problem of being self-refuting. The early Greek skeptics claimed that the senses could not be trusted and then argued from the senses used in seeing an oar which looked bent when under water—optical illusions, etc. Evidently, the senses could be trusted to establish that the senses could not be trusted! The 17th- and 18th-century skeptics likewise made such self-refuting statements. They had certain knowledge that no certain knowledge was possible. They put forth the absolute that there are no absolutes. They knew that no one knew anything. Once the contradictory metaphysical assumptions were uncovered, skepticism could not stand up to itself.

By the middle of the 19th century, people had grown bored of a dry and sterile empiricism or skepticism. They could not live or die comfortably with the idea that men were but machines in a mechanistic world. They began to realize that man's personality was somehow tied to his being more than was a machine's or animal's. There was something noble about man which indicated that there was more to him than a collection of cells.

When Darwin's *Origin of Species* (1859) was published, it was viewed as yet another attack on supernaturalism, Christianity, and the immortality of the soul. Darwin's theories provoked people into seeking "scientific" evidence for supernaturalism. Darwin's book did more to alarm people than did the work of Hume.

The first book which started to turn the public interest to the existence of an afterlife was *The Coming Race* by Bulmer-Lytton. His work influenced such writers as Mathers, Yeats, Crowly, and Waite. But the direction to which he was turning them was not to Christian supernaturalism but back to the older occult practices which dominated Europe before the entrance of Christianity. His works made the occult fashionable in British society for the first time.

The initial spark which ignited the occult flame was the widely reported séances conducted by the Fox sisters. The Foxes lived in Hydesville, N.Y., and on the night of March 31, 1848, they conducted a séance in which a spirit who called itself William Duesler claimed to have been murdered in that house by a former owner. If they dug up the basement, they would find his body. When they dug it up, they found the corpse.

Since the spirit at the Fox house communicated by a rapping noise on the table, it became known as "table rapping." It soon became a fad to have séances and to try to contact the spirit. The Ouija board also became quite popular as a séance tool. It could be found in parlor rooms all across America and England.

Lest anyone think that this occult revival was something which only infected the uneducated masses, it must be noted that some of the greatest poets, writers, politicians, philosophers, and scientists of that age became firm believers in an afterlife through the occult.

The Society for Psychical Research (SPR) was organized in 1882 by some of the great men of that day. Henry Sedgwich, the noted philosopher at Cambridge, was particularly instrumental in gathering top minds into the SPR. The membership included such men as William Gladstone (past prime minister), Arthur Balfour (future prime minister), Alfred Lord Tennyson (the poet), Lewis Carroll (author of *Alice in Wonderland*), Sir Arthur Conan Doyle (creator of the Sherlock Holms series), William James (the father of utilitarianism), and C. D. Broad (the philosopher). The American chapter of the SPR had such famous members as Samuel Clemens (Mark Twain).

The purpose of the SPR was to investigate occult experiences in a scientific manner to uncover fraudulent claims (as it did with Madame Blavatsky, the founder of Theosophy), or to establish claims which must be deemed valid according to reason and science. In their search they dealt with over 17,000 cases. Out of this number, they dismissed all but 1,684. This figure represented those cases which seemed to them to be valid paranormal experiences.

The SPR investigated mediums and their séances, the appearance of ghosts, haunted houses, reports of levitation or apparition, materialization, Indian mystics and their feats, etc. They sought to find evidence that the spirit or mind of man survived death and that we could communicate with the departed by occultic means.

The fad of occult practices such as séances died out in the early part of the 20th century. People grew tired of ghost stories and tales dealing with the objects of the occult arts. The secular humanists reasserted themselves by developing new forms of empiricism and skepticism which denied an afterlife.

Materialism or naturalism reached its climax in the development of Marxist dialectical philosophy in which all morality, ethics and religion are denied and the freedom, dignity and worth of human beings rejected. It is essentially a philosophy of negation in which all concepts which have to do with something which cannot be weighed and measured are rejected. Since materialism has nothing to offer in a positive way in the marketplace of ideas, it has gained ascendency over entire nations only by the tyranny of a bayonet. Since it cannot compete with other systems, it simply outlaws them. Thus the Marxists have so far liquidated over 100 million people in their drive to eradicate belief in morality, ethics, religion, and the freedom, dignity and worth of man. Materialism always leads to oppression and tyranny because in and of itself it cannot create values or morals.

The philosophy of materialism suffers as well from self-refutation. "Vulgar" materialism taught that ideas are merely "secretions" of the brain and there is no such thing as "mental energy," or "thought," or "mind." If this were true, then the concept of materialism is itself a secretion of someone's brain, and why is it essentially better than someone else's secretion? Would not the Christian's secretions be just as "valid" as the materialist's? And we must point out that the basic metaphysical principles which underlie the philosophy of materialism are not material in nature. Hence, if they are right, they are wrong. If they are wrong, then they are wrong. Either way, materialism is a system which cannot be viewed as valid. We will touch on this issue later.

The other forms of empiricism and skepticism which have flourished in the 20th century are existentialism, linguistic analysis, and behavioral psychology. Each of these systems in turn must be viewed as being self-refuting. Each system was based upon a foundational principle which disproves the system once the principle is turned on the system itself. For example, if all behavior, including thinking, is determined by such things as irrational genetic and environmental factors, then the concept that all ideas are determined by irrational genetic and environmental factors is itself the result of irrational forces. Upon what ground is the theory or idea of behavioral psychology exempted from being itself the result of irrational determination? If the idea of behavioral psychology is itself irrational and determined by mindless forces, upon what grounds can it claim to be valid?

While Western secular humanists became secure in their belief that they had successfully removed the idea of a conscious afterlife from scientific and philosophic discussion and relegated it to religion and superstition, one scientist began a search in 1930 which would ultimately produce the present popularity of ideas concerning a conscious afterlife. This man was Joseph Banks Rhine.

Rhine was born in Juniata County, Pa. in 1895. He grew up in a rural environment and had a strong religious background. At one point in his life, he expressed the desire to become a Protestant pastor. He received his doctorate in biology from the University of Chicago. The educational process which he passed through to gain his doctorate included attacks on his religious beliefs by professors who were hostile to Christianity. He was forced into a reluctant skepticism by peer pressure. At that time scientism was at its height of unquestioned authority. Its dogmas were not challenged because to do so was to be ostracized from the scientific community. Science had become a "sacred cow," and the scientists had become the priests who officiated at its services and punished all those deemed "heretical" in not holding to popular scientific dogma.

The most significant change in Rhine's life occurred when he listened to some lectures on spiritism and the occult by Sir Arthur Conan Doyle. Conan Doyle was a zealous propagator of the occult, and it was he who planted in Rhine's mind the idea of discovering "scientific" proof for a conscious afterlife. If Rhine could only "prove" by scientific means that the mind was still conscious after the death of the body, then the scientific community would be forced to accept the supernatural.

Rhine started to work on his own by visiting countless séances, trying to find a "true" medium who would prove to be an irrefutible contact with the Beyond. He eventually gave up this search because the mediums were too interested in their own professional success and, hence, were not reluctant to use fraud and deceit.

He became friends with William McDougall who invited him to join the faculty at Harvard. They both became involved with Dr. Prince who, along with McDougall, was a member of the SPR. McDougall even served as the president for both the British and American SPR groups! Rhine became deeply involved with the SPR and its attempt to demonstrate a conscious afterlife through occultic practices.

Later, when SPR president McDougall moved to Duke University, he arranged for Rhine to join him there and to set up a separate department on psychic studies. The two would work together to further the goals of the SPR.

Rhine's first task was to develop new terminology. He was aware that the scientific community was prejudiced about the terms "occult," "mediums," "séances," "witchcraft," "sorcery," etc. The only way to get by this word barrier was to rename or relabel the subjects which the SPR had researched for years. Once he could bypass the word barrier, maybe the scientific community would listen. Thus it was Rhine who coined the term ESP—extrasensory perception. ESP simply means that man can have knowledge or perception of things which are not material in nature. ESP thus would describe the ability of one person to read the mind of someone else, or describe the ability of someone to foresee the future.

Rhine and others later developed other terms such as "paranormal psychology" or "parapsychology," which would serve as convenient ways to dish out old concepts as "new evidence." Since the scientific community was not forewarned that the "new" science of J. B. Rhine was actually the old occult ideas of the SPR,

Rhine's work began to be viewed as something new and exciting.

Even though he was able to cause some initial excitement over his "discoveries" of ESP, his initial "proofs" of ESP did not win over the scientific community because Rhine allowed himself to be deceived. For example, he attempted to prove the existence of telepathy or mind reading by submitting as evidence a horse which could supposedly read the mind of his master. Rhine actually put forth this telepathic horse as proof of psychic abilities in the 1930s. Later, to his chagrin, it was discovered that the horse had been receiving signals from the owner.[3]

Rhine's work with professional mediums, mind readers, etc., came to a close. They had tried to deceive him one time too many. So, he decided to use ordinary people who did not have any psychic or professional reputation to protect. It was in this line of research that he began to make headway in the scientific community.

Rhine believed that everyone had ESP to some degree. It was out of this conviction that he began to experiment with such things as cards to demonstrate the existence of ESP. We must point this out, because Rhine's position did not arise out of his scientific research but his research arose out of his position. He was seeking to prove his theories when he conducted his experiments.

Using cards in research seemed to pay off in the 1950s. The scientific community's interest was aroused when Rhine published results which seemed to reveal that some people had the ability to know what card was next in the deck or was being held in the hand. Subsequent research, however, has dismissed Rhine's experiments as unscientific and probably fraudulent.

The cards had various symbols such as circles, squares, wavy lines, etc. These symbols were drawn with a dark ink which soaked through to the other side of the card to such a degree that a faint outline of the symbol could be seen. When the card was held up, anyone looking at the back of the card would be able to "discern" correctly what symbol was on the other side by merely observing the faint outline.

Even though Rhine's experiments were not given in a controlled manner and lacked any scientific merit, by the 1960s excitement over ESP began to snowball. By the mid-seventies it had reached the college campuses and attained "fad" status. By the end of the seventies and the beginning of the eighties, the mass media was featuring parapsychological experiments on TV and radio and in popular magazines like the *Reader's Digest*. Once again the public was fascinated by "ghosties and ghoulies and things that go bump in the night."

The public interest was also stirred when the Soviets supposedly released their findings on psychic research. These findings were popularized in *Psychic Discoveries Behind the Iron Curtain*, published by Prentice Hall in 1970. For materialists to admit that "mind over matter" can take place means that the "mind" cannot be viewed as a material object such as the brain. The fact that some Soviet atheistic materialists were willing to accept parapsychology or ESP encouraged the secular humanists in the West to accept it as well. Even the atheist Ducasse became a believer in occult supernaturalism *a la* parapsychological experiments.[4] While such atheists rejected Christianity because of its supernaturalism, they were yet willing to accept the occult because of ESP.

Another influence which figures strongly in the present popularity of parapsychology is the "Life After Life" teaching.[5]

In 1972, Drs. Moody and Kübler-Ross wrote the book *Life After Life*, published by Bantam Books. It was condensed by *Reader's Digest* in 1977 and became a bestseller. Another book quickly followed in 1977, *Reflections on Life After Life*, published by Bantam Books as well. Their thesis was that various individuals had an out-of-body experience when they apparently died. When the body died, the person's "mind" or "soul" was able to float around the room and observe from different angles the efforts of the medical staff to revive them. In some cases the body was revived and the person felt himself drawn back into his body. Other people left the room and traveled through a tunnel of light and caught a glimpse of a city of light which was interpreted by some of them as "heaven." Others saw what they described as "hell." Regardless of what they saw, they were told that they had to return to their bodies because their time had not yet come. After they regained consciousness in the hospital, they could vividly remember their out-of-body experience.

The work of Moody and Kübler-Ross generated a multitude of books, articles, debates and discussions. Dr. Maurice Rawlings presented case histories of people whose out-of-body experiences clearly paralleled Christian teaching on the afterlife. His book *Beyond Death's Door* was published by Thomas Nelson, Inc. In 1981, the TV show *That's Incredible* featured some of his case histories.

The third influence which has helped to popularize the concept of a conscious afterlife is the amazing growth of belief in the theory of transmigration or reincarnation.

The original concept of transmigration states that man must go through a series of lives in order to be cleansed of moral evil and of the illusion of a physical reality. Man's chief problem is that he is self-conscious and that he thinks in terms of a dichotomy between himself and the world, himself and God. Based on a monistic absolute idealism, Eastern forms of transmigration have always assumed that reality is ultimately One and that all distinctions, such as between man and the world, are to be viewed as illusion.

The Eastern transmigration theory is not particular about what kind of body into which one is reborn at death. One's "soul" may migrate into the bodies of insects, animals or human beings. One can be reincarnated (or re-in-fleshed) into the body of a worm, a clam, a pig, or a man! The law of Karma determines the kind of life one is born into according to the kind of suffering that is demanded to pay for evils done in past lives.

During the late 19th century, the occult revival included a resurgence of belief in the theory of reincarnation. The SPR investigated reincarnational recall in which individuals claimed to remember their previous lives. Their consciousness of past lives arose either spontaneously or due to hypotic regression techniques. Madame Blavatsky, the founder of Theosophy, did much to revive the concept of reincarnation in the United Kingdom. It was also at this time that various Indian mystics and gurus began to arrive in England and the U.S. seeking converts. It was hoped that the recall experiences would prove that the soul is conscious after death even if it is viewed as something which is repeatedly born again and again into different bodies.

When the occult revival faded out in the early 20th century, the theory of reincarnation fell into decline. Attempts were made to revive the teaching of reincarnation, but all of them failed to bring it back into the concern and interest of the public until *The Search for Bridey Murphy* was published in 1956.

An amateur hypnotist put Ruth Simmons, a housewife, into a trance. While under hypnosis, Mrs. Simmons said that she had lived in Ireland in the 19th century in a previous life and that her name at that time was Bridey Murphy. She told stories of old Ireland and even spoke in an Irish brogue. She described in great detail the home she lived in and the church she attended. Since Mrs. Simmons had never been to Ireland or spoken in an Irish dialect, the hypnotist wrote a bestseller which claimed that Mrs. Simmon's regression to a past life, through hypnotic recall, "proved" the theory of reincarnation. The book was also made into a movie and caused a good deal of public excitement.

Subsequent research has uncovered the fraudulent character of the Bridey Murphy story. She claimed to have been born in 1798 in County Cork, Ireland. The parish records have been searched and there is no evidence that Bridey Murphy was ever born in County Cork. She also claimed that she and her parents attended St. Theresa's Church. But that church was not even built until 1911, and she could not have attended there as a child. She also said that she lived in a wooden house called The Meadows, but the houses in that part of Ireland are built of stone or brick, and no record exists of a wooden house called The Meadows.[6]

When a search in Ireland proved negative, investigations were made into Mrs. Simmons' history. It was discovered that until the age of three she lived with her Irish-speaking grandmother and part-Irish grandfather. Her grandmother spoke in an Irish brogue and told her granddaughter stories of old Ireland. Professional hypnotists concluded from these facts that Berstein, the amateur hypnotist, had only caused Mrs. Simmons to recall what she had learned while living with her grandparents.[7]

Recent research has also discovered that when Mrs. Simmons was a child, her next-door neighbor was named Bridey Murphy![8] This clearly explains the source of the name. Childhood memories were mixed and confused and converted into a reincarnational recall by the suggestions of the hypnotist.

It wasn't until the mid-1960s that the theory of reincarnation began to enjoy some popularity again. This popularity was to a great degree created by the works of Edgar Cayce. He became an "American guru" for many young people in the drug culture of the sixties and seventies.

Cayce's grandfather was known for his psychic ability to find water and to make brooms dance. It is felt by some that Edgar inherited his psychic abilities from his grandfather.[9]

The popularity of Cayce was confined mainly to the college and university campuses during the late sixties and early seventies. Then the base of his popularity began to spread out into the general public until now his books can be found in the homes of people who were never in the drug culture.

Cayce was called the "Sleeping Prophet" because he would place himself in a trance and give either a medical reading in which he would diagnose the physical ills of someone and then prescribe a cure, or he would give a life reading in which he would describe the person's previous incarnation.

The important contribution that Edgar Cayce made was to westernize the Eastern concept of transmigration. According to Cayce's theory, one could be reborn only into a human body. He rejected the Eastern concept of migration into insect or animal bodies. Reincarnation was limited to a series of lives within human bodies.

After Cayce, the public's interest was stirred by the publication of more hypnotic recall experiences along the same lines as *The Search for Bridey Murphy*. The American SPR leader, Dr. Ian Stevenson, put forth "Twenty Cases Suggestive of Reincarnation" in Vol. 26 of the *Proceedings of the Society*. These cases were later published and caused a great deal of excitement. During the late seventies and early eighties, self-realization seminars were held across the country which supposedly placed an entire group into a trance and regressed everyone in that group back to his past life. For the mere sum of $400, one could lie on a living room floor and together with a dozen or more people supposedly regress into past lives.

Once again, no initial research was done to confirm or to disprove the reincarnational recall experiences which were developed in the self-realization seminars. The material was rushed into print without a shred of evidence.

Since we have examined in detail the evidence for and against the theory of reincarnation in our book *Reincarnation and Christianity* (Bethany House Pub., 1980), we will not give any further analysis except to point out that the theory of reincarnation is incompatible with the Jewish and Christian Scriptures and that it was condemned by the early Christian Church as being in direct conflict with the atoning work of Jesus Christ. The genius of the Christian view of the atonement is that Jesus Christ has paid the full price for the redemption of His people. Christ's death on the cross means that there is no need for Karmic rebirth in which one must suffer for his own sin. Christ has suffered all that is necessary for man's salvation. Also, when one examines all of the arguments that the reincarnationists use in order to support their position, one finds that these arguments are totally devoid of any historic, scientific, philosophic, or religious merit. For the details of our analysis, please consult our book on the subject.

CONCLUSION

What is important for us to understand about the present situation in which we find ourselves is that we must realize that although the claim is repeatedly made that a "new" science has been discovered which is based on "new" evidence, it is only the terminology which is new. The concepts are the same occultic practices which the SRP researched in the 19th century. The facts are that *no* new powers have been discovered and *no* new energy has been tapped. Wilson and Weldon in their *Occult Shock and Psychic Forces* (Master Books, 1980) demonstrate that the so-called "new" energy forces are actually the same old occultic forces. Just as a rose by any other name smells the same, even so, occult practices by any other name are still occult practices. A new name does not mean a new source of energy.

The Christian Church should present its position on the afterlife with humble boldness and crystal clarity. Christianity has something to offer the world which is far superior to what the mediums and parapsychologists can offer. While they can only guess about what lies beyond death, biblical Christianity is unashamedly based on One who went there and came back and told us what lies beyond the grave.

In the following chapters, we will develop the Christian's response to materialism, annihilationism, Universalism and occultism, because Christians must not only proclaim biblical truth but also defend it (Jude 3).

NOTES

1. See: *A Treatise of Human Nature*, published in 1739.

2. D. Walker, *The Decline of Hell* (Chicago: University of Chicago Press, 1964), p. 3.

3. D. Cohen, *ESP* (New York: Harcourt Brace Jovanovick, Inc., 1973), pp. 74f.

4. *A Modern Introduction to Philosophy* (ed. Edwards & Pap; New York: The Free Press, 1965), pp. 248–260.

5. M. Hellwig, *What Are They Saying about Death and Christian Hope?* (New York: Paulist Press, 1978), p. 8.

6. *Strange Stories, Amazing Facts* (New York: *Reader's Digest*, 1976), pp. 384–390.

7. Ibid.

8. C. Wilson, *The Occult* (New York: Random House, 1971), p. 514.

9. K. Kock, *Occult ABC* (Germany: Literature Mession Aglasterhausen Inc.), pp. 57f.

Chapter 7

MATERIALISM

The word "materialism" has several different meanings in the 20th century. First, there is the popular usage of the word which refers to those who are guilty of greed and avarice. A "materialist" in this sense refers to someone whose life revolves around his material possessions. Second, the word "materialism" is used in a philosophical and technical sense to refer to those who reduce or limit reality to material objects. Their creed is, "Everything that is, is material." By this, they mean that anything which is not of a material nature does not exist; it is only a figment of man's imagination. Man himself is only a material machine. There is no "soul" or spiritual essence in the machine which we call "man." "Everything that is man is material." It is in this second sense that we use the word "materialism" in this chapter.

MATERIALISM AND EMPIRICISM

As a philosophic world view, materialism assumes the validity of the theory of empiricism. Thus materialism is a view of being which depends on a certain view of knowing.

Empiricism states that knowledge must be restricted to those objects which can be perceived by our senses. Thus we cannot "know" nonmaterial objects. The materialists go one step further and state that since we cannot know nonmaterial things, we must conclude that these things do not exist. It is therefore a waste of time to discuss such meaningless words as "God," "soul," "mind," "self," because "meaning" is restricted to what we can "know," which is reduced to "material objects" which can be perceived by the five senses.

Now, we must point out that the relationship between materialism and empiricism is not a logical one in which one is validly deduced from the other. The materialists' argument, "Since we cannot know anything about nonmaterial objects, therefore they do not exist," is invalid. The most one could validly deduce from the principle of empiricism is that nonmaterial things are unknowable. To say that nonmaterial things do not exist is to know too much. Rather, materialism and empiricism are related on a presuppositional level where both are faith assumptions. And they are also related historically in that the popularity of empiricism paved the way for the acceptance of materialism.

A BRIEF HISTORY

The philosophic world view of materialism first appeared in the writings of Democritus (460–360 B.C.), who was called "the Father of Materialism."[1]

"Everything that is, is made of atoms" was his creed. He was the first true materialist because he denied that the atoms were acted upon by forces such as "mind," "love," and "hate."

While Empedocles and Anaxagoras believed in nonmaterial forces, Democritus believed that atoms moved because of their own innate powers. He thus denied the existence of any nonmaterial forces.

Materialism did not reappear until the 17th-century Renaissance when the Greek classics were rediscovered. They influenced such writers as Gassendi (1592–1655) and Hobbs (1589–1679). Hobbs was the more consistent of the two in that he denied the existence of all nonmaterial things, including God, souls, angels, etc.

In the 18th century, Julien de Le Mittrie (1709–1751) crystalized the concept that man was a machine. The anti-Christian materialist d'Holback (1723–1789) sought to establish the eternity of matter to escape the theistic implication of creation *ex nihilo*. Materialism began to experience popularity during this century for the first time.

During the 19th century, such materialists as Buchner (1855) taught that there is no force without matter and no matter without force. The evolutionist Huxley did much to popularize a materialistic view of the origin of life that involved spontaneous generation, i.e., life out of nonlife.

When the 20th century dawned, the philosophy of materialism began to exercise an iron grip on state universities and colleges. Such writers as Gilbert Ryle attempted to refute the idea that there is a "ghost," i.e., a "soul" or "mind," in the machine which we call man.[2] Not until the 1970s–1980s did the grip of materialism begin to weaken under the assault of modern brain research, parapsychological experiments and quantum mechanics.

For a detailed study of materialism, see the classic work, *The History of Materialism*, by Frederick Lange (London, 1925).[3]

AN ANALYSIS OF MATERIALISM

As a philosophy, or world and life view, materialism must satisfy the same demands of reason and experience which are demanded of any other philosophy. No amount of special pleading can exempt materialism from a rigid philosophical analysis.

Since we have elsewhere developed the kind of questions which should be applied to all systems of thought, we will apply some of these questions to the philosophy of materialism.[4]

Our analysis will have three sections or divisions. First, we will analyze the internal integrity of the theory of materialism. Thus, we will be examining the theory in and of itself. Second, we will analyze the theory as it relates to the world around us. Third, we will analyze the theory as it relates to its understanding of man.

The Internal Integrity of Materialism

The materialists have never solved or worked out all the inherent self-refuting elements and defects which can be found in their system. When confronted by the lack of any internal integrity in their system, most modern materialists reply that materialism is not really a system but only the best "guess" available. They have become "shy" about their materialism. This is in stark contrast to the bold dogmatics of the materialists who went before them. The reason for the modern insecurity is the growing awareness of inherent problems in the theory itself.

First, materialists fail to recognize that their system is based on hidden metaphysical assumptions.

Every system has its "first principles" or foundational presuppositions upon which it is based. Materialism has its presuppositions as well. Yet, because these presuppositions are not material in nature or demonstration, materialists become very nervous when confronted by them. What are the leading faith assumptions or presuppositions of materialism?

1. Materialism assumes the doctrine of human autonomy. Human autonomy is the theory that man starting from himself and by himself can understand man and the world around him without any supernatural revelation or information. It is the assumption that "man is the measure of all things" and that man can build a unified system of knowledge by which everything can be explained.

The tragic history of philosophy, in which each system refutes the ones going before it, should have taught them the invalidity of the theory of human autonomy. Human autonomy always ends in skepticism.

2. Materialism assumes that the theory of empiricism is true. They fail to see that empiricism is self-refuting in nature. The theory that all knowledge is limited to what can be empirically known is

itself incapable of being known or demonstrated on empirical grounds. Thus, it is a self-refuting presupposition of materialism.

3. Materialists assume that we are living in a closed universe in which everything in principle is explainable in material categories. They end up arguing in a circle when confronted by evidence for nonmaterial realities by assuming that such things do not exist because they do not exist. A closed universe leads to a closed system and a closed mind in which one discovers the attitude, "Don't confuse me with the facts; my mind is already made up."

4. Materialists also assume the doctrine of ontological thinking. They assume that reality must conform to what they "think" it to be. Anything which is "unthinkable" to them cannot exist. Reality is thus reduced or limited to what their finite minds think it to be. Since they philosophically reduce reality to material objects, they assume that nonmaterial objects cannot exist because they are "unthinkable" in material categories.

Once the metaphysical assumptions of materialism are uncovered, its true religious nature is revealed. It is a religious commitment to a mechanistic, closed universe. Their presuppositions are groundless because they are not rooted in human experience. They are leaps of faith. While they reject metaphysics, they cannot escape building their system upon it.

Second, as a theory, materialism is self-refuting.[5]

C. S. Lewis, in *Miracles*, reveals the self-refuting character of the main premise of materialism:

> . . . no account of the universe can be true unless that account leaves it possible for our thinking to be a real insight. A theory which explained everything else in the whole universe but which made it impossible to believe that our thinking was valid would be utterly out of court. For that theory would itself have been reached by thinking, and if thinking is not valid, that theory would, of course, be itself demolished. It would have destroyed its own credentials. It would be an argument which proved that no argument was sound—a proof that there are no such things as proofs—which is nonsense.
>
> . . . no thought is valid if it can be fully explained as the results of irrational causes.[6]

But Naturalism, as commonly held, is precisely a theory of this sort. The mind, like every other particular thing or event is supposed to be simply the product of the Total System. It is supposed to be that and nothing more, to have no power whatever of going on to its own accord. And the Total System is not supposed to be rational. All thoughts whatever are therefore the results of irrational causes, and nothing more than that. . . . The Naturalist will have to admit that thoughts produced by lunacy or alcohol or by the mere wish to disbelieve in Naturalism are just as valid as his own thoughts. What is sauce for the goose is sauce for the gander. The Naturalist cannot condemn other people's thoughts because they have irrational causes and continue to believe his own which have (if Naturalism is true) equally irrational causes.

Thus the Freudian proves that all thoughts are merely due to complexes—except the thoughts which constitute this proof itself. The Marxist proves that all thoughts result from class conditioning—except the thought he is thinking while he says this.[7]

If all thoughts have irrational causes, then that thought itself has an irrational cause. So why should we believe it? If all thoughts are irrational chemical secretions or electrical charges, then why should the thought of materialism be viewed as rational and reasonable?[8] As Lewis eloquently pointed out, the materialists want to refute Christian thoughts by tracing them supposedly to irrational causes such as chemical determinism, behavioral conditioning or class consciousness. But they exempt themselves. This they cannot logically or rationally do.

Third, materialism is not coherent.

The theory states that reality is solely made of "matter" or "material objects" which have "material properties." The whole theory turns on the word "matter" or "material." Yet, this is exactly where materialism's incoherence reveals itself. No one seems to know what "matter" or "material properties" mean. They cannot define the word "matter."[9]

Modern physicists have long abandoned the artificial Newtonian models of atoms and molecules. Modern physics has led us to a crisis in which no one seems to know what "matter" is. As a theory, materialism was coherent in the 19th-century context of a belief in "celestial ether," but it is quite incoherent in the context of modern physics.

Fourth, materialism uses circular reasoning.[10]

When confronted by evidence of nonmaterial realities, it "refutes" such evidence by merely redefining it in materialistic terminology. Just because one redefines something does not mean that he has refuted it. Yet, this is the common practice of materialists.

For example, when a materialist was confronted by the sober testimony of a credible witness who had experienced an angelic visitation, the materialist did not refute the experience nor the person's understanding, but only redefined the experience in materialistic terms. What the materialist failed to recognize is that *giving* an alternate explanation is not the same as *proving* that alternate explanation.

Fifth, materialism cannot validly speak of the world or the universe as a totality.

If our knowledge is limited to what our sense can perceive, who has ever been able to see all of reality in one-sense perception? Who can step outside of the cosmos to look at it objectively? Are we not part of this reality? How can the materialists talk about "ultimate reality" without contradicting their own position? Have they ever seen it?

In summary, materialism has inherent within itself the seeds of its own destruction. James Balfour stated it beautifully in 1895 when he said:

> What sort of a system is that which makes haste to discredit its own premises? In what entanglements of contradictions do we not find ourselves involved by the attempt to rest science upon observations which science itself asserts to be erroneous?[11]

Materialism and the World

Materialism attempts to give a plausible explanation of the origin and nature of the universe. Popular TV series such as Carl Sagan's *Cosmos*, Kenneth Clark's *Civilization*, and David Attenborough's *Life on Earth* are all examples of a dogmatic materialistic world view. Virtually every college and high school textbook presents the theory of materialism as a "fact" and ignores any other viewpoint. They assume that their world view is the only plausible one and that it alone should be presented in secular education. As a system, it seems to generate arrogant and pretentious attitudes among its adherents, which prevents them from being open to contrary evidence.

While the materialists assume that they have developed a completely satisfying explanation of the world around them, there are five major defects in their world view which render it highly questionable.

First, materialism is simplistic.[12] To sweep away all the complexities of this world and to put forth the maxim "Whatever is, is matter" is to be guilty of the grossest simplicity. The universe is far too complex and varied to be the dull world of matter which the materialists make it out to be.

Second, materialism is guilty of reductionism.[13] Reductionism is the method or process in which one element of reality is selected to be absolutized and the rest of reality is reduced to that one category. Anything not reducible is relegated to nonexistence. In this way, man is reduced to no more or less than a stone. Everything has the same material nature. There are no qualitative distinctions between objects.

While idealists like Berkeley reduce reality to "mind" and deny the existence of "matter," the materialists reduce reality to "matter" and deny the existence of "mind"! Yet, both are guilty of assuming that reality must be of only one being. They both assume the metaphysical theory of monism. They are both guilty of reductionism. On what grounds do they assume that reality must be of only one kind or being? Why cannot reality be of both matter and mind? Why do they demand that we must choose one over the other?

Third, materialism is not adequate to explain the origin of the universe.[14]

First, if, as the materialists claim, all knowledge is restricted to what our senses can perceive, then they cannot logically talk about the origin of the universe or life because they were not there to perceive it. When they talk about origins, they have entered the realm of religion and metaphysics. Second, the materialists have yet to develop an adequate explanation as to why we should accept the astounding premises they put forth to account for the origin of the universe and life. They would have us accept:

Everything ultimately came from nothing
Order came from chaos
Harmony came from discord
Life came from nonlife
Reason came from irrationality
Personality came from nonpersonality
Morality came from amorality

It takes far greater faith to believe the above claims of the materialist than to believe that a personal, infinite, rational God created this universe.

Fourth, materialism does not correspond to reality.[15]

The world appears to be more than matter. Materialism simply denies what it cannot explain. Simple denials carry very little weight with the thinking person.

If all is matter, then where did the idea of "mind" come from? If all is matter, then why and how do we account for such emotional states as intention or memory? Why are the materialists kept busy trying to explain away all the experiences people have in which they come into contact with the supernormal or supernatural?

Fifth, the findings of modern physics, particularly in the field of quantum mechanics and Heisenberg's principle of indeterminancy have raised serious doubts about the scientific validity of materialism's understanding of the nature of reality.[16]

Many young physicists are rapidly moving in the direction of Eastern idealism in which reality is assumed to be "mind" and "matter" does not exist! There is a growing fascination with Taoism or Buddhism as a religious framework for modern physics.[17] The sterile character of Western materialism has driven people into the seductive arms of Eastern mysticism. The pendulum is beginning to swing from the extreme of materialism to the extreme of idealism.

Dr. Bernard Ramm foretold this shift toward idealism in modern physics in a book he wrote in 1953. His prophetic words are worth considering.

> Both Nevius and Hocking believe that the current shift in physics from the older Newtonian physics to the new relativity and atomic physics is seriously damaging to the naturalistic program. . . . If the contentions of such men as H. Weyl, A. Compton, J. Jeans, W. Carr, A. Eddington, and F. Northrop are correct, then it is conceivable that fifty years of science will see an abandonment of the naturalistic program by the scientists. . . . The slight breeze in the direction of idealism may turn to prevailing winds.[18]

Anyone familiar with modern physics knows that there is a growing movement toward idealism which is fearless and aggressive.

As an attempt to explain the world, materialism is beset by a simplistic and reductionistic methodology which renders it philosophically unacceptable.

Materialism and Man

We now come to the most difficult part of the theory of materialism. Its adherents would have us believe that man is only an electrochemical machine. Everything man is and does can be explained solely in terms of the movement of particles of matter. Man does not have a "mind," "self," or "soul" which is different or distinct from his body, particularly his brain. Qualitatively speaking, man is no different from bricks or bats. He does not have anything more and he is not any greater than any other material object. Is this view of man true? Does it satisfy the demands of reason and human experience? What are the implications for society if it is true?

First, materialism is once again guilty of reductionism. Mark Cosgrove explains:

> Reductionism is a way of viewing man that reduces him to an explanation of his parts, i.e., man equals a collection of individual brain and body processes. But reductionism is unable to answer why the whole man seems to be more than the sum of his physical parts.[19]

One way to highlight what the materialists are saying is to point out that a man and a rock are exactly the same if the materialistic theory is true. Neither man nor rocks possesses "mind" or "soul." Both are simply a collection of atoms. If this is so, then it should be easy for them to explain why rocks do not think, feel and make decisions, while man does these things. Or, since materialism views man as being qualitatively no different from animals, it should be just as easy to explain why animals do not experience self-awareness, religious worship, aesthetic feelings, and moral motions. The materialists have yet to explain why and how man does what rocks or animals cannot do.

We must conclude that man cannot be artificially reduced to a random collection of atoms and be placed in the same category as rocks or dogs. The materialists reduce man to the category of rocks by simply denying all those things which distinquish man from the rest of the creation. This is clearly understood by such materialists as B. F. Skinner, who stated in *Beyond Freedom and Dignity*, p. 200: "To man Qua man we readily say good riddance."

Second, materialism cannot adequately explain man.

A philosophy must be adequate to explain reality as it is perceived by man. Materialism does not correspond to what man is or does.

1. Materialism has never successfully refuted Descartes' argument for the existence of "self." To doubt or deny the existence of "self" really proves its existence, because the activity of doubt demands the existence of the doubter. Materialists are like the man who searched his house, and finding no one, declared, "No one is at home." He evidently forgot that he was at home. Or again, materialists are like the child who replied, "No one is here," awareness as a response to the question, "Is anyone home?" Man's self-awareness is intuitive and necessary to thought itself. To deny it is to prove it.

2. Materialism has never developed a plausible theory for the origin or survival of man's morality, aesthetic appreciation, religious drive, rationality, personality, pride, sense of responsibility, and self-awareness.

In the classic work, *The Foundations of Belief*, Arthur James Balfour cogently argues that, given the materialists' evolutionary premise of the survival of the fittest, man's ethics, aesthetics, and reason should have been bred out of humanity long ago.[20] The materialists have never explained why or how man enjoys good music or a beautiful sunset. Neither can they explain why or how aesthetic feelings fit into the materialists' world. Rocks and cats do not appreciate the beauties of art or of this world. Balfour applies this same argument in respects to ethics and reason. If materialism is true, such things should not exist. Since they do, materialism is erroneous. And since the denial of the consequence is always valid in logic, Balfour's argument has never been answered.

3. Materialism fails to deal with the evidence that reason tran-

scends neurology, morality transcends stimulus, memory transcends time, and freedom transcends causality.[21]

The materialists assume that their theory is true. They do not reduce it to a "secretion" born out of the random motion of nonrational atoms. They themselves assume that their reason transcends neurology.

If stimulus is the source of morality, then the self-gratification of the pleasure zones of the brain would be the basis of ethics. But ethics is based on universal principles which call upon man to deny self-gratification for the good of others. Hence, morality transcends stimulus.

The fact that man remembers the past, perceives the present, and anticipates the future reveals that he is a transcendent self as well as a body. People with major brain damage still have a transcendence above time in which they talk about the past, present, and future. Seeing that the past is no longer in existence and the future has not come into being, if thoughts are the result of the present motion of nonrational atoms, how and why does man remember the past and anticipate the future? Since there is no "past" or "future" stimulating the brain, from whence does memory or anticipation come?

If man is a machine, then all of his thoughts, words and deeds are predictable and capable of being conditioned. Since we can condition a dog to salivate at the ring of a bell, if materialism is true, we can train all men to secrete the thoughts of materialism at the ring of a bell. But man is not predictable and cannot be totally conditioned.

If mechanistic conditioning were possible, how can the resistance of such men as Solzhenitsyn to Soviet conditioning be explained? The millions of people suffering in Communist concentration camps reveal the failure of the materialists to condition people, even when the materialists have unlimited political power and the use of all forms of conditioning from drugs to torture. By their failure, the Soviet materialists have demonstrated that man is unpredictable and cannot be programmed like a computer or conditioned like a dog. Man's freedom transcends causality.

Third, materialism's simplistic identification of man's mind as his brain does not correspond to the findings of modern brain research.

Human intuition has always resisted identifying the "mind" or "self" with some part of the body. There is an intrinsic awareness that while the "self" has a body, the "self" is not the body. A man can lose his hand or foot in an accident and yet feel no loss of "self." One Vietnam veteran who had lost both arms and legs stated that he did not feel his "self," "ego," or "soul" was in any way affected by the loss of bodily parts. The "self" or "mind" cannot be identified as the body or simply some process of the body.

Following the realization that the loss of bodily parts does not affect man's awareness of his "self" or "mind," modern materialists selected only one part of the body to be identified as the "self," "mind," or "ego." They chose the organ we call the brain.

It was assumed that "mind" was simply a descriptive word for how the brain worked. Thus, the "mind" did not exist in some nonmaterial way; it was only the result of the random motion of nonrational atoms in the brain. The mind and the brain were one. What one did, the other did also.

The materialists committed a major medical or anatomical error when they identified the mind as the brain. They failed to see that man's "mind" or "self" is in the brain much like a hand may be in a glove. William James compared the relationship of the mind to the brain by the analogy of light shining through a prism.[22] To identify the light as the prism or the mind as the brain is nonsense.

The father of modern brain research, Sir Charles Sherrington, started out believing in materialism's identification of the mind as the brain. As the result of his lifelong research on the brain, he concluded, in *Man on His Nature* (Cambridge University Press, 1963), that it was an error to equate the mind with the brain. He concluded his years of research by saying:

> That our being should consist of two fundamental elements offers, I suppose, no greater inherent improbability than that it should rest on one only.[23]

One of the greatest neurosurgeons of Canada is Dr. Wilder Penfield. His brain research in connection with epilepsy provided some startling evidence that the mind is not the brain.

Penfield discovered that the mind is not a computer but has a computer—the brain. The mind of man is related to the brain in the same way that a computer programmer is related to a computer. Or again, the mind is related to the brain much like the viewer is related to the TV he is watching. Thus, man has a mind and a brain.

What led Penfield and others to reject the materialist's identification of the mind as the brain? An entire host of evidence has been collected by Penfield in *The Mystery of the Mind*, and by Popper and Eccles in *The Self and Its Brain*.[24] Perhaps one illustration of the kind of evidence which is documented in these books would be helpful at this point.

In treating a patient with epilepsy, after a local anesthetic, the scalp was lifted away, and the cranium opened to allow the surgeon direct access to the brain tissue. Using an electrical probe, he touched that part of the brain which made the right hand move or twitch.

As the hand moved, he said to the patient, "You just moved your hand." The patient replied, "I didn't move it, you did." Evidently, man's self-awareness is not directly related to the brain.

The surgeon then directed the patient to will in his mind not to let his right hand move. The patient agreed to resist moving it in his mind and as the hand began to twitch due to the application of the electric probe, the patient's left hand reached over and stopped the right hand from moving. The physician could control the brain and make it move the right hand, but the mind of the patient, which was transcendent above the brain, moved the left hand to stop it! If the patient's mind and brain were identical, then the surgeon would have been able to control the patient's mind as well as his brain. But the patient's mind was free from the control of the physician and the manipulation of the brain.

The materialists' identification of the mind as the brain may have seemed plausible in the 19th century when brain research was in its primal stage, but it simply cannot stand up to modern brain research. Cosgrove comments:

> A simple materialistic explanation for all that man is and does will not fit with human experience or with what we know about the human brain.[25]

Fourth, materialists cannot live what they believe.

Materialists cannot logically believe in "love," yet they fall in love and marry. They cannot believe in "mind," yet they cannot avoid using "mind" terminology in their speech when referring to themselves or others. They believe that man is a random swarm of nonrational atoms no different than stones, yet they value people and relationships. They cannot treat their children or mates as random atoms. What they say in the classroom is therefore contradicted by how they live in the home. They experience the mysteries and beauty of this world and man while denying that such things exist. Materialism is not a faith to live by or die by. It is unlivable on a consistent basis because it is merely a philosophy of negation in which anything that is worth living for or dying for is negated.

Fifth, materialism leads to the denial of all those social values and ethics which have formed the basis of human worth, freedom and democracy.

The materialists from the left or the right are committed to destroying the freedom and worth of man. The world they envision was prophetically portrayed in Orwell's *1984* and graphically described by Solzhenitsyn in the *Gulag Archipelago*.

It is a frightening world of oppression and terror. An elite group attempts to control the masses by torture, drugs, etc. In effect, the whole world becomes one vast Nazi concentration camp. One can almost smell the smoke of the ovens as one reads Skinner's *Beyond Freedom and Dignity*. No wonder C. S. Lewis entitled his analysis of materialism's view of man as *The Abolition of Man*. Our generation will do well to heed Francis Schaeffer's observation in his book, *Back to Freedom and Dignity*. He stated:

> If we follow Skinner, we are left with a total skepticism in regard to all knowledge and knowing. Further, if the only way man is able to function in either knowledge or values is as Skinner does by acting on the basis of that which he and his system destroy, are we not left with Skinner himself as a pitiful man— not as a rat or a pigeon pushing levers but as a poor, optimistic rat or pigeon pushing levers?[26]

CONCLUSION

As a world view, materialism is not philosophically acceptable. It carries within itself the seeds of its own destruction. It does not correspond to what the world is. It does not describe man as he is or does. It is unlivable on an individual level and unbearable on a political level. It must be viewed as the attempt of rebel sinners to suppress the truth of their ultimate accountability to God (Rom. 1:18f.).

While they suppress the truth in unrighteousness, says the Apostle Paul, they themselves know it in their heart of hearts. May God hasten the day when materialism will be viewed as the philosophical absurdity that it really is.

NOTES

1. E. Zeller, *Outlines of the History of Greek Philosophy* (New York: Meridian Books, 1967), pp. 80–86; D. Runes, *Dictionary of Philosophy* (New Jersey: Littlefield, Adams & Co., 1967), p.75.

2. G. Ryle, *The Concept of Mind* (London: Oxford Press, 1949).

3. *The Encyclopedia of Philosophy* (ed. Paul Edwards; New York: Macmillan Pub. Co., 1907); W. Windlebond, *A History of Philosophy* (New York: Harper & Row Pub., 1958).

4. R. Morey, *A Christian Handbook for Defending the Faith* (New Jersey: Pres. & Ref., Pub. Co., 1979).

5. P. Badham, *Christian Beliefs About Life After Death* (New York: Barns & Noble, 1976), p. 4; *King's College Lectures on Immortality* (London: University of London Press, 1920), p. 130.

6. C.S. Lewis, *Miracles* (New York: Macmillan, 1966), pp. 20, 21.

7. Ibid., pp. 21–23.

8. *A Modern Introduction to Philosophy* (ed. Edwards & Pap;

New York: The Free Press, 1965), p. 177.

9. *Encyclopedia of Philosophy*, Vol. 5, p. 179.

10. *A Modern Introduction to Philosophy*, p. 177.

11. A. Belfour, *The Foundations of Belief* (New York: Longmans, Green, and Co., 1895), p. 113.

12. B. Ramm, *The Christian View of Science and Scripture* (London: The Petermaster Press, 1964), p. 39.

13. Ibid., p. 40.

14. *Scientific Studies in Special Creation* (ed. W. Lammerts; Pres. & Ref. Pub. Co., 1971).

15. B. Ramm, *Protestant Christian Evidences* (Chicago: Moody Press, 1966), pp. 59, 60.

16. M. Cosgrove, *The Essence of Man* (Grand Rapids: Zondervan/Probe, 1977), p. 34.

17. Gary Zukav points the way to Zen-Buddhism in his popular book, *The Dancing Wu Li Masters* (New York: Bantam Books, 1979). See also *The Tao of Physics* (Berkeley: Shambhala, 1975).

18. B. Ramm, *Protestant Christian Evidence*, p. 58.

19. Cosgrove, p. 28.

20. Balfour, pp. 4–86.

21. Ramm, pp. 61–70.

22. *Recent Philosophy* (ed. Gilson, Langin & Maurer: New York: Random House, 1966), p. 674.

23. Quoted by A. Custance, *The Mysterious Matter of the Mind*, p. 55.

24. W. Penfield, *The Mystery of the Mind* (Princeton: Princeton University Press, 1975); Popper & Eccles, *The Self and the Brain* (New York: Springer-Verlag, 1977).

25. Cosgrove, p. 25.

26. F. Schaeffer, *Back to Freedom and Dignity* (Ill.: InterVarsity Press, 1973), p. 47.

Chapter 8

ANNIHILATIONISM

Perhaps the best way to study the theory of conditional immortality or annihilationism is to give a brief overview of its history and then a theological analysis of its arguments.

A BRIEF HISTORY

The theory of annihilationism in which the wicked pass into nonexistence either at death or the resurrection was first advanced by Arnobius, a 4th-century "Christian" apologist, according to standard reference works such as *Baker's Dictionary of Theology* (p. 184).

Before his baptism, Arnobius wrote seven books which presented his "Apology of Christianity" to the Gentiles. They were probably written around A.D. 303, and it is these works which have been preserved for posterity.

As we read Arnobius' seven books in Vol. 19 of the *Anti-Nicene Christian Library: Translations of the Writings of the Fathers Down to A.D. 325*, we had to agree with the historian Phillip Schaff's assessment of Arnobius' work. Schaff points out that it is

> Meager and unsatisfactory. Arnobius seems as ignorant about the Bible as Minucius Felix. He never quotes the Old Testament, and the New Testament only once. He knows nothing of the history of the Jews and the Mosaic worship, and confounds the Pharisees and Sadducees.[1]

Given Arnobius' ignorance of the Bible, and that these works were written before he had the opportunity of even becoming a member of the Christian Church, it is no wonder that Arnobius viewed man in terms of the philosophy of materialism instead of through the Scriptures. Phillip Schaff points out:

> As to man, Arnobius . . . denies his immortality. The soul outlives the body but depends solely on God for the gift of eternal duration. The wicked go to the fire of Gehenna, and will ultimately be consumed or annihilated.[2]

Schaff's sober assessment of the low quality of Arnobius' work is in sharp contrast to Froom who calls him "one of the bright anti-Nicene lights."[3]

The contrast between Froom's view of church history and that of professional historians is also highlighted in that the historians call Arnobius the first propagator of annihilationism, while Froom calls him "the last Anti-Nicene Conditionalist Spokesman."[4]

After Arnobius, no significant church father took up the doctrine of annihilationism. The position of Tertullian, Hippolytus, Cyprian, Ambrose, Chrysostum, Jerome, Augustine, etc., was clearly in favor of the doctrine of a conscious afterlife and eternal punishment.

Both conditionalism and Universalism were formally condemned as heresy as early as the Second Council of Constantinople in A.D. 553 (see: *The Seven Ecumenical Councils*, p. 320).

Even Froom is forced to admit that no Christian thinker can clearly be claimed as conditionalist until the 12th century.[5] There were thus eight hundred years between Arnobius and the Waldenses, when the conditionalist faith was clearly viewed as heresy by the Christian Church.

In his section on "The Revival of Paganism," Schaff points out that the period of A.D. 1294–1517 witnessed the rise of secular humanism which viewed classic pagan philosophy as superior to Christianity.

Among those who embraced a pagan philosophy of materialism was a philosophy professor named Pietro Pomponazzi. He denied the existence and immortality of the soul in 1516 and was burned for it in Venice. He was one among many who turned to the philosophy of materialism. This ultimately led to the 5th Lateran Council, where the immortality of the soul was reaffirmed and materialism condemned.[6]

Once again, Schaff's classification of Pietro among the materialistic humanists is in contrast to Froom who claims that he was one of the greatest "Christian" scholars.[7]

During the pre-Reformation period, there seems to be some indication that both Wycliffe and Tyndale taught the doctrine of soul sleep as the answer to the Catholic teachings of purgatory and masses for the dead.[8]

We must pause at this point to call attention to the fact that just because someone believes that the soul is not conscious between death and the resurrection does not mean that this person must necessarily or logically be committed to the view that the wicked remain in a state of unconsciousness after the resurrection. Thus, there are occasions in church history when someone clearly believed that all souls were unconscious until the resurrection, but after the resurrection, the wicked go into eternal, conscious torment and the righteous into eternal, conscious bliss. Froom and other annihilationists always assume that if someone believes in soul sleep, this necessarily means that he also believes that the wicked, after the resurrection, will pass into nonexistence. On this basis, Froom is able to include many people on his massive lists in Vol. 2 of the *Conditionalist Faith of Our Fathers*, which, although he can quote evidence that they believed in soul sleep, there is no indication that they went on to believe in the eternal extinction of sinners.

At the beginning of the Reformation, even Luther himself toyed with the idea of soul sleep as a quick and clean answer to the Catholic teaching of purgatory. But later writings reveal that he changed his mind.

Luther's commentary on Genesis is a good indication of his latter views on the subject:

> When after this poor life, we shall join the choirs of the angels, we shall worship God in perfect holiness and righteousness.[9]

Other statements in his commentary speak of a conscious afterlife:[10]

> In the interim [between death and resurrection], the soul does not sleep but is awake and enjoys the vision of angels and of God, and has converse with them.[11]

Commenting on Gen. 35:18, Luther states that when Rachel died, she "was received into the glory of heaven."[12]

The opinion of Calvin is clear in that the first book he wrote was *Psychopannychia*, which was a treatise against the doctrine of soul sleep. He does not mention Luther as a propagator of soul sleep, but all references are intended against the Socinians and the Anabaptist groups.

All the Protestant creeds which flowed out of the Reformation are committed to the orthodox position, and in many of them there is a direct rejection of soul sleep and annihilationism.

> The bodies of men, after death, return to dust, and see corruption: but their souls, which neither die nor sleep, having an immortal subsistence, immediately return to God who gave them: the souls of the righteous, being then made perfect in holiness, are received into the highest heavens, where they behold the face of God in light and glory, waiting for the full redemption of their bodies. And the souls of the wicked are cast into hell, where they remain in torment and other darkness, reserved to the judgment of the great day. Beside these two places, for souls separated from the body, the Scriptures acknowledge none. (WCF XXX2.1)
>
> The end of God's appointing this day is for the manifestation

of the glory of his mercy, in the eternal salvation of the elect: and his justice in the damnation of the reprobate, who are wicked and disobedient. For then shall the righteous go into everlasting life, and receive the fullness of joy and refreshing, which shall come from the presence of the Lord: but the wicked who know not God, and obey not the gospel of Jesus Christ, be cast into eternal torment, and be punished with everlasting destruction from the presence of the Lord, and for the glory of his power. (WCF XXXIII.2)

In the above statements of the Westminster Confession of Faith, we have an example of how the great Protestant creeds all committed themselves to the doctrines of a conscious afterlife and eternal punishment.

The great evangelical revivalists such as Edwards, Whitefield, Wesley, Spurgeon and Moody were all committed to the orthodox position.

While there were noted individuals now and then who became conditionalists, for the most part, it was only among Adventists, Jehovah's Witnesses, Christadelphians, etc., that the doctrines of soul sleep and the annihilation of the wicked were believed. The mainstream of historic Christianity has never deviated from its commitment of a conscious afterlife and eternal torment. This has been repeatedly pointed out by all orthodox theologians.

Froom spends over 1,000 pages listing individuals which he claims believed in soul sleep and annihilationism. While his work is impressive, the fact that he includes such neo-orthodox theologians as Paul Tillich and Karl Barth is surprising when one considers the fact that most neo-orthodox and liberal thinkers such as Barth are Universalists and not annihilationists.[13]

The inclusion of such individuals as Karl Barth in Froom's list causes us to question Froom's classification system. An overview of all the individuals he claims were on the conditionalists' side reveals numerous instances of individuals who were simply against orthodoxy. This is a major defect which, if Froom were alive, we would request that he remedy.

At the present time, the doctrines of soul sleep and annihilationism are primarily propagated among evangelicals by cultic groups such as Jehovah's Witnesses and denominations such as the Seventh-Day Adventist Church.

A case in point is Verdict Publications, an organization started by Seventh-Day Adventists in Australia who wanted to make inroads into the evangelical community. At that time, they published a magazine called *Present Truth*, which was mailed free of charge to thousands of pastors in Australia and the U.S. The group never identified its relationship with the Adventist church. This was finally exposed by D. C. Shelton and others. Once it became known that *Present Truth* was a covert Adventist operation, the magazine was abandoned.[14] After the difficulties in Australia, some members of the organization moved to the U.S. and have revived their efforts again with *Verdict* magazine. There is one important difference which has transpired since the move from Australia to the U.S. By this time, some of the crucial leadership had severed official ties with the Seventh-Day Adventist Church. This severing would enable them to escape the problems which arose in Australia, and it also reflected the fact that they had begun to rethink the Adventist theology concerning the doctrine of justification.

While Verdict Publications no longer has any official Adventist ties, it is still heavily Adventist in theology, particularly in regard to Ellen G. White's doctrine of soul sleep and annihilationism. They published *The Fire That Consumes* in 1982, which is a brief summary of Froom's massive work. Their hope is that this work will introduce Adventist theology into evangelical circles.

Froom's work also influenced John W. Wenham, Warden of Latimer House, Oxford. In his book, which was published by InterVarsity Press, he reveals that after reading Froom and a few other conditionalists, he no longer feels "obligated to defend the notion of unending torment" (*The Goodness of God*, p. 41).

Wenham assumes that Froom's research is historically accurate, which it isn't. He even claims that no orthodox scholar ever refuted the arguments of the conditionalists (p. 40)!

By the above statements and his bibliography at the back of his book, Wenham reveals that he came to a conditionalist position through grossly inadequate research. There are over a dozen evangelical works which have fully answered the conditionalist arguments. For example, Robert Landis spent 508 pages refuting them in 1859; W.G.T. Shed wrote against annihilationism in 1886; Harry Buis did this again in 1957; and Walter Martin, in his book *The Truth About Seventh Day Adventism*, gave a telling criticism of Adventist doctrine in 1960. (For these works, please consult the bibliography at the end of this book.)

That InterVarsity Press would publish a work of such woefully inadequate research as Wenham's *The Goodness of God* reveals that the liberal *zeitgeist* is being felt even in what was once considered an unimpeachable orthodox publisher.

As the pressures of liberalism continue, we expect to see more neo-evangelicals moving either into Universalism or annihilationism, either of which are acceptable to those who hold a liberal theological position. This is regretably the result of a weak view of Scripture which has been developing in certain evangelical circles over the last 25 years.

A THEOLOGICAL ANALYSIS

Just as the philosophy of materialism has expressed itself in secular terminology, it has also expressed itself in religious terminology. One Western religious expression of materialism is popularly known as conditional immortality or annihilationism.

Both the secular and religious forms of materialism view man as being explainable on material principles alone. They both deny that man has an immaterial soul and that man's soul or spirit survives the death of the body. They are both guilty of reductionism in that they reduce man to his body.

Since the orthodox position has gained creedal acceptance in all major Protestant churches as well as in the Church of Rome, except for a few rare individuals, the doctrinal position of annihilationism is propagated primarily by the Seventh-Day Adventists and cultic groups such as the Watchtower and the Worldwide Church of God.

While it is admitted without reservation that one can be a true Christian and yet hold to annihilationism, we must point out that it is generally in connection with cultic or neo-cultic organizations that this belief is found.

A case in point would be the Seventh-Day Adventist Church, which has done much to overcome its cultic origins.[15] Although there are some danger signs that it may slip back into a cultic mentality, particularly in its exalted views of Ellen G. White.[16] Yet, there are multitudes of Adventists who rest in Christ's work alone for their salvation. We have had the pleasure of fellowshipping with such "evangelical" Adventists and do not hesitate to view them as fellow Christians.

We wish to thank, at this point, those Adventist pastors who were willing to examine our presentation of the arguments for annihilationism and to verify that we have indeed understood their position and the arguments which they use.

While our research has involved every conditionalist work, in or out of print, that is accessible today, the Adventist scholar, Leroy Froom, has written the classic work in favor of annihilationism. Since the appearance of *The Conditionalist Faith of Our Fathers* in 1965, all subsequent works in favor of conditionalism have been pale summaries of his massive work. He has done the difficult work of summarizing all of the works that went on before him.

Because of the importance of Froom's work, we have given special attention to his arguments throughout our entire study. It was felt that his arguments should be dealt with in their respective contexts. The fact that we did not make reference to other conditionalists' books is not to be taken that we did not research them.

Since Froom's work is the classic work and summarizes all the arguments that were given before him, we have made all references to his work as the primary expression of the conditionalist faith.

While we have dealt with the arguments of annihilationism in every chapter, perhaps a brief survey of these arguments and our answers to them would be helpful to the reader. In some cases, we will refer the reader to the appropriate chapter where the exegetical details were given.

Argument #1

In *The Fire That Consumes*, we read that "the Conditionalist arguments have never been squarely met. . . . This subject has not been discussed in the open by the best minds and methods of mainstream evangelical scholarship. . . . The Conditionalist arguments . . . have simply been ignored."[17] The author goes on to label the orthodox as "traditionalists" and to refer to them as such throughout his book to give the impression that the only reason why the orthodox believe in eternal punishment is because of the influence of church tradition.

Answer

When we read such an argument in *The Fire That Consumes*, we immediately turned to its bibliography. No mention or reference was found of the works of such evangelical scholars as Bartlett, Boettner, Grant, A. Hodge, Hovey, Landis, Stuart, Martin, etc., all of whom wrote extensively on the subject of conditional immortality and gave a detailed refutation of it.

As a matter of fact, we have consistently found that none of the annihilationists, Froom included, seem acquainted with the classic orthodox treatments of the subject. Thus, their argument at this point is based on faulty and inadequate research. It is a specimen of *argumentum ad ignorantiam*.

Argument #2

The Scriptures teach the doctrine of soul sleep. When man dies, he does not go to heaven or hell, but passes into a state of unconsciousness called "sleep." Since the first death is a state of unconsciousness, then the second death will be eternal unconsciousness.[18]

Answer

It would be appropriate at this point to deal with the doctrine of "soul sleep," which is continually surfaced by the annihilationists in order to refute conscious torment in both the intermediate and eternal state.

First, it is always argued that the mere fact that the Bible refers to death by the word "sleep" is absolute proof that there is no conscious life after death. That this is an erroneous argument is seen from the following facts.

1. The word "sleep" is a metaphor describing the appearance and posture of the body.[19] Even Froom admits that it is a metaphor.[20]

2. The word was also used by the Greeks, Egyptians, etc., to describe their dead.[21]

Since these surrounding cultures indisputably believed in a conscious afterlife, their use of the word "sleep" to describe their dead obviously cannot mean that they believed the dead were unconscious. Thus, the mere presence of the word "sleep" in Scripture as a metaphor for death cannot logically be used as an argument for soul sleep. As Jeremias stated:

> The notion of soul-sleep is just as foreign to the N.T. as to Judaism; the image of sleep is introduced . . . simply as an euphemistic description of death.[22]

Second, the Scriptures clearly teach that after death, man is conscious either in the bliss of heaven or the torments of Hades. Since the second death is patterned after the first death, both deaths refer to separation, not annihilation.

In addition to the many passages which have already been put forward in previous chapters, the following passages in their respective contexts fully demonstrate that the soul or spirit of man is conscious in the intermediate state.

Matthew 17:1–3

> **And six days later Jesus took with Him Peter and James and John his brother, and brought them up to a high mountain by themselves. And He was transfigured before them; and His face shone like the sun, and His garments became as white as light. And behold, Moses and Elijah appeared to them, talking with Him.**

When Christ was glorified on the mountain, two historical figures appeared. While Elijah like Enoch had never tasted death (2 Kings 2:11; cf. Heb. 11:5), Moses had died and God had buried him (Deut. 34:5, 6). Even though he was dead, Moses was completely conscious and able to converse with Christ and Elijah on the mountain.

Some annihilationists respond by stating that the transfiguration did not really take place. The historicity of this event is denied on the grounds that it is called a "vision" (KJV) in Matt. 17:9. But as Hendriksen and others have pointed out, the Greek word *orama* in verse 9 does not refer to a hallucination but to something which they saw with their own eyes.[23] Thayer defines *orama* as "that which is seen, a sight, spectacle: Acts 7:31; Matt. 17:9."[24]

Other annihilationists speculate that Moses had been resurrected already as a special blessing. Yet, there is not a single verse in the Bible which speaks of such a resurrection.

That Moses was still alive and conscious in the afterlife will always prove an embarrassment to conditionalists. Bishop J. C. Ryle, commenting on this passage, said:

> There is no such thing as annihilation. All that have ever fallen asleep in Christ will be found in safe keeping. . . . Though unseen to us, they all live to God. . . . Their spirits live as surely as we ourselves. . . .[25]

Luke 23:42, 43

> **And he was saying, "Jesus, remember me when You come in Your kingdom!" And He said to him, "Truly I say to you, today you shall be with Me in Paradise."**

In response to the dying thief's request, Christ assured him that on that very day he would be with Him in Paradise.

First, as Bishop Ryle points out,

> It is clear proof of the separate existence of the soul when the body is dead. We shall live and have a being, when our earthly tabernacle is mouldering in the grave. The thief's body was that day to be broken and mangled by Roman soldiers. But the thief himself was to be with Christ.[26]

Second, at that stage of the process of revelation, "Paradise" was understood to refer to that part of Hades which was reserved for the righteous dead.[27] It did not mean "heaven" as it was later understood in 2 Cor. 12:2–4. It referred to the place of conscious bliss in Sheol, or Hades, popularly known at that time as Abraham's bosom (Luke 16:19–36).

The annihilationists have always been troubled by this text. Ignoring the rules of grammar and syntax, they erroneously state that the word "today" should modify Christ's words "I say" instead of referring to the thief's entrance into Paradise. Thus they attempt to translate verse 43 as follows:

> Verily, I say to you today, you shall be with me in paradise.[28]

The whole point of their rearranging the punctuation is to remove the fact that the thief was going to Paradise on that day. Lange points out that this is gramatically "senseless."[29] Meyer calls it an "idle and unmeaning" attempt to avoid the emphasis in the original.[30] Modern commentators such as Lenski do not see any grammatical grounds whatsoever for rearranging the punctuation.[31]

In the midst of his suffering, the thief was comforted to know that he would be with Christ in Paradise by the end of that day. The emphasis is on the where (Paradise) and the when (today).

Since it is rather obvious that Christ was speaking to the thief on that day and not "yesterday" or "tomorrow," there would be no reason for Christ to state, "I say to you today." Instead, the word "today" modifies when the thief would enter Paradise.

Acts 7:55–60

> But being full of the Holy Spirit, he gazed intently into heaven and saw the glory of God, and Jesus standing at the right hand of God; and he said, "Behold, I see the heavens opened up and the Son of Man standing at the right hand of God." But they cried out with a loud voice, and covered their ears, and they rushed upon him with one impulse. And when they had driven him out of city, they began stoning him, and the witnesses laid aside their robes at the feet of a young man named Saul. And they went on stoning Stephen as he called upon the Lord and said, "Lord Jesus, receive my spirit!" And falling on his knees, he cried out with a loud voice, "Lord, do not hold this sin against them!" And having said this, he fell asleep.

In this remarkable account of Stephen's martyrdom, Luke gives us the last words which were uttered by Stephen. These words revealed that his death was a triumph and not a defeat. No doubt, the Apostle Paul himself remembered these striking words as he was an eyewitness to Stephen's death.

What is important for us to consider is that Stephen did not ask the grave to receive him, but Christ, whom he saw in heaven, to receive or take unto himself his spirit or soul.

When Stephen said, "Lord Jesus, receive my spirit," he used the word *dexomai* in its aorist middle imperative tense. As A. T. Robertson pointed out, Stephen was urgent and emphatic in his prayer to the heavenly Christ that Jesus would take his spirit into heaven at that very moment.[32]

Stephen did not look down at death to an unconscious existence in the grave. Instead, he looked up into heaven itself and asked Christ to take him up to be with Him. Lenski comments:

> That prayer was heard. Stephen's spirit, the immaterial part of his being, left his body and was received by Jesus into the

glory and the bliss of heaven, there to await the last day when his body would be raised up to be again united with his soul and to participate in its heavenly joys.[33]

Or again, as Calvin stated:

This verse clearly testifies that the soul of man is not a vanishing breath, according to the ravings of some madmen, but that it is an essential spirit, and survives death.[34]

In Thayer's lexicon (p. 130), we find that *dexomai* in Acts 7:59 can only be grammatically understood in terms of "receive to thyself in heaven my spirit [author's paraphrase]." After his spirit departed to be with Christ, Stephen's body "fell asleep," awaiting the day of its awakening from the grave.

2 Corinthians 5:1–8

For we know that if the earthly tent which is our house is torn down, we have a building from God, a house not made with hands, eternal in the heavens. For indeed in this house we groan, longing to be clothed with our dwelling from heaven; inasmuch as we, having put it on, shall not be found naked. For indeed while we are in this tent, we groan, being burdened, because we do not want to be unclothed, but to be clothed, in order that what is mortal may be swallowed up by life. Now He who prepared us for this very purpose is God, who gave to us the Spirit as a pledge. Therefore, being always of good courage, and knowing that while we are at home in the body we are absent from the Lord—for we walk by faith, not by sight—we are of good courage, I say, and prefer rather to be absent from the body and to be at home with the Lord.

This passage has generated much discussion down through the centuries. It is difficult to interpret because of its unique vocabulary and the mixed metaphors which are used.

There are two basic approaches to this passage. First, a few commentators view it as describing the resurrection body and the second coming of Christ. They deny that it describes the intermediate state between death and resurrection.[35]

This position is usually taken by those who believe that Paul thought Christ would return at any moment in his own lifetime. Meyer states that Paul "was convinced for himself that he would live to see it."[36]

We must point out, Paul knew that Christ could not return as long as Peter was alive and that he himself had yet to go to Rome as Christ prophecied (John 21:18, 19; Acts 23:11).

There were other prophecies which Paul knew had to be fulfilled before the coming of Christ could be considered possible. Had

not Christ prophesied the destruction of the temple? (Matt. 24:1,
2). Was not the gospel to go forth unto all nations? (Matt. 24:14).
Did not Paul himself place the final apostasy and the Antichrist as
necessary preludes to the second coming? (2 Thess. 2:1–3).

We fail to be convinced that the Apostle Paul was a victim of
eschatological delusions.

A few commentators also put forth the idea that in this passage
the Apostle reveals his fear and dread of death. Paul hoped to
remain alive until the resurrection because he wished to avoid death.

We cannot accept such an idea, because whenever the Apostle
spoke of death elsewhere in his epistles, there is no indication that
he had a fear or dread of it. To Paul, death was a triumphant departure into the immediate presence of the heavenly Christ (2 Tim.
4:6; Phil. 1:23). Indeed, it was the Apostle Paul himself who guaranteed that even death could not separate us from the fellowship
and enjoyment of the love of Christ (Rom. 8:38, 39; 1 Thess. 5:10).

It is also argued that 2 Cor. 5:10 clearly speaks of the judgment
of Christ and therefore verses 1–8 refer to the resurrection.

The problem with this interpretation is that verse 10 directly
modifies verse 9, in which believers are told to be pleasing unto
Christ because they will have to stand before Him one day. Thus
the judgment of Christ is introduced for the first time in this passage
as a motivation for godly living.

The majority of commentators have always interpreted verses
1–8 as referring to the intermediate state between death and resurrection.[37]

First, since 5:1 begins with "for we know," we must begin the
context with chapter 4. In 4:11, 12, 16, etc., it is clear that the Apostle
is discussing death and not the second coming.

Second, in 4:16, Paul describes man in a dualistic sense of being
composed of a perishable body (outer man) and a transcendent soul
(inner man) which goes on after death.

Third, the place of dwelling is something which the believer
has right now in the heavens (v. 1); "we have a building," not *will
have*. Where in Scripture are we told that our resurrection body is
already created and waiting in heaven for us? The only rational
answer is that Paul is speaking of the soul's dwelling in heaven.

Fourth, in 5:1, the body is described as the place where the
transcendent "inner man," or soul, resides. Death is described as
the leaving of the soul to dwell in another place. The parallel is not
in the word "body" but in the word "habitation," i.e., place of
dwelling, as seen by the repetition of the word "habitation" in verse
2. The place of dwelling while alive is on earth, while the place of
dwelling after death is in heaven (v.1).

In Scripture, heaven is described as a city, house or mansion with many rooms (John 14:2; Heb. 11:10; Rev. 21:10). Therefore, the metaphor of a heavenly dwelling place after death is perfectly proper.

In contrast, when Christ returns, the saints do not go to dwell in heaven. Instead, they come "with Him" out of heaven to dwell on a new earth (1 Thess. 4:14; Rev. 21:10).

Nowhere in Scripture is the resurrection an event which refers to dwelling in heaven or receiving a body out of heaven. The resurrection bodies are always pictured as coming out of earthly graves and never out of heaven (John 5:28).

That Paul was referring to the intermediate state is also clear from 2 Cor. 5:4, where he uses the metaphor of being "unclothed" or "naked"; soul was a well-known metaphor used by Plato and other Greek writers.[38] It always referred to the disembodied state. It never had reference to resurrection.

Lastly, Paul describes the dwelling place after death as "in the heavens" (v. 1) where Christ is present (v. 8). At the second coming, Christ is on earth and no longer in heaven (Matt. 25:31), and we receive our bodies from the grave and not out of heaven. Elsewhere the Apostle speaks of his desire to ascend to the immediate presence of Christ in heaven after death (Phil. 1:23).

In the light of these facts, 2 Cor. 5:6 can only be interpreted as meaning that while in the body, we are absent from the immediate presence of Christ in heaven. But the moment we are absent from the body, we will be in the presence of the heavenly Christ. Thus, regardless if we are "home" or "absent," i.e., in or out of the body, we will always seek to please Him (v. 9).[39]

Philippians 1:21–23

Perhaps the best way to begin our study of this passage is to use Lightfoot's translation of it.

> **Others may make choice between life and death. I gladly accept either alternative. If I live, my life is one with Christ: if I die, my death is gain to me. Yet when I incline to prefer death, I hesitate: for may not my life—this present existence which men call life—be fruitful through my labours? Nay, I know not how to choose. I am hemmed in, as it were, a wall on this side and a wall on that. If I consult my own longing, I should desire to dissolve this earthly tabernacle, and to go home to Christ; for this is far better.[40]**

This is the clearest passage in the New Testament which speaks of the believer going to be with Christ in heaven after death.[41]

This context deals with Paul's desire to depart this earthly life for a heavenly life with Christ. There is no mention or allusion to the resurrection in this passage.[42]

The tense Paul uses in verse 21 when speaking of death "denotes not the act of dying but the consequence of dying, the state after death."[43]

Notice Paul's use of the pronoun "I." Paul's ego, self, or soul, dwells in his body while alive, departs from it at death, and immediately after death is in the presence of Christ in heaven.[44] As Lange put it:

> Unless Paul believed that the death which released him from the trials of this life was to introduce him at once to the presence of Christ and a state of blessedness, we see no adequate reason for the struggle between his desire to depart and be with Christ, and his anxiety to labor still for the advancement of the Redeemer's Kingdom on earth. If he believed that he was to remain for an indefinite time without consciousness in the grave, his zeal for men's salvation and his contempt of personal dangers and trials in the pursuit of that object, would lead him to desire to live as long as possible, on account of the importance of his ministry to mankind. On the other hand, if we suppose him to have regarded his attainment of the joys and rewards of heaven as simultaneous with his departure from this world, we have then an adequate explanation of this perplexity.[45]

Given the context and the grammatical construction of the passage, there is no legitimate way to escape the truth that Paul desired to depart this life and to be with Christ.[46]

Hebrews 12:22–24

> **But you have come to Mount Zion and to the city of the living God, the heavenly Jerusalem, and to myriads of angels, to the general assembly and church of the first-born who are enrolled in heaven, and to God, and Judge of all, and to the spirits of righteous men made perfect, and to Jesus, the mediator of a new covenant, and to the sprinkled blood, which speaks better than the blood of Abel.**

In order to emphasize the superiority of Christianity over Judaism, the author uses the rabbinic imagery[47] of a heavenly Jerusalem to draw a contrast between what the Jews experienced at Mount Sinai under Moses to what believers experience at the heavenly Jerusalem under Christ (vv. 18–24).

The author's choice of tenses and his use of nouns without definite articles have been noted by grammarians as an example of the author's expertise in the Greek language.[48]

In verse 22, he uses the perfect tense to indicate that the believers had been ushered into citizenship in and fellowship with the heavenly Jerusalem. The perfect tense indicates that it was at conversion that these saints were ushered into citizenship.[49]

This grammatical observation refutes the erroneous argument of the annihilationists who state that this passage concerns a future scene after the resurrection. As F. F. Bruce has pointed out, there is no reference whatsoever to the resurrection in this passage.[50] He goes on to say:

> No distinction in meaning can be pressed between "spirits" here and "souls" there. . . . It is plain that, for him, the souls of believers do not need to wait until the resurrection to be perfected. They are perfected already in the sense that they are with God in heavenly Jerusalem.[51]

In this glorious picture described by the author, the earthly saints join in the worship which resounds from myriads of angels and disembodied spirits of fellow saints who have departed this life. These saints were justified through faith while on earth and are now perfected and completed in heaven.

That the author is describing the blest condition of departed saints who now worship God before the throne is so clear that we must agree with the commentators that it cannot be questioned or doubted.[52] As Alford stated, this passage is indisputable proof that the souls of departed believers "are not sleeping, they are not unconscious, they are not absent from us: they are perfected, lacking nothing . . . but waiting only for bodily perfection."[53]

The conditionalists have never adequately dealt with the grammar and syntax of this passage, because the "spirits of justified men now perfected" who are worshiping at God's throne are obviously the conscious souls of believers during the intermediate state. The fact that they would merely wave it aside as a future event despite the grammar of the Greek text is an indication of their inability to grapple with this passage.

1 Peter 3:18–20

> For Christ also died for sins once for all, the just for the unjust, in order that He might bring us to God, having been put to death in the flesh, but made alive in the spirit; in which also He went and made proclamation to the spirits now in prison, who once were disobedient, when the patience of God kept waiting in the days of Noah, during the construction of the ark, in which a few, that is eight persons, were brought safely through the water.

In this highly controversial passage, Peter tells us that between Christ's death and resurrection, Jesus descended into Hades and there preached to "the spirits now in prison" (v. 19).

While there remain many unanswered questions which have never been fully resolved by any commentator in two millenniums, the phrase "the spirits now in prison" clearly speaks of disembodied spirits in the netherworld.

> That by spirits in prison is meant souls of men separated from their bodies and detained as in custody in the underworld, which the Greeks call Hades, the Hebrews Sheol, can hardly be doubted.[54]

The commentators are unanimous in their agreement with Rosenmuller's statement. Whether the passage speaks of Christ's preaching through Noah to his generation or Christ's descent into Hades, all interpreters are agreed that "the spirits in prison" are disembodied conscious spirits or souls.

We recommend Lange's discussion of Christ's descent into Hades as the most able treatment known.[55]

Revelation 6:9, 10

> **And when He broke the fifth seal, I saw underneath the altar the souls of those who had been slain because of the word of God, and because of the testimony which they had maintained; and they cried out with a loud voice, saying. "How long, O Lord, holy and true, wilt Thou refrain from judging and avenging our blood on those who dwell on the earth?"**

First, there can be no doubt that the scene described took place in heaven (Rev. 4:1, 2).

Second, that John "saw" these souls does not mean that they must have had resurrected bodies—as the annihilationists claim—anymore than it would require God the Father and the angels to have bodies because John "saw" them as well.[56] As Meyer points out, John's sight is mystical and visionary, not sensuous and physical, and the idea that the souls would have to have physical bodies to be seen is unnecessary as well as false.[57]

Third, the souls are the disembodied spirits of the martyrs who cry out to God for vengeance on their enemies. The attempt to reduce these souls to lifeless and unconscious bloodstains on the altar is incorrect as well as ridiculous.[58]

The blood mentioned in 6:10 explains how the souls got to the altar and why they are crying out for vengeance. To reduce the souls to bloodstains is impossible, because these same martyrs are described elsewhere in John's vision as conscious beings who worshiped God (6:11; 7:9–17).

This passage has always proven a great difficulty to those who deny that believers ascend to heaven at death. But John's language is clear that these souls were conscious and active in heaven.

Summary

The passages which we have surveyed are clear enough to reveal to the honest reader that the doctrine of soul sleep is erroneous. When a believer dies, he immediately ascends to the presence of Christ and experiences conscious bliss. This is in obvious contrast to the wicked who descend to the murky darkness of Hades and experience conscious torment.

Argument #3

That death is a state of unconsciousness is clear from such passages as Ps. 6:5; 88:10, 11; 115:17; Eccles. 9:5, 10. The dead are unconscious and are incapable of knowledge, wisdom or activity.[59]

Answer

As we have already pointed out in our chapter on hermeneutics, an undue dependence upon Old Testament texts is a characteristic of the way annihilationists argue. Instead of understanding the vagueness of the Old Testament and appreciating the clarity of the New Testament, they prefer to list a dozen passages where the dead are said not to participate in the joys and activities of this life as if this proves their doctrine of soul sleep.

First, in such places as Ps. 6:5; 88:10, 11; 115:17, the psalmist used those Hebrew words which are virtually always used in respect to public worship in the house of God in the midst of the congregation. The Hebraist, John Gill, comments:

> These passages only respect praising God before men, and in the church militant, as is done by saints in the land of the living.[60]

For example, in Ps. 6:5, David laments that if the Lord does not deliver him out of his depression by destroying his enemies (vv. 3, 10), he would die. Once in Sheol, he could not give "thanks" (*yadah*) unto the Lord. So, the Lord should deliver him in order to receive David's thanksgiving.

The word *yadah* in its various forms is found 103 times in the Hebrew Old Testament. Almost without exception, it is the word used for public worship in congregational meetings and refers to public testimonies, praise, thanks, etc.[61]

The psalmist is simply saying that once he is dead, there will be no further opportunities to give public praise in the midst of the congregation.

Third, the book of Ecclesiastes has always been a favorite source of proof texts for the doctrine of soul sleep. Yet, an analysis of its basic message reveals that it should not be treated in this way.

Perhaps the best way to understand Ecclesiastes is to compare it to the book of Proverbs. Both books are found within the poetical section of the Old Testament. The five poetical books of Job, Psalms, Proverbs, Ecclesiastes and Song of Songs deal with the practical issues of life instead of such things as prophecy, history or theology. They are also called "Wisdom literature" because they seek to educate us about life and how to live it.

Although Proverbs and Ecclesiastes are both wisdom literature, they teach us about life in two totally different ways. Proverbs begins with the assumption that there is a personal God who gives meaning to all of life (Prov. 1:7). In contrast, Ecclesiastes begins with the assumption of "the man under the sun," i.e., autonomous man without God (Eccles. 1:16, 17).

Proverbs begins with God and asks the question, "How should we live?" Ecclesiastes begins without God and asks, "Why should we live?"

Proverbs is positive, while Ecclesiastes is negative and pessimistic. Proverbs promises us that life will be wonderful if we begin with God (1:1–7). Ecclesiastes warns us that life is empty and without meaning if we begin without God (1:2).

In Proverbs, wisdom is more important than money (3:13–18). In Ecclesiastes, money is more important than wisdom (10:19; 1:17, 18).

In many other ways, Ecclesiastes reveals the warning that without God, nothing in life will have any meaning or significance.[62]

The texts seized upon by the annihilationists to prove their doctrine of soul sleep must be interpreted in the context of the basic theme and message of Ecclesiastes.

After giving the perspective of autonomous man for eleven chapters, the author concludes by bringing the Creator into the picture (12:1), defining death as the ascent of the spirit to God (12:7), and the necessity of beginning with God and the keeping of His commandments (12:13, 14).

As we mentioned in our chapter on hermeneutics, the annihilationists fail to realize that the context of a book as a whole must be taken into consideration in the interpretation of any given verse in that book.

Argument #4

Since the words Sheol and Hades are translated "grave" in the KJV, therefore the fate of all men is to descend into the grave at death. There is no intermediate state, but the soul perishes with the body at death and both are consumed in the grave.[63]

Answer

There are good lexicographical and exegetical reasons for rejecting any attempted identification between Sheol/Hades with the grave. This evidence is given in the chapters on the soul and Sheol.

Argument #5

The Scriptures speak of the fate of the wicked in terms of their being "destroyed," "consumed," etc. The wicked are said to "perish" forever. These terms must mean that they pass into nonexistence.[64]

Answer

We examined such terms in the chapter on eternal punishment and have demonstrated that there is no lexicographical or exegetical evidence to support the conditionalists' assumption that such terms mean annihilation. The way such terms are used in Scripture reveals that they cannot mean annihilation. For example, W. E. Vine's *Expository Dictionary of New Testament Words* (p. 302) states that the idea behind such words as *apollumi* "does not mean extinction but ruin, loss, not to being, but of well-being. This is clear from its use."

Argument #6

"Eternal life" means unending physical immortality or existence. Since only the righteous receive "eternal life" at the resurrection, the wicked must pass into nonexistence. Otherwise, they too would be recipients of "eternal life."[65]

Answer

In our chapter on immortality, we demonstrated that "eternal life" which the righteous receive is a quality of divine life which the wicked never experience. The righteous receive this eternal life at regeneration and do not have to wait for it until the resurrection. It does not mean "unending existence" but "eternal well-being."

Argument #7

Only God has immortality according to 1 Tim. 6:16. Therefore man is not immortal.[66]

Answer

Only God has absolute immortality, seeing He has no beginning or end. While this argument is fully answered in the chapter on immortality, we must point out that since the annihilationists view themselves as possessing some kind of immortality, there are obviously different kinds of immortality.

Argument #8

The worms and fire in a dump consume the garbage until it is no more. They do not torment the garbage but consume it. Thus the worms and fire of Gehenna consume the wicked until they no longer exist. Then the fire and worms die out.[67]

Answer

Gehenna is discussed in the chapter which deals with Sheol and Hades. See also the chapter on eternal punishment. Since the worms are said to be "undying" and the fire "eternal" and "never extinguished," something more substantial than annihilation is called for. The rabbinic metaphor which was used by the Jews clearly meant torment (see our discussion of Judith 16:17, Eccles. 7:16, 17).

Argument #9

The words *olam, aion,* and *aionios* do not mean eternity, because they are used of such temporal things as mountains. Therefore, "eternal punishment" need not mean that the punishment is eternal in duration, but only in result.[68]

Answer

When we observe the contexts where *olam, aion,* and *aionios* are used, they do indeed mean eternal in duration when speaking of the final state. The lexicographical and exegetical evidence for this is given in the chapter on eternal punishment.

Argument #10

The doctrines of a conscious afterlife and eternal torment are pagan concepts and are the result of Platonic influence. Because they are pagan, they are satanic in origin.[69]

Answer

Froom's constant charge that anyone who believes in a conscious afterlife and eternal punishment is influenced by Plato's philosophy reveals that he did not understand Plato's philosophy or the orthodox position. For example, Plato believed in the preexistence of the soul in the heavenly World of Ideas. This obviously has nothing to do with the orthodox position. While Plato believed in natural immortality, the orthodox have always viewed life in this world or in the next as a gift of God. That orthodoxy is not "Platonic" in its view of man or death is demonstrated in the chapter on body, soul and spirit. The conditionalists' argument at this point is a species of argument *ad hominem*.

Argument #11

All the Jewish and early patristic literature demonstrates that conditional immortality was the true position of the Jews and early Christians. The orthodox position was a later incursion of Greek philosophy into the church.[70]

Answer

In the chapters on the soul, Sheol and eternal punishment, Jewish and patristic material is submitted which reveals that such conditionalists as Froom constantly overstated their claim. The claim that there is no literary evidence for the orthodox position is erroneous.

Argument #12

Since God created man as a being with a body, it is impossible for him to exist in a disembodied state. Without a body, man's spirit could not think or speak. Thus death must be a state of unconsciousness.[71]

Answer

This philosophic objection is dealt with in the chapter on immortality. The mere fact that God and the angels are conscious though bodiless reveals that a bodiless state need not be unconscious. Also, this argument ignores the implications of the fall and is based solely on implications drawn from the creation.

CONCLUSION

In our brief overview of the arguments for conditionalism, we have hopefully demonstrated that most of them are based on faulty assumptions or false reasoning. They have been weighed and have been found wanting.

It is to be regretted that every few generations, the conditionalists' arguments must be answered all over again. This is necessary because the conditionalists will forget that they have been answered and will attempt to convince the church that their arguments have never been dealt with fairly or openly. Throughout our study and particularly in this chapter, we have covered all the arguments for conditionalism and annihilationism that is to be found in the literature on this subject. No stone was left unturned in our search to find out what the Scripture teaches and what we should believe as to our fate after death and the resurrection.

NOTES

1. P. Schaff, *History of the Christian Church*, Vol. II, pp. 858f.
2. Ibid., pp. 859f.
3. Froom, I, p. 917.
4. Ibid.
5. Ibid, II, p. 63.
6. Schaff, Vol. VI, p. 610.
7. Froom, II, p. 60.
8. W. Martin, *The Truth About Seventh Day Adventism*, pp. 117f.
9. M. Luther, *Commentary on Genesis* (Grand Rapids: Zondervan Pub. Co.), Vol. I, p. 52.
10. See his comments on Gen. 2:7; 4:9, etc.
11. Luther's Works, Vol. XXV, p. 321.
12. M. Luther, *Commentary on Genesis*, p. 223.
13. Froom, II, p. 1034.
14. See Shelton's exposé in Baptist Reformation Review, Spring 1975, Vol. 4, no. 1, pp. 14ff.
15. W. Martin, *The Truth About Seventh Day Adventism*.
16. G. Paxton, *The Shaking of Adventism*, Baker Book House, 1977.
17. Fudge, XVI, pp. 48, etc.
18. Froom, I, pp. 34, 35, 155; *Let God Be True*, pp. 60, 61; *Is This Life All There Is?* p. 38.
19. H. Alford, *The State of the Blessed Dead* (New York: Randolph & Co., p. 11; J. Gill, *Body of Divinity* (Georgia: Turner Lassetter, 1965), p. 598; R. Stover, *What Do We Know About Life After Death?* (Grand Rapids: Zondervan Pub. Co., 1941), p. 24.

20. Froom, I, p. 468.

21. Gill, ibid., p. 598; Alford, ibid., p. 11; *Expositor's Greek Testament* Vol. II, p. 204.

22. *Theological Dictionary of the New Testament* (ed. Kittel), Vol. I, p. 147.

23. W. Hendriksen, *The Gospel of Matthew*, p. 609.

24. Thayer, p. 451.

25. J. Ryle, *Expository Thoughts on the Gospels* (Zondervan Pub. Co., 1969), Vol. I, p. 207.

26. Ryle, ibid., Vol. II, pp. 476, 477.

27. Alford, Vol. I, pp. 661, 662; Lange, *Luke*, p. 376; Meyer, *Luke*, p. 566.

28. Froom, I, pp. 278f.

29. Lange, *Luke*, p. 376.

30. Meyer, *Luke*, p. 567.

31. Lenski, *The Interpretation of St. Luke's Gospel* (Minnesota: Augsburg Pub. House, 1963), p. 1145; *Expositor's Greek Testament*, Vol. II, p. 641.

32. A.T. Robertson, ibid., Vol. III, p. 99.

33. R. Lenski, *The Interpretation of the Acts of the Apostles* (Minnesota: Augsburg Pub. House, 1963), p. 309.

34. J. Calvin, *Acts*, p. 222.

35. See: Froom, Alford, Hughes, and Meyer.

36. Meyer, *I and II Corinthians*, p. 507.

37. Ephraem, Hervius, Aquinas, Photius, Anselm, Valcin, Thomas, Lyra, Wolf, Calovins, Morus, Hofmann, Lange, Rosenmuller, Starke, Rerger, Stanley, Tasker, Lightfoot, Vincent, etc.

38. Crat., 403 13; Repub. 577B, etc.

39. See Hodge's *Commentary on II Corinthians* for further details.

40. J. Lightfoot, *Saint Paul's Epistle to the Philippians* (Zondervan Pub. Co., 1965), pp. 91, 92.

41. Martin, ibid., pp. 124, 125.

42. *Expositor's Greek Testament*, Vol. III, p. 429.

43. Lightfoot, ibid., p. 93.

44. Ibid.

45. Horatio Hackett in Lange's *Commentary on Philippians*, p. 26.

46. See: Martin, W., ibid., pp. 122–125, for an extended treatment of this passage.

47. II Baruch 4; IV Ezra 7, 8, etc.

48. R. Lenski, *The Interpretation of Hebrews* (Minnesota: Augsburg Pub. House, 1963), p. 451.

49. F.F. Bruce, *Commentary on the Epistle to the Hebrews* (Grand Rapids: Wm. B. Eerdmans Pub. Co., 1964), p. 372.

50. Ibid., p. 328.

51. Ibid.

52. See: Calvin, Owen, Brown, Lenski, etc.

53. Alford, Vol. IV, p. 255.

54. Rosenmuller, quoted by Alger, *A Critical History of the Doctrines of a Future life* (W.J. Widdleton Pub., 1966), p. 221.

55. Lange, *Revelation*, pp. 372f., Ellicott, Vol. VIII, pp. 421f.

56. Lenski, *The Interpretation of St. John's Gospel* (Minnesota: Augsburg Pub. Co., 1963), p. 232; Alford, Vol. IV, p. 618.

57. Meyer, *Revelation*, p. 228.

58. See: Lenski, Meyer, etc.

59. Ibid., Froom, *Let God Be True*, etc.

60. J. Gill, ibid., p. 600.

61. See; Ps. 9:1, 2; 18:49; 35:18; 43:4; 71:14–16, etc.

62. F. Grant, *Facts and Theories as to a Future State* (New York: Loizeaux Bros., 1889), pp. 49, 138; A. Hovey, *The State of the Inpenitent Dead* (Boston: Gould & Lincoln, 1859), p. 11; S. Kellog, *From Death to Resurrection* (New York: Anson D.F. Randolph & Co., 1885), p. 26; H. Theissen, *Lectures in Systematic Theology* (Grand Rapids: Eerdmans Pub. Co., 1963), p. 489.

63. Froom. I, pp. 39f.; *Let God Be True*, p. 73.

64. Froom, I, pp. 105f.; Fudge, pp. 90f.; *Let God Be True*, p. 278.

65. Froom, I, pp. 113f., 196, 290, 320, etc.; *Let God Be True*, p. 278.

66. Froom, I, pp. 319f.; *Let God Be True*, p. 64.

67. Froom, I, pp. 117f.; Fudge, pp. 161f.; *Let God Be True*, pp. 76f.

68. Froom, I, pp. 288f., 931f.; Fudge, pp. 37f.

69. Froom, I, pp. 111, 529–680; *Let God Be True*, p. 79; *Is This Life All There Is?*, pp. 43–46.

70. Froom, I, pp. 632–740, 928–1079.

71. In Vol. II, Froom documents that many modern philosophers state that a body is necessary for consciousness. No evidence is submitted for such a position. See also Cullman's *Immortality of the Soul or Resurrection*.

Chapter 9

UNIVERSALISM

A BRIEF HISTORY

The idea that all men find themselves ultimately in an eternal state of bliss was originally propagated by some of the Gnostic sects such as the Basilidians, Carpocrations, etc.[1]

It was picked up by Clement of Alexandria (A.D. 150–220), one of the founders of the Alexandrian schools of theology which tried to reconcile Christianity and Greek philosophy by creating a synthesis between the two.[2] Although there is a possibility that he later came to believe in eternal punishemnt,[3] it is generally conceded that Clement was the first to teach Universalism in the Christian Church.[4]

Clement's star pupil, Origen (A.D. 185–250), was the first to develop a systematic treatment of salvation which included the ultimate reconciliation of Satan and his demonic hosts as well as all men. According to Origen, the fires of hell were not punitive but corrective. Through their sufferings, all demons and men would exercise their free will and seek reconciliation with God.

Origen appealed to the Scriptures as teaching Universalism. Then using a highly allegorical hermeneutic, he proceeded to spiritualize away all those biblical passages which referred to a coming resurrection, judgment day, eternal torment, etc. His method of interpretation was Gnostic in character and ignored the grammar and syntax of Scripture. He did to Christianity what Philo had done to Judaism. He paganized it.

Origen's Universalism was condemned by the Christian Church in the East at (1) a synod at Alexandria (A.D. 394), (2) a synod at Cyprus, and (3) a synod at Rome. It was later condemned at the general 5th Lateran Council in A.D. 649.[5]

After Universalism was officially declared a heresy by the Christian Church, except for a few rare individuals such as Eusibius, it did not reappear until the Reformation, and then only among some of the Anabaptist sects.[6]

It was condemned as heresy by the Lutheran church in the Augsburg Confession XVII as well as by the Reformed confessions.

It was condemned in the 42 articles of Faith of the Church of England. When the articles were reduced to 39, the Article condemning Universalism was dropped.

In Europe, Universalism was put forth by the Socinians, who also rejected most orthodox doctrines such as the Trinity. While Universalism never developed into a separate denomination due to the state-church structure, liberal theologians within state churches such as Schleiermacher rejected the orthodox position on hell as well as on most other topics.[7]

In England, Universalism was not popularly preached or taught until James Kelly (1750). He had been one of Whitefield's preachers at the Tabernacle and had originally been a Calvinistic Baptist.

After the revival was disrupted by the Calvinist-Arminian debate, many people such as Kelly abandoned Whitefield's theology and followed Wesley's views instead.[8]

Kelly's antagonism to Calvinism ultimately led him beyond Wesley's Arminianism. "If Christ died for all, then all are saved" became Kelly's driving obsession. He spent the rest of his life preaching and writing in defense of Universalism. Since he was not an organizer but spent his time preaching, no permanent work came out of his labors.

One of Kelly's converts was a Methodist preacher by the name of John Murray. He arrived in America in 1770 and is called the "Father of American Universalism."[9]

As Murray worked to spread Universalism among Methodists, Congregationalists, Episcopalians, etc., Elhanan Winchester (1781) started a work among the Baptists. Formerly a Calvinistic Baptist, Winchester formed the "Universal Baptist Church" in opposition to the general Calvinistic Baptist churches of his day.

We must point out that Kelly, Murray and Winchester held to orthodox views on all subjects except eternal torment. They were not Unitarians, because they believed in the Trinity. They believed in the necessity and vicarious nature of the atonement. They taught that the Bible was inspired. They believed in the deity and bodily resurrection of Christ. They felt that temporary punishment after death was necessary to satisfy the law and justice of God.

In 1790, with Murray present, The Philadelphia Convention of Universalists issued a statement of faith. They set forth that they believed: (1) the Bible is "a revelation of the perfection and will of God, and the rule of faith and practice"; (2) there is only one God; (3) Christ was God and man and that His death "will finally restore the whole human race to happiness"; (4) the person and work of the Holy Spirit; (5) the moral law is the rule of life.[10]

While the founding fathers of American Universalism were orthodox except as to eternal torment, within a generation, the

Universalists abandoned nearly all orthodox doctrines and became basically Unitarian in theology. It would be instructive to observe how this happened.

In defense of Universalism, the early Universalists such as Murray argued that the nature of God forbade the existence of an eternal hell. Also, man's "good" nature and free will rendered an eternal hell unthinkable because man was "free" to repent in hell itself! The horrors of hell guaranteed that any who went there would repent and be saved. Thus, man was at liberty to be saved even after death.

By moving the basis of Universalism to the nature of God and the free will of man instead of resting it solely on the atonement of Christ, the early Universalists actually undercut the rest of their orthodox theology.

The first Universalist to see this clearly was Hosea Ballou (1771–1852).[11] Raised a Calvinistic Baptist, Ballou later embraced Universalism.

At first, Ballou was orthodox in respect to the Trinity, vicarious atonement, etc., but then his thinking began to change. If the nature of God, i.e., God's goodness, grace, mercy, etc., renders hell impossible, and renders the salvation of all men a necessity; and if man's nature, i.e., his goodness, equally renders hell impossible and renders the salvation of all men ultimate, then the orthodox teaching on the vicarious nature of the atonement is really unnecessary. God's nature is sufficient in and of itself for salvation.

Once the necessity and vicarious nature of the atonement is rejected, why is there any reason for belief in the deity or resurrection of Christ? Why is there any need for a Trinity? Ballou concluded that there is no reason for belief in the fall of man, the necessity of the atonement, salvation by faith alone, etc. Once hell is thrown out, there is nothing to be "saved" from. Then why talk about salvation in the orthodox sense?[12]

Hosea Ballou lived to see his total repudiation of historic Christianity become the norm for Universalists. The orthodox elements in Kelly's and Murray's thinking were completely exorcised out of Universalist theology within a generation.

The Universalist movement grew as more and more people abandoned their Calvinistic heritage. Chancy's *The Salvation of All Men* (1784) sparked a debate which produced over seventy-five books and articles before it ran its course. Not even Jonathan Edwards and Timothy Dwight were able to stop the tide of Universalist theology.[13]

The evangelist Charles G. Finney was forced to debate Universalists on several occasions. His answer, which many evangelicals today still think to be the best defense, was to reject the Reformed concept that Christ actually accomplished atonement on the cross by infallibly securing salvation for the elect, and to posit in its place the idea that Christ made salvation "possible." Christ did not secure salvation for "the elect," as the Calvinists claimed, or for "all men," as the Universalists claimed. Finney saw that Universalism made use of the Reformed view of the nature of the atonement as its own basis. By attacking the Calvinistic concept of the atonement, Universalism was refuted. Finney relates one such incident in his memoirs where he was asked to refute Universalism.

> In this state of things, Mr. Gale, together with some of the elders of his church, desired me to address the people on the subject, and see if I could not reply to the arguments of the Universalist. The great effort of the Universalist was of course to show that sin did not deserve endless punishment. He inveighed against the doctrine of endless punishment as unjust, infinitely cruel and absurd. God was love; and how could a God of love punish men endlessly?
>
> I arose in one of our evening meetings and said, "This Universalist preacher holds forth doctrines that are new to me, and I do not believe they are taught in the Bible. But I am going to examine the subject, and if I cannot show that his views are false, I will become a Universalist myself." I then appointed a meeting the next week, at which time I proposed to deliver a lecture in opposition to his views. The Christian people were rather startled at my boldness in saying that I would be a Universalist if I could not prove that his doctrines were false. However, I felt sure that I could.
>
> When the evening came for my lecture, the house was crowded. I took up the question of the justice of endless punishment, and discussed it through that and the next evening. There was general satisfaction with the presentation.
>
> The Universalist himself found that the people were convinced that he was wrong, and he took another tack. Mr. Gale, together with his school of theology, maintained that the atonement of Christ was the literal payment of the debt of the elect, a suffering of just what they deserved to suffer; so that the elect were saved upon principles of exact justice; Christ, so far as they were concerned, having fully answered the demands of the law. The Universalist seized upon this view, assuming that this was the real nature of the atonement. He had only to prove that the atonement was made for all men, and then he could show that all men would be saved; because the debt of all mankind had been literally paid by the Lord Jesus Christ, and Universalism would follow on the very ground of justice; for God could not justly punish those whose debt was paid.
>
> I saw, and the people saw—those who understood Mr. Gale's position—that the Universalist had gotten him into a tight place. For it was easy to prove that the atonement was made for all

mankind; and if the nature and value of the atonement were as Mr. Gale held, universal salvation was an inevitable result.

I then appointed to lecture on the Universalist's argument founded on the Gospel. I delivered two lectures on the atonement. In these I think I fully succeeded in showing that the atonement did not consist in the literal payment of the debt of sinners, in the sense which the Universalist maintained; that it simply rendered the salvation of all men possible, and did not of itself lay God under obligation to save anybody; that it was not true that Christ suffered just what those for whom He died deserved to suffer; that no such thing as that was taught in the Bible, and no such thing was true; that, on the contrary, Christ died simply to remove an insurmountable obstacle out of the way of God's forgiving sinners, so as to render it possible for him to proclaim a universal amnesty, inviting all men to repent, to believe in Christ, and to accept salvation; that instead of having satisfied retributive justice, and borne just what sinners deserve, Christ had only satisfied public justice, by honoring the law, both in his obedience and death, thus rendering it safe for God to pardon sin, to pardon the sins of any man and of all men who would repent and believe in Him. I maintained that Christ, in His atonement, merely did that which was necessary as a condition of the forgiveness of sin; and not that which cancelled sin, in the sense of literally paying the indebtedness of sinners.

This answered the Universalist, and put a stop to any further proceedings or excitement on that subject.[14]

By the time of the fundamentalist-liberal debates of the 1920s, it was assumed that liberal theologians were Universalists, while those who believed in the inspiration of Scripture taught the doctrine of eternal torment. Thus, in *Christianity and Liberalism*, Machen assumed that Universalism was part of liberal theology which denied the Trinity, the virgin birth, the deity and resurrection of Christ, the vicarious atonement, the inspiration of Scripture, etc.[15]

In his classic critique of liberalism, Machen demonstrated that it is actually a form of humanism and is not really Christian in any sense except that the liberals take Christian words and pour into them humanistic meanings. Thus, liberal theologians should not be viewed as fellow Christians but as humanists who have invaded the Christian Church.

After the controversy in the 1920s died down, the average Bible-believing Christian assumed that the doctrine of eternal torment was an essential part of evangelical theology. This assumption continued until the 1960s when the neo-evangelical movement began.

The neo-evangelical movement was the attempt to introduce the neo-liberal theology of Karl Barth into evangelical colleges and seminaries by individuals who had once been orthodox in theology.[16]

Although they had long since rejected evangelical theology, these individuals retained their teaching positions by simply calling their new liberal theology "evangelical." Thus, while they called themselves "evangelicals," they actually rejected those very doctrines which historically made someone an evangelical, such as the inerrancy of Scripture.[17]

Karl Barth, the founder of the "new Modernism," was raised with a Calvinistic heritage. Blending together some of this heritage—particularly the doctrine of irresistible grace—with elements of liberal theology—universal salvation—he was able to produce a theology which he hoped would be a "new evangelicalism." What he actually did, according to C. Van Til, was to produce a "new Humanism."[18]

Barth was guilty of reductionism in that he absolutized the objective elements in salvation such as election and denied the existence, or significance of the subjective elements such as faith and repentance. He absolutized God's sovereign grace and spoke of it as "triumphing" in the salvation of all men.

That Barth was a Universalist—although he publicly denied it like Farrar—is clear from what he wrote.[19] Even Berkouwer pointed out that Barth's refusal to admit his Universalism "cannot be reconciled with the fundamental structure of his doctrine of election."[20]

Barth objectified the entire process of salvation to ensure that man would not be involved in it at any point. Christ himself is the electing God and the man elected. Christ alone is elected and accepted by God. He was reprobated by a divine "no" and elected by a divine "yes." Thus the "yes" and "no" of salvation is taken entirely out of man's hands and put into Christ's hands alone.

Since Christ as man is elect, then all men in Christ will be saved. Human faith or unbelief are not necessary for election or reprobation. Therefore, they are not necessary for the triumph of grace.

The only difference between the Christian and the non-Christian according to Barth is that the Christian "knows" that he is saved, while the non-Christian doesn't. They are like a group of people stranded on a raft. The raft is actually floating in four feet of water, but only two of the group "know" it. The rest think that they are in danger of drowning.

The church's mission, according to Barth, is to joyously proclaim that Christ has saved all men. Thus, "unbelief" is impossible, because it will be conquered by triumphant grace. The "yes" and "no" decision of salvation does not belong to man but to Christ alone.

Although many hailed Barth's theology as something new, he

was actually following in the footsteps of Joseph Huntington (1762–1794), who wrote *Calvinism Improved* in 1796. Also, two Scottish theologians, Hastie and Paterson, at the turn of the century, tried to use Calvinism as a vehicle for Universalism. They all tried to combine the Calvinistic doctrine of irresistible grace with the Universalistic salvation of all men.[21]

The great Princeton theologian, B. B. Warfield, dealt with the attempt to use Calvinism as the vehicle for Universalism in his *The Plan of Salvation* (pp. 69–86). Many of his cogent remarks could be applied to Barth's Universalism today. The two Scottish theologians, Hastie and Paterson, assumed (1) that only Calvinism contained the dynamics of election and irresistible grace which could guarantee universal salvation. They realized that since Calvinism guaranteed the salvation of some, then it could, if revamped, guarantee the salvation of all. In their opinion, which of course would be hotly contested by many, Arminianism as a system left salvation in question because it placed it entirely in man's hands. (2) They assumed that election and predestination concern all men and believed that all men were elect. (3) They then came to the conclusion that we must begin with the assumption that all men are actually saved.

Warfield points out that the attempt to use Calvinism as a vehicle for Universalism will always be a failure:

1. The Calvinistic doctrines of election and irresistible grace have meaning only in the context of Calvinism's particularism.

2. Once election and grace are placed in the corporate system of Universalism, they lose their meaning, significance, and effectiveness.

3. Hastie and Paterson are actually assuming that God owes man salvation. Thus grace would no longer be grace, but debt.

4. These men have a weak view of sin. Universalism has always suffered from such a light view of sin.

Warfield's final answer is to point out:

> The real solution to the problem that is raised in respect to the distribution of the divine grace is, then, not to be sought along the lines either of the denial of the omnipotence of God's grace . . . or of the denial of the reality of his reprobation with our neo-Universalists, but in the affirmation of his righteousness. The old answer is after all the only satisfying one: God in his love, saves as many of the guilty race of man as he can. . . . Being God and all that God is, he will not permit even his ineffable love to betray him into action which is not right. (p. 74)

Barth's Universalism was built basically upon the same line of argument that had been developed by Hastie and Paterson.

Barth in his Universalism even redefined the wrath of God and made it a means of grace. Van Til explains:

> For Barth, man, as sinner, is, to be sure, under the wrath of
> God, but this wrath is, itself, a form of the all-overreaching grace
> of God. There is no eternal punishment awaiting for those who
> are not in Christ [because] there are no men who are not in
> Christ. . . . This is Barth's "biblical Universalism." It is his Christ
> Event.[22]

The most honest and biblically rigorous assessment of Barth's
theology is Van Til's *Christianity and Barthianism.* He critiques all
other assessments such as Berkouwer's *The Triumph of Grace in the
Theology of Karl Barth.* His argument that Barth is actually a humanist
has never been answered.

The neo-evangelicals drifted toward Barthianism because it was
acceptable to the liberals. Seeking to remain within the evangelical
community, they maintained their positions in churches and educational institutions. Slowly but surely, they have influenced many
students to think that Barth was an "evangelical." Thus one can at
this time call himself an "evangelical" and yet deny the inerrancy
and historicity of Scripture, the orthodox view of the person and
work of Christ, the vicarious atonement, and eternal torment!

One modern attempt to spread Barthian Universalism among
evangelicals and reformed Christians is Neil Punt's *Unconditional
Good News* which was published by Eerdmans in 1980. Beginning
with the Barthian reduction of salvation to its objective elements,
Punt declares: "It is an error to think that there is anything that
must be done to inherit eternal life."[23] He goes on to reject the idea
that sinners must repent and believe the gospel in order to be saved.
They should be informed that they are saved—not exhorted to be
saved by faith and repentance.

Punt was raised with a Calvinistic heritage in the Christian
Reformed Church. After rejecting the Calvinism and orthodoxy of
his forefathers, he has elected to remain in his church and spread
Barthian Universalism even though such beliefs are condemned by
his church's standards of faith.

Surprisingly, Punt's book received favorable reviews in some
evangelical magazines! Evidently, the level of theological discern-
ment is so low today that some reviewers did not even understand
what Punt was really saying.

We fear that unless fundamental and evangelical colleges and
seminaries take a strong stand against neo-liberal professors in their
midst who are peddling Barthian Universalism, within a generation
or two, these institutions will be denying the Trinity, the vicarious
atonement, the inspiration of Scripture, etc.

History has a nasty habit of repeating itself. Just as the descendants of Kelly and Murray ultimately became humanists and joined with the Unitarians in 1961, the descendants of the neo-evangelicals will be Unitarian in theology within a generation or two. Let us hope that evangelicals will remember this sad fact of history and return yet to the orthodoxy of their fathers.

One last consideration which must be pointed out is that the breakdown of belief in the inspiration of Scripture and the growing peril of Universalism and annihilationism are preparing the way for future descendants of the evangelical church to be swept into the world of the cults and occult.

A THEOLOGICAL ANALYSIS

Throughout our study, we have dealt with most of the Universalists' arguments in their proper context. Yet, a summary of their chief arguments and the biblical answers to them would be helpful.

Before we give an overview of Universalist arguments, it would be helpful to take note that there are three basic kinds of Universalism.

First, there is "cheap Universalism" which is the kind of street theology which one finds on college campuses. It is the sentimental idea that there is no hell because God would never hurt anyone. God is usually pictured as being a kindly old grandfather with a "boys-will-be-boys" attitude, who is either indifferent or powerless about evil.

Cheap Universalism has no theological or philosophic base, but it is simply an expression of hope or wish fulfillment that God will not judge men for their sins.

Second, there is "philosophic Universalism" in which man is viewed as part of the divine essence. In Eastern philosophy and Western mind cults, man ultimately returns to being "one" with God.

Since we have dealt with this concept in connection with our study of reincarnation,[24] it is sufficient to point out that the biblical doctrine of creation undercuts all such pantheistic beliefs. The radical distinction between the Creator and the creature cannot be dissolved.

Third, there is "pseudo-christian Universalism" which tries to find a biblical basis for the hope that all men will be saved. It has expressed itself in a multitude of ways.

Some feel that there is no punishment for sin whatsoever but all ascend to heaven at death. Then there are those who feel that there must be a temporary period of suffering after death in order to cleanse the wicked of their sins. Others place this temporary suffering after the resurrection.

Some speak of all men as ultimately being saved in the future, while others state that all men are saved already.

It is this last kind of Universalism that is attempting to invade the evangelical church. Because of this, we will limit our analysis to those arguments which are put forward as proving pseduo-christian Universalism.

Argument #1

The nature of God, i.e., His love, goodness and mercy, means that all men will be saved. These same attributes also exclude any idea of eternal punishment.

Answer

The attempt to use God's love to disprove the doctrine of hell is futile for several reasons.

First, we must recognize that the Scriptures speak of the wrath of God as well as His love (John 3:36; Rev. 6:16, 17, etc.). We cannot pick and choose when it comes to God's attributes. As Machen pointed out:

> The New Testament clearly speaks of the wrath of God and the wrath of Jesus Himself; and all the teachings of Jesus presuppose a divine indignation against sin. With what possible right, then, can those who reject this vital element in Jesus' teaching and example regard themselves as true disciples of His? The truth is that the modern rejection of the doctrine of God's wrath proceeds from a light view of sin which is totally at variance with the teaching of the whole New Testament and of Jesus Himself.[25]

Second, this argument would set at variance God's love and His justice. We must remember that God is holy, righteous and just, as well as loving and kind, and that all His attributes control his actions. B. B. Warfield stated in this context:

> God is not part God, a God here and there, with some but not all the attributes which belong to true God: he is God altogether, God through and through, all that God is and all that God ought to be.[26]

Third, when the Univeralists speak of God's love, mercy and goodness, they do not speak of these things in terms of God's attributes as revealed in Scripture. A. W. Pink explains:

> There are many today who talk about the love of God, who are total strangers to the God of love. The Divine love is com-

monly regarded as a species of amiable weakness, a sort of good-
natured indulgence; it is reduced to a mere sticky sentiment,
patterned after human emotion.[27]

Fourth, merely to assert that God's love excludes eternal punishment but guarantees salvation does not prove anything. Where
is this ever stated in Scripture? Nowhere. Is this revealed in nature?
Hardly. The results of God's punishment for man's sin are visible
on every hand.

The attempt to base man's salvation solely upon God's attributes, such as His love or goodness, is unscriptural, for the Bible
never speaks of God's love except in the context of Christ's vicarious atonement (John 3:16; Rom. 5:8). Thus God's love, in and of
itself, cannot save anyone, much less all of humanity. None of
God's attributes, in and of themselves, can save anyone. Because
this is everywhere assumed in Scripture, Christ's atonement was
viewed as being absolutely necessary. After all, it is the manifes-
tation of God's love in Christ that saves sinners, not "love" as mere
sentiment.

Argument #2

The nature of man, i.e., his innate goodness and the possibility
of salvation in hell itself, guarantee that all men will be saved. It
also renders an eternal hell unthinkable, because all men will seek
reconciliation with God in the next life after they experience temporary punishment for their sins.

Answer

First, the Scriptures nowhere speak of any innate goodness in
man. After the historic fall of man into sin, all of humanity is viewed
as being sinners with no inherent goodness.

> As it is written, "There is none righteous, not even one; there
> is none who understands; there is none who seeks for God; all
> have turned aside, together they have become useless; there is
> none who does good, there is not even one. Their throat is an
> open grave, with their tongues they keep deceiving, the poison
> of asps is under their lips; whose mouth is full of cursing and
> bitterness; their feet are swift to shed blood, destruction and
> misery are in their paths, and the path of peace have they not
> known. There is no fear of God before their eyes. For all have
> sinned and fall short of the glory of God." (Rom. 3:10–18, 23)
> Therefore, just as through one man sin entered into the world,
> and death through sin, and so death spread to all men, because
> all sinned. (Rom. 5:12)
> And you were dead in your trespasses and sins, in which

> you formerly walked according to the course of this world, according to the prince of the power of the air, of the spirit that is now working in the sons of disobedience. Among them we too all formerly lived in the lusts of our flesh, indulging the desires of the flesh and of the mind, and were by nature children of wrath, even as the rest. (Eph. 2:1–3)

The Universalists always make light of sin and reduce it to "slips" or "mistakes" instead of viewing it as it really is—horrible rebellion against God.

Second, the Scriptures never speak of a second chance for repentance after death or resurrection. Instead, after death comes the judgment (Heb. 9:27). James Orr points out that the final judgment in Scripture "is decisive in its issues. Not a single suggestion is given of a reversal of its decisions in any future age."[28]

In Christ's parable in Luke 16:19–31, He clearly taught that there was no way for the rich man to escape his sufferings because between the wicked and the righteous "there is a great chasm fixed, in order that those who wish to come over from here to you may not be able, and that none may cross over from there to us" (v. 26).

Christ goes on to warn the rich man that his living brothers only had the opportunity of repentance while they were alive (vv. 29–31).

Throughout Scripture, the issue of salvation is limited to the lifetime of the hearer (Heb. 9:27; 3:15—4:11, etc.).

The urgency of the issue of salvation which was pressed on sinners in apostolic preaching cannot be ignored (2 Cor. 6:1, 2). This urgency can only be understood as being rooted in the conviction that once death takes place, there is no further opportunity for repentance or salvation. As Carl Henry states, the Scriptures are crystal clear that "a man's fate is finally settled at death and that eternal punishment awaits the wicked."[29]

While the Universalists claim that there is "hope" for those who died as unbelievers, the Apostle Paul states that for unbelievers there is "no hope" after they have died (1 Thess. 4:13). There can be written across the tombstone of every unbeliever the sobering words, "NO HOPE."

Third, the Universalists turn hell into a kind of purgatory where the wicked are cleansed or reformed by their sufferings. As Carl Henry has pointed out, the Scriptures never speak of hell as a kind of neo-Protestant purgatory, but always as the ultimate state of the lost.[30]

Fourth, after the fall, man no longer has an absolute "free will" because his will along with the rest of his nature is in bondage to sin. When man fell in sin, his whole being fell with him.

The Reformed doctrine of total inability or depravity does not mean that man is as evil as he can be. God's common grace prevents that from happening. Neither does it negate the kind acts which men do one for another.

What the Reformers, such as Luther in *The Bondage of the Will*,[31] were saying was that man is not able to please God while still in an unregenerate state. Man as sinner cannot merit or earn salvation. God does not owe salvation to anyone because he earned it through good works. Salvation is a free gift to ill-deserving as well as undeserving sinners (John 8:34; Rom. 8:7, 8; Eph. 2:1–3, 8, 9, etc.).

Reformation theology did not deny human responsibility or an objective choice set before sinners through the preaching of the cross. They are simply pointing out that both faith and repentance are the gifts of God, not the contributions of man (Acts 11:18; 18:27; Phil. 1:29; 2 Tim. 2:25).

Leaders of the Reformation, such as Luther and Calvin, interpreted the Scriptures as saying that we are not saved on the basis of the exercise of our wills. As a matter of fact, they claimed that this is directly contradicted in such Scriptures as the following:

> Who were born not of blood, nor of the will of the flesh, nor of the will of man, but of God. (John 1:13)
> So then it does not depend on the man who wills or the man who runs, but on God who has mercy. (Rom. 9:16)

Regeneration is an act of God alone and not a decision of man. Thus it was claimed that we are saved by God's grace and not by our own efforts.

> For by grace you have been saved through faith; and that not of yourselves, it is the gift of God; not as a result of works, that no one should boast. (Eph. 2:8, 9)

Thus, working from a Reformed view, repentance and faith are exercises of God's grace and not the result of man's will. Then there is no possibility that unregenerate sinners in hell will repent or believe. If God did not give them the gift of repentance and faith in this life which are necessary to come to Christ (John 6:45, 65), where is there any scripture to indicate that He is going to give such gifts to them in the next life?

The Universalists who appeal to their view of man's "free will" as the basis for salvation reveal that they actually believe in autosoterism, i.e., man alone can save himself without God's grace or assistance. This, historic Christianity, both Calvinist and Arminian, has always denied. Autosoterism is nothing more than heathenism according to B. B. Warfield:

> There is fundamentally only two doctrines of salvation; that

salvation is from God, and that salvation is from ourselves. The former is the doctrine of common Christianity; the latter is the doctrine of universal heathenism.[32]

Ultimately, the basis of man's salvation is not the exercise of his will but the unmerited grace of God which is established through the work of Christ. For had Christ not died, had provision for sin not been made, then faith or no faith, repentance or no repentance, man could not have been saved. This grace is nowhere in Scripture said to extend to the wicked in hell. While the *means* of man's salvation is his repentance and faith, nowhere in the Scriptures is it said God will honor such in hell. On the contrary, there is "no hope" after death (1 Thess. 4:13).

Argument #3

The words *olam, aion,* and *aionios* do not mean eternity or endlessness. Therefore "everlasting punishment" only means a temporary period of punishment.

Answer

We have dealt with this objection in our chapter on eternal torment. Like the annihilationists, the Universalists cannot accept the simple statements of scriptures such as "eternal punishment."

No one approaching the New Testament without preconceived opinions could get any other impression from the language on this subject than that the punishments of the wicked in hell are to be everlasting.[33]

Argument #4

We should approach the Scriptures with the initial assumption that all men are now saved. In this way, many tests of Scripture will be seen as supporting Universalism.

Answer

The argument of Barth, Punt and others that we should begin with the assumption that all men are saved[34] is erroneous because it is arbitrary and decides the issue before the text of Scripture is consulted.

Why should we arbitrarily assume that none, some or all men will be saved before checking the Scriptures? If hermenuetics mean anything, then we should not begin with any preconceived assumptions beyond that the Scriptures will answer our questions on this subject.

But there is actually a deeper assumption that the Universalists are making. Warfield explains:

> This question is certainly not to be facilely resolved by the simply assumption that God's mercy must be poured out on all alike, since otherwise not all men can be saved. The fundamental presupposition of such an assumption is no other than that God owes all men salvation, that is to say, that sin is not really sin and is to be envisaged rather as misfortune than ill-desert.[35]

Argument #5

The grace of God is triumphant and will issue in the ultimate salvation of all men.

Answer

This argument, which was popularized by Barth, is the attempt to use the Calvinistic concept of grace as a vehicle for Universalism.

In addition to the remarks already made in connection with the history of this attempt, the following points should be considered.

First, the Universalists have an unscriptural definition of grace. Grace is particularized in Scripture in terms of this or that sinner being the object of grace. When this particularism is removed and a corporate universality injected, grace loses its meaning.

In addition to this, grace loses its "gift" status when it is injected into the Universalists' scheme. Berkouwer explains:

> The error of universalism does not lie in glorifying God's grace, but in interjecting grace into a system of conclusions which is in conflict with grace as a sovereign gift.[36]

Once grace becomes something which God owes to all men, then it loses its "gift" character and takes on a "debt" significance. But the Scriptures are clear in their definition of grace that grace must be a free gift and not a debt (Rom. 4:1–5; 11:6).

Second, Universalism ignores the transition from wrath to grace which is everywhere described in Scripture (John 3:36; Eph. 2:1–4; 1 Thess. 1:10, etc.). Van Til comments:

> The criticism made by Reformed theologians may well be said to find its center in the idea that, in Barth's view, there is no transition from wrath to grace in history. . . . In other words, Barth's theology is said, in effect, to reject historic Christianity. The death of Christ on the cross is not that by which he, as our substitute, saves us from the wrath to come, for there is no wrath

in God that could issue in man's eternal death. The resurrection of Christ is not that event in history by which Christ arises from the dead for our justification; we are already justified in Christ. Thus, there is no place in history where God and man really confront one another.[37]

Third, Barth's concept of a universal and triumphant grace leads to insurmountable problems.

1. It is reductionistic because it absolutizes the objective elements in salvation and ignores the subjective elements.

2. It removes the significance of both faith and unbelief.

3. It takes away the urgency of the gospel by not calling men to a "yes" or "no" decision. It places this decision only in God's hands and proclaims that the decision has already been made.

4. It ignores the threat of the gospel that if sinners do not repent and believe, they will perish. Barthian Universalism cannot make any real threats.

5. The offense of the cross is removed because the exclusiveness and necessity of calling on Christ as the only way of salvation is rejected. Thus no offense remains.

6. There is no motivation for evangelism or missions if all men are already saved.

7. Biblical ethics is based on "the negative sanctions of eschatological penalty."[38] A coming eternal judgment is treated as a real future event in Scripture. Once this judgment is viewed as already being decided beforehand in Christ for all men, there is no eschatological judgment to avoid. The judgment becomes a "paper tiger."

8. If all are saved, how could we know that this salvation is gracious and not a necessity of God's nature? If He has done only what He has to do, then no glory ascends to God for this salvation.

9. The biblical distinctions between the saved vs. the lost; the sheep vs. the goats; the elect vs. the reprobate; those not under God's wrath vs. those under it; the church vs. the world; etc, make no sense whatsoever if Universalism is true. No attention is paid to passages such as Rom. 9:14–23, where Paul states that all of God's attributes are revealed and glorified because of the fact that there are two ultimate classes of people—those who repent and those who continue in their rebellion. Just as the eternal salvation of the "vessels of mercy" reveals the goodness, mercy and grace of God (Eph. 2:7), even so the eternal perdition of the "vessels of wrath" reveals the righteous wrath and power of God.

Argument #6

Church history reveals that the Jews and early Christians did not believe in eternal torment but in universal salvation.

Answer

We have dealt with this argument in the chapter on eternal torment. Pusey's refutation of Farrar still stands unanswered.

Argument #7

In Matt. 25:46, the word *kolasis* (punishment) refers only to temporary corrective suffering and not to eternal, punitive punishment. This is the meaning of the word in the Greek language.

Answer

Kolasis, according to Thayer (p. 353), "brings with it or has connected with it the thought of punishment." Arndt and Gingrich agree with Thayer (p. 441). There is no lexicographical evidence that *kolasis* in the Koine Greek of the New Testament reflects the rare meaning of correction which is found in Classical Greek. The argument is based on an ignorance of the distinction between Koine and Classical Greek.[39]

Argument #8

Christ died for all men; therefore all are saved. If Christ has truly redeemed all men and paid all that divine justice demands, then there is nothing more to be done.

Answer

When orthodox theologians speak of "Christ dying for the world" and "Christ died for man," they are speaking of the infinite sufficiency of Christ's death. After all, it is rather obvious that Christ's death is sufficient for all men. Being incarnate deity, His death has infinite merit. His atonement would be sufficient for a million worlds.

When the Universalist says "Christ died for all men," he illogically tries to draw the conclusion that all are saved. But there is no biblical or logical warrant or necessity that the infinite sufficiency of the atonement must result in an infinite application. Sufficiency and application are two different things.

A case in point is that while Origen and other early Universalists believed that Christ's death redeemed Satan and his demonic host, most modern Universalists do not extend the atonement to fallen angels. They are forced to accept the orthodox position that such passages as Heb. 2:16 indicate that Christ did not come to atone for the sins of angels but human beings. Thus Christ took upon himself a human nature—not an angelic nature.

No logical conclusion can be drawn from the sufficiency of the atonement beyond that it is sufficient.

When it comes to the subject of the extent of the atonement, regarding who will be saved, orthodox theologians disagree among themselves. Yet, even here the real issue is once again the sufficiency of the atonement.

When some theologians say that the extent of the atonement embraces all of humanity, they mean that it is hypothetically possible for all men to be saved, i.e., Christ has made salvation possible for all men because His death has infinite merit. They are not saying that salvation has been realized by the actual securing of the salvation of all men. Salvation is sufficient for all, but not divinely secured for all.

Other theologians hesitate to embrace the phrase, "Christ died for all men," out of fear that such language will lead to Universalism. But many theologians do not quarrel with this phrase, owing to such passages as 1 Tim. 2:4–6, 1 John 2:2 and 2 Pet. 3:9.

All orthodox theologians, both Calvinist and Arminian, believe in the free and universal offer of the gospel. The gospel is preached to all men because it is understood that salvation is sufficient for all and that God truly desires the salvation of all men. It is when we come to the extent of the application of the atonement that there are deeper conflicts within orthodoxy.

All orthodox systems agree that on the human side, the extent of the application of the atonement, is limited to those who believe in Jesus Christ. There is no way to avoid the hundreds of passages in Scripture where sinners are told that if they believe, they will not perish and if they don't believe, they will perish (see John 3:16).

The real issue now surfaces. While the Universalist absolutizes the objective elements of salvation such as election and grace and then repudiates the subjective elements such as the necessity of repentance and faith, we must not, in extreme reaction to this, absolutize the subjective elements such as faith and repentance. Both extremes do not do justice to the balance found in Scripture between divine sovereignty and human responsibility.

The Scriptures do not limit salvation to its objective or subjective elements but embrace both. God is sovereign but man must believe the gospel. The human and divine elements are often placed side by side in Scriptures. For example, in John 1:12, 13, we read:

> But as many as received Him, to them He gave the right [privilege] to become children of God, even to those who believe in His name, who were born not of blood, nor of the will of the flesh, nor of the will of man, but of God.

First, there is the subjective element of the necessity of receiving Christ in order to be given the privilege of becoming a child of God.

The Universalists should here note that all men are not the children of God, and God is not the Father of all men. Becoming a child of God is not a "right" which God owes man, but a "privilege" reserved for those who believe in Christ. The New Testament is clear that becoming a child of God is something which is determined on whether one believes in Jesus Christ. For example, in Gal. 3:26, we read, "For you are all sons of God through faith in Christ Jesus."

Second, there is also the objective element of God's grace in regeneration which does not depend on human action or will. Notice that in this text, both the human and divine elements are placed side by side. This indicates that the author did not feel any great contradiction or conflict between the two.

Or again, in John 6:37, we find the divine and human elements placed together once again, "All that the Father gives Me shall come to Me; and the one who comes to Me I will certainly not cast out."

All the ones who have been given to Christ will come to Him in faith because God is sovereign. The certainty of their coming does not negate the necessity that they must come individually, and no one who comes will be cast out.

Notice also that in this text, salvation is spoken of corporately and individually. In the text, we read that "all" will come to Christ. This does not negate that they must come "one by one."

Universalists always emphasize the corporate aspects of salvation. They deny that there is an individual aspect at all. They say that all men are elect in Christ and all men are saved in Christ in a corporate way. There is no necessity for each individual to come to a saving knowledge of Jesus Christ.

As an extreme reaction, some orthodox theologians have emphasized the particular or individual aspects of salvation to the exclusion of the corporate aspect. Since there are Scriptures which speak of sinners coming one by one, i.e., individually, they deny that God deals with His people corporately.

In the above text, we find that the Scripture never presents us with the dilemma of choosing between viewing salvation corporately or individually. The biblical position is that God's people are one and many at the same time.

We are once again faced with the philosophic problem of the one and the many. Hence, once again, there are those who reduce one to the other and present us with the dilemma of viewing God's people as one or many. But the Scriptures do not present such a dilemma. God's people are one and many at the same time.

The only biblical solution is to balance the objective and subjective elements in salvation. Divine sovereignty and human responsibility are both clearly taught in Scripture. There is no reason to reduce one to the other. The human and divine sides of salvation must be held together.

For centuries theologians have debated and sought to formulate a solution to the seeming conflict between the two sides of salvation. While some orthodox theologians believe this area is still open for discussion, many others such as Warfield have sought to demonstrate that no solution is clearly offered in Scripture and is actually insoluble. Many orthodox scholars would therefore urge us to accept the biblical balance in faith remembering that faith can swim when reason can no longer touch bottom.

Argument #9

Why would God punish finite sins with infinite torment? Doesn't it make better sense to give finite punishment for finite sins?

Answer

The problem with this argument is that we are not speaking of a finite God. The God of Scripture is infinite and since His salvation is eternal, even so His wrath is eternal. It is no more inconceivable that God rewards finite unbelief with infinite wrath than that He rewards finite faith with infinite bliss. To shut hell would be to shut heaven if this argument were true.

Argument #10

The New Testament clearly teaches Universalism in the following passages: John 1:9, 29; 12:32; Acts 3:21; Rom. 5:18; 1 Cor. 15:22, 28; 2 Cor. 5:19; Eph. 1:4, 10; Phil. 2:9, 10; Col. 1:19, 20; 1 Tim. 2:4; 4:10; Titus 2:11; Heb. 2:9, etc.

Answer

As we approach these passages, it would be helpful to remember that we must not take a text out of context but let Scripture interpret Scripture. It does not impress us, therefore, when Universalists like Andrews merely quote over a hundred texts in support of Universalism.[40] The mere quoting of a text does not establish anything.

First, there are texts which really do not have anything to do with the issue of how many sinners will be saved. For example,

John 1:9 which speaks of Christ being the only light, i.e., revelation, which man will ever have, does not, in the context, refer to Christ saving anyone, much less all men.[41]

Second, there are passages where the Universalist interpretation depends solely upon the simplistic and naïve assumption that the biblical words "all" and "world" mean every human being who ever lived or shall ever live (John 1:29; 12:32, etc.).

What the Universalists fail to observe is that biblical words should be interpreted in terms of how they are used. Once it is admitted that the words "all" and "world" are used in passages where they cannot mean all of humanity, the simplistic assumption of the Universalist must be rejected.

We must stress the importance of hermeneutics at this point. A word must not be arbitrarily defined. Its meaning must be established on the basis of its usage by the biblical authors.

The Universalist pours his own meaning into the biblical words "world" and "all." Whenever the Bible says that Christ died for "all" or for "the world," the Universalist will insist that these verses teach that Christ actually, completely redeemed or saved every sinner everywhere in all generations, including those in hell at the time Christ died. But to decide what these words mean without checking Scripture is to pour his own meaning into them.

When we examine how the Bible uses the words "all" and "world," we find that these words hardly ever refer to every sinner who ever lived. There are too many places where the words cannot mean this by any stretch of the imagination. In the following verses (KJV), wherever the words "all" and "world" appear, substitute them with the following Universalistic definition: "All sinners everywhere in all generations, past, present and future, including those in heaven and hell at the time Christ, died."

A. "world"

> And it came to pass in those days, that there went out a decree from Caesar Augustus, that all the world should be taxed. (Luke 2:2)
>
> He was in the world, and the world was made by him, and the world knew him not. (John 1:10)
>
> For there is no man that doeth any thing in secret, and he himself seeketh to be known openly. If thou do these things, shew thyself to the world. (John 7:4)
>
> If the world hate you, know that it hated me before it hated you. (John 15:18)
>
> I pray for them: I pray not for the world, but for them which thou hast given me; for they are thine. (John 17:9)
>
> Love not the world, neither the things that are in the world. If any man love the world, the love of the Father is not in him. (1 John 2:15)

And we know that we are of God, and the whole world lieth in wickedness. (1 John 5:19)

B. "all"

Then went out to him Jerusalem, and all Judea, and all the region round about Jordan, and were baptized of him in Jordan, confessing their sins. (Matt. 3:5, 6)
And ye shall be hated of all men for my name's sake: but he that endureth to the end shall be saved. (Matt. 10:22)
And there went out unto him all the land of Judea, and they of Jerusalem, and were all baptized of him in the river of Jordan, confessing their sins. (Mark 1:5)
And they came unto John, and said unto him, Rabbi, he that was with thee beyond Jordan, to whom thou barest witness, behold, the same baptizeth, and all men come to him. (John 3:26)

These verses should prove beyond any doubt that no one has the right to assume that such words as "all" or "world" mean every sinner who ever lived.

Third, there are passages which speak of Christ defeating His enemies and subduing all opposition to His kingdom (1 Cor. 15:22–28).

How the defeat of His enemies can be turned into their salvation is never explained by the Universalists. That He will subdue all men and demons cannot logically be used to argue that He will save all men and demons.

Fourth, there are passages which if read in the original language cannot be used legitimately by the Universalists.

In Acts 3:21, we read of "restoration of all things." The Universalists ever since Origen have seized upon the word *apokatastasis* in the text to teach that all men will be "restored," i.e., saved. Many Universalists have even called themselves "restorationists."

When we checked the lexicographical evidence, we found that *apokatastasis* does not mean that all men will be saved. The Greek word simply refers to God fulfilling all of those things which He had promised to do in the Old Testament Scriptures. In other words, Peter is referring to the coming of the messianic theocracy and the fulfillment of Old Testament prophecy (Thayer, p. 63). Thus, as J. A. Alexander pointed out, the word refers to the fulfillment of what God had spoken and not to the salvation of all sinners.[42]

Or again, in Phil. 2:10, we read that "every knee should bow." Notice that the text does not say "shall bow" but "should bow." The Universalists usually quote it as saying "shall" instead of "should" in order to interpret the passage as saying that all men will be saved.

In the original, the word *kamptw* is found in the third person singular aorist subjunctive mood. In this passage it is used in connection with *hina*, which means that *kamptw* is not describing a future event, but simply what ought or should take place. When the subjunctive is used with *ean*, then it refers to a future condition. But here, in Phil. 2:10, it is used with *hina*, which means a wish or desire on Paul's part that all men should acknowledge Christ.[43]

And, let us hasten to add, even if one chooses to ignore the grammar of the Greek text and state that all men "shall bow their knees" and acknowledge that Jesus Christ is Lord, this cannot logically be assumed to mean that they will bow their knees in salvation. They could be bowing in defeat as they acknowledge Christ's lordship as they go off into eternal perdition. If they will not acknowledge Him as Lord now, then they will do so on the "hot pavement" of hell.

The same thing can be said for the Universalists' attempt to use Heb. 2:9. While the English text states that Christ tasted death for "every man" (KJV), the Greek has no noun after the word "every."

What should we put into the empty space after the word "every"? Hermeneutically, we must recognize that the author did not place a noun at that point because he assumed that the reader would keep in mind of whom he had been previously speaking.

In the context, the author had been speaking of the people of God. He referred to them as "heirs of salvation" (KJV) in chapter 1:14 and later describes them as "sons" (Heb. 2:10), "brethren" (vv. 11, 12), "children" (vv. 13, 14), "the people [of God]" (v. 17), etc.

If we allow the context to supply the missing noun, then it would be "every heir," "every son," etc. There is nothing in the passage which would give any reason for a Universalistic interpretation.

Fifth, how do we interpret those passages where Christ is said to "sum up all things" (paraphrase; Eph. 1:10) and "reconcile all things" (Col. 1:20)?

In their respective contexts, these passages do not speak of the ultimate salvation of all men. The context reveals that Christ has accomplished all that is necessary for completing God's plan of salvation. He will return the natural order or reconcile it to the state of perfection and bliss in fulfillment of Old Testament prophecy. Thus, these passages merely speak of the coming of the Messianic Kingdom and figurative language is used to speak of its universal sway.

Sixth, many of the passages used by the Universalists cannot stand up to an exegetical analysis.

For example, it is said that Christ is called "the Savior of all men" in 1 Tim. 4:10. It is then urged, "How could Christ be called the Savior of all men if He has, in fact, not saved all men?"

First, in the context, it is God the Father and not Christ, who is described as the Savior (cf. 1 Tim. 1:1).

Second, this text refers to the work of the Father and not to the work of the Son. Therefore, there is no warrant to assume that Christ's atonement is being referred to at all.

Third, in the context, it is the Father's providential care or preservation of all men that is in focus. Thus God the Father is "the preserver" of all men, the providential ruler and preserver of all life. This has been pointed out by such commentators as Calvin, Fairbairn, and A. T. Robertson.

In summary, if all the passages which the Universalists use in their attempt to prove their position are examined in their respective context, and sound hermeneutical principles are utilized, the case for Universalism evaporates. They consistently ignore the grammar and the syntax of the Greek text and arbitrarily pour their own meanings into words.

Argument #11

What about the heathen? Surely God will not condemn them! For them faith and repentance are not essential for salvation. All men will be saved regardless if they are atheists, pantheists, or idolators.

Answer

The Universalist attempts to escape the necessity of repentance and faith by hurling what he thinks is an unanswerable objection to historic Christianity: "But, what about the heathen? Are you telling me that all those innocent people are going to hell? Even when they didn't have a chance?"

To many Universalists, the question of the heathen serves as a challenge to Christianity as well as an escape hatch from the claims of the gospel on their own conscience. If the heathen can make their way to heaven without believing in Jesus, the Universalist smugly assumes that he also can make his way to heaven without becoming a Christian.

The neo-orthodox takeover of the major denominations with their colleges and seminaries has flooded the liberal world with the teaching of Universalism. At the same time, neo-evangelicals have embraced and are propagating a semi-Universalism in which any sincere heathen who lives up to the light he has will be saved. They argue that God is too loving to damn those for whom Christ died and who never had a chance. We have talked with individuals from prominent evangelical colleges and seminaries who do not believe in the historic doctrine of the damnation of all unbelievers, including the heathen.

Perhaps the best way to begin is to clarify the question of the heathen.

> Can a sinner be saved from hell even though he does not believe in the true God or in Jesus Christ? Or, upon what grounds can a sinner claim admittance to heaven other than repentance toward God and faith in the Lord Jesus Christ? Are repentance and faith essential for salvation?

The popular Universalist answer is that the heathen will be saved from hell even though they do not believe in Jesus Christ. The supposed grounds of the heathen's claim to heaven rests upon three arguments.

1. If a sinner is sincere in whatever religion he believes in and he lives up to the light he has, it would be unjust for God to condemn him to hell.

2. If a sinner never heard the gospel, this means that he never had a chance to be saved. Therefore, it would be unjust for God to condemn someone who never had a chance.

3. We are condemned if and when we reject Jesus Christ and His gospel. It is obvious that those who have never heard of the gospel cannot be condemned for rejecting it! Therefore, it would be unjust for God to condemn the heathen.

The issue can be further clarified by observing that all unbelievers without exception can be placed into one of the following categories which describe the circumstances of their unbelief.

1. Ignorance: The geographic area in which the unbelievers live is so remote that the gospel message has never penetrated it. The unbelievers have absolutely no opportunity to hear the gospel even if they wanted to do so.

2. Neglect: The gospel has penetrated the area and is present and available to all, but some unbelievers neglect to hear or study it. Thus they are still ignorant of the gospel and are not saved due to their neglect.

3. Nominal acquaintance: The gospel is vaguely understood, but there is no true saving belief in it. The unbeliever denies or rejects the gospel and clings to his own pagan ideas and religion.

4. Nominal acceptance: The unbeliever professes to accept the gospel and to believe in Jesus Christ, but this profession is false.

Now, according to the popular conception of the issue, the question of the heathen concerns only the first case where sinners are ignorant of the gospel because there is absolutely no opportunity to hear it. The Scriptures are very clear that if we neglect, deny or only nominally accept the gospel, we cannot be saved (1 John 2:18, 19).

Another point that should be made is that the proper definition of "heathen" is any and every unbeliever. We must not allow people to assume that the word "heathen" refers only to the primitive peoples of the Third World. The unbelievers who live in New York City or London constitute the heathen just as much as the Hindus or Australian bushmen.

The basic and foundational issue in the heathen question is whether or not the Scriptures view ignorance due to neglect or to the absence of the gospel as constituting sufficient grounds for salvation. And, also, whether or not the lack of faith constitutes unbelief as well as the rejection of faith.

With these introductory remarks in mind, let us begin by setting forth several opening principles which shall guide us in our study.

Principle 1: The Scriptures alone can tell us of the eternal destiny of all those who do not believe in the person and work of Christ (Isa. 8:20; 2 Tim. 3:16).

Principle 2: We must be careful to avoid the three typical non-Christian approaches to this issue.

1. The person who is a rationalist thinks that his reason or logic can tell him where the heathen go at death. He usually begins his position by saying: "I think that . . ." "It is only logical that . . ." "The only intelligent answer is . . ."

2. The person who is experience-centered thinks that stories and testimonies which relate human experience will decide the issue. He usually will tell some groundless story which is incapable of verification about some heathen somewhere who supposedly worshiped the true God without actually knowing who or what He really was, or who had angels or Jesus appear to him in dreams or visions. He usually begins his position by saying, "Have you heard the story about . . ."

3. The person who is a mystic will trust his subjective emotions or feelings to tell him the truth. He usually begins his position by saying, "I feel that . . ."

Principle 3: Defend God at all costs.

Whatever God does is right and just. Do not the Scriptures teach us that "Shall not the Judge of all the earth deal justly?" (Gen. 18:25). God is not unjust or unloving because He casts the wicked into hell. He is sovereign in His wrath as well as in His grace (Rom. 9:13–23).

Some people defend man at all costs even to the degradation of God. "Rather, let God be found true and every man be found a liar" (Rom. 3:4).

Principle 4: Never tone down a biblical doctrine because it offends people.

The gospel itself can be offensive to unbelievers (1 Cor. 1:18–23). Should we abandon it because the unregenerate think it foolish?

The disciples came to the Lord Jesus and told Him that He had offended the Pharisees. His reaction shows us the proper attitude when the truth offends people.

> Then came his disciples, and said unto him, Knowest thou that the Pharisees were offended, after they heard this saying? But he answered and said, Every plant, which my heavenly Father hath not planted, shall be rooted up. Let them alone: they be blind leaders of the blind. And if the blind lead the blind, both shall fall into the ditch. (Matt. 15:12–14, KJV)

Principle 5: Take one step at a time.

There are many issues involved in the heathen question which must be answered before the final answer is given.

Principle 6: Determine in your spirit to believe whatever God says in His Word, for "if any man is willing to do His will, he shall know of the teaching, whether it is of God" (John 7:17).

We must be careful that we approach the heathen issue with an open mind and a humble heart in utter submission to the authority of Scripture.

With these opening principles completed, we will now set forth the central propositions of our position.

Proposition 1: All men are lost sinners and in need of salvation.

This first proposition is so basic to the Christian gospel that it is impossible to deny its scripturality. Carefully read Rom. 1—3, for we find in this passage a full exposition of the just condemnation of God which rests universally upon all men, "for all have sinned"; and "the wages of sin is death" (Rom. 3:23; 6:23).

Proposition 2: General revelation is not sufficient for salvation.

General revelation is that mute nonverbal witness of the creation that points men to the existence and power of God and to man's own creatureliness and sinfulness. General revelation confronts all men at all times through the world around them and the voice of their conscience within them (Rom. 1:18–28; 2:14, 15).

While general revelation is sufficient to condemn all men because it leaves all mankind "without excuse" (Rom. 1:20), the Scriptures never speak of it as being sufficient to save anyone. In the Bible, salvation is tied to the gospel and the gospel comes to us only in God's special revelation, the Holy Scriptures (Rom. 10:17).

It must be further pointed out that the Bible teaches that no sinner has ever perfectly lived up to the light of general revelation. All men suppress and reject the light of creation and worship the creature instead of the Creator (Rom. 1:18, 21–25, 28). Thus, there never has been and there never shall be a sinner who lives up to all the light he receives from general revelation (Rom. 3:10–18).

Proposition 3: The fact of judgment is determined on the basis of the nature and the actions of the person in question.

Because all men are "by nature" sinners, all men are under the wrath of God (Eph. 2:3).

The doctrine of original sin involves the imputation of Adam's sin to all mankind. This imputation is followed by the condemnation of God and the judgment of death (see Ps. 51:5; 58:3; Rom. 5:12–21; 1 Cor. 15:22). It is, of course, recognized that some Christians would consider Ps. 58:3 as hyperbole, and interpret it as meaning that man chooses to "go his own way" by consciously yielding to temptation when an age of accountability or moral understanding is reached.

Many theologians believe that we sin because we are sinners, and that what we are by nature determines the fact of judgment. Whether this "nature" is acquired by sin, or sin is committed because of this nature, all agree that it is wrong to teach that we are lost only if and when we reject Christ. The gospel is preached to those who are already lost and perishing (1 Cor. 1:18). Judgment will come because of what you are and what you have done.

The heathen are condemned because of what they are and what they do, i.e., their nature and their deeds. They are sinners. Therefore, they are under God's wrath.

Proposition 4: The degree of punishment is determined on the basis of the light and life of the person in question.

As we pointed out in a previous chapter, because God is just, there will be degrees of punishment in hell. All sinners in hell will be perfectly miserable but not equally miserable.

In determining the degree of punishment in hell, our Lord takes into account the words (Matt. 12:36, 37) and works (Matt. 16:27; Rev. 20:11–15; 22:12) of sinners.

Disobedience and unbelief due to ignorance do not deliver one from punishment, for ignorance of the Law is no excuse (Lev. 5:17). But sins done in ignorance will not receive as much punishment as sins done consciously in violation of known law (Luke 12:47, 48).

The more one knows, the more responsible he is to live up to that light. The greater the responsibility, the greater the punishment. Certain cities were liable to more divine punishment because they actually saw and heard the Christ, yet refused Him (Matt. 10:5; 11:20–24). The writer to the Hebrews speaks of some people receiving more punishment than others (Heb. 10:29). The sin of the Pharisees was made greater by their contact with Christ (John 15:22).

While the fact of judgment is determined by what we are, i.e., our nature, the degree of punishment is determined on the basis of the amount of true knowledge we have received and the quality of life that we lived (Rom. 2:3–6).

Proposition 5: The explicit teaching of Scripture is that the only way to escape the wrath of God is to believe in the Lord Jesus Christ. (All following quotations taken from KJV.)

> Look unto me, and be ye saved, all the ends of the earth: for I am God, and there is none else. (Isa. 45:22)
>
> He that believeth on the Son hath everlasting life; and he that believeth not the Son shall not see life; but the wrath of God abideth on him. (John 3:36)
>
> I am the door: by me if any man enter in, he shall be saved. (John 10:9)
>
> Jesus saith unto him, I am the way, the truth, and the life: no man cometh unto the Father, but by me. (John 14:6)
>
> Neither is there salvation in any other: for there is no other name under heaven given among men, whereby we must be saved. (Acts 4:12)
>
> Whom God hath set forth to be a propitiation through faith in his blood, to declare his righteousness for the remission of sins that are past, through the forebearance of God; to declare, I say, at this time his righteousness: that he might be just, and the justifier of him which believeth in Jesus. Seeing it is one God, which shall justify the circumcision by faith, and uncircumcision through faith. (Rom. 3:25, 26, 30)
>
> For other foundation can no man lay than that is laid, which is Jesus Christ. (1 Cor. 3:11).
>
> For there is one God, and one mediator between God and men, the man Christ Jesus. (1 Tim. 2:5)

Proposition 6: All non-Christian religions are condemned in Scripture because they: (a) are idolatrous. Pagan religions are not man's search for God, but they are actually man's rejection of God (Rom. 1:18–25); (b) actually give worship to Satan and his demons (1 Cor. 10:19–22); and (c) fail to find God through the wisdom of this world (1 Cor. 1:18–31).

The heathen are not worshiping the true God in their pagan religions. We reject the false idea that all religions are just different roads to God. All unbelievers are idolators.

Proposition 7: The absence of special revelation does not in any way relieve the heathen from perishing, as they have already willfully rejected whatever light they have previously received (Rom. 1:18–32).

The fact that they die physically reveals that God views them as sinners and that they face a Christless eternity in the second death. (All quotations from KJV.)

> For there is no respect of persons with God. For as many as have sinned without law shall also perish without law. In the

day when God shall judge the secrets of men by Jesus Christ according to my gospel. (Rom. 2:11, 12, 16)

For all have sinned, and come short of the glory of God. (Rom. 3:23)

Wherefore, as by one man sin entered into the world, and death by sin; and so death passed upon all men, for that all have sinned. (Rom. 5:12)

For the wages of sin is death; but the gift of God is eternal life through Jesus Christ our Lord. (Rom. 6:23)

Proposition 8: The Scriptures teach that all unbelievers will be cast into the lake of fire when Jesus returns in glory and power (see Matt. 25:41, 46; Rev. 21:8).

2 Thess. 1:8 tells us about the fate of those who do not know God.

> And to you who are troubled rest with us, when the Lord Jesus shall be revealed from heaven with his mighty angels, in flaming fire taking vengeance on them that know not God, and that obey not the gospel of our Lord Jesus Christ: who shall be punished with everlasting destruction from the presence of the Lord, and from the glory of his power; when he shall come to be glorified in his saints, and to be admired in all them that believe (because our testimony among you was believed) in that day. (2 Thess. 1:7–10, KJV).

Proposition 9: Unbelievers must hear or read of the Lord Jesus Christ through a human instrumentality in order to be saved.

The gospel does not come to us from angels, visions, or dreams. God has committed unto the church the privilege and responsibility of spreading the gospel (Matt. 28:19, 20; Acts 1:8; Rom. 10:13–17).

Proposition 10: God will always send the gospel by a human instrument to those whose hearts are open to the gospel message.

Cornelius is a good example of how God will send the gospel to those who respond to even limited light.

The angel which came to Cornelius did not give him the gospel, for unto angels this ministry was never committed. The angel told Cornelius to send for Peter so that Cornelius would hear the gospel and be saved.

> And he shewed us how he had seen an angel in his house, which stood and said unto him, Send men to Joppa, and call for Simon, whose surname is Peter; who shall tell thee words, whereby thou and all thy house shall be saved. (Acts 11:13, 14, KJV)

Cornelius obeyed the angel, and when Peter came and preached the gospel, then, and not until then, was Cornelius saved (Acts 10:44–48). Cornelius was a moral and God-fearing man (Acts 10:1,

2). Yet, he was not saved until the gospel came and he placed his faith in Jesus Christ.

Proposition 11: If salvation is possible through ignorance or neglect of the gospel, then Jesus Christ died in vain, i.e., for nothing.

His death was unnecessary and a mockery if salvation can be obtained by any other manner than by believing in Him (Gal. 2:21).

Proposition 12: A survey of the history of redemption reveals that ignorance, neglect, and nominal acquaintance or acceptance were never sufficient grounds to deliver anyone from the just wrath of God against sin.

A. *The Flood.*

Man sinned (Gen. 6:1–5, 11–13) and God's judgment came upon him for his sin (Gen. 6:6, 7, 13, 17). Only the believer Noah and his family were delivered from God's wrath (Gen. 6:8–10, 14–16, 18–22).

Question: Were there any ignorant, sincere and neglectful people in Noah's day? What happened to them? If we asked Noah about the fate of all unbelievers in his day regardless if they were ignorant or neglectful, what would he say? Is the Flood a pre-picture of the judgment day at the second coming of Jesus Christ? (Matt. 24:37–39; 2 Pet. 2:5, 9). Since all the heathen (unbelievers) without exception perished under the flood waters of God's wrath, what does this tell us about God's judgment on unbelievers when Christ returns? All unbelievers will perish regardless if they are ignorant or neglectful.

B. *The Tower of Babel.*

Man sinned and God's judgment came upon him (Gen. 11). This judgment took two forms.

First, human language was diversified. Second, the human race was scattered.

Question: Were there any sincere, ignorant or neglectful people working on the tower? What happened to them? Is it not the case that the two major reasons why some men are ignorant of the gospel correspond exactly to God's two judgments, i.e., different languages and mankind's having been scattered over the face of the earth?

C. *Sodom and Gomorrah.*

Man sinned (Gen. 18:20, 21; 19:1–9) and God's judgment came upon him (Gen. 19:10, 11, 23–29). Only the believer Lot and his two daughters were delivered from the fire and brimstone.

Question: Were there any sincere, ignorant, and neglectful people living in these cities? What happened to them? Abraham said that "Shall not the judge of all the earth deal justly?" (Gen. 18:25). What did God do with all the unbelievers in Sodom and

Gomorrah? If we asked Abraham and Lot about the eternal fate of all unbelieving sinners, what would they say? Is the destruction of these cities a pre-picture of the coming destruction on the day of judgment? (Luke 17:28–30; 2 Pet. 2:5–9; Jude 7). What significance does this have on the heathen question?

D. *The history of God's people.*

1. God's judgment upon Egypt at the time of the Exodus. Were there any sincere, ignorant, and neglectful Egyptians? Were they saved from the judgment plagues of God? Were only the firstborn of these who believed God's warning safe from the angel of death, or did the angel pass over any houses where the people were sincere, ignorant, or neglectful?

2. God's commandment to Israel. Was idolatry allowed in Israel? What was the penalty for idolatry? (Deut. 13). Was there any difference in the sight of the law whether the idolator was sincere, ignorant, or neglectful? (Lev. 5:17). If sincere or ignorant idol worship saved one from the judgment of God, this would make true worship meaningless. How would Moses answer the question of the heathen?

3. God's destruction of the Canaanites. To what fate did God assign the Canaanites? (Josh. 9:24, etc.). Were there any sincere, ignorant or neglectful Canaanites? What happened to them? How would Joshua answer our question?

4. God's deliverance of Rahab. Was Rahab a Canaanite? Why was she delivered while the rest were destroyed? (Josh. 2:8–13). Were the only ones delivered from destruction those who believed in Jehovah? How would Rahab answer our question?

5. God's view of the nations. How did Israel view the idolatrous nations around them? (Ps. 9:17). What happens to those who do not bow to Jehovah? (Ps. 2:11, 12).

6. The conversion of Ruth. How, and why, did Ruth join the people of God? Does she not serve to show how Gentiles were saved in Old Testament times? How could they be saved? How would Ruth answer the heathen question?

E. *Jonah and Nineveh.*

Were there any sincere, ignorant, or neglectful people in Nineveh? What fate had God assigned them? Why did the judgment turn away? How would Jonah answer the question of the heathen?

F. *Jesus Christ.*

Did He ever claim to be the only way of salvation? (John 14:6). What did He call false religious leaders? (John 10:8). Did He state that only faith in Him will deliver one from the judgment of God? (John 3:16, 36). How would He answer if we asked Him about the heathen?

G. *The Apostles.*

Did they teach that only faith in Christ saves? (Acts 4:12; 10:43; 16:31; Rom. 5:1; 10:9–13). Did they ever teach that there is no salvation outside of the gospel? (Rom. 10:14–17). Is Christ the only mediator between God and man? (1 Tim. 2:5). How would they answer the question of the heathen?

H. *Missions.*

Are we commanded to preach the gospel to all men? (Mark 16:15, 16). Why? Do they need it? If the ignorant and sincere can be saved as long as they don't hear the gospel, do missionaries actually damn more than they save? Would it not be cruel to introduce the gospel to ignorant people? If men were not already lost and without hope, would missions make any sense?

Here are some answers to those who think God unjust in condemning the heathen.

1. We dare not accuse God of being unjust in whatever He does! The Apostle Paul rebukes such a rebellious attitude in Rom. 9:11–24.

If the righteous Judge of all the earth has revealed in His Word that all the heathen will be cast into the lake of fire (Rev. 20:15), who is the man that can condemn God? For if human governments recognize the necessity of preserving law and order by judgment upon law-breakers, how much more must "the Judge of all the earth!"

2. Sincerity in living up to some of the light one has will only make one a candidate for further light as it did for Cornelius in Acts 10. But Cornelius had to be saved through the gospel given by a human messenger (Acts 11:14). Not even the angel could tell Cornelius the gospel. Sincerity in and of itself is not enough, though, as in the case of Cornelius, God will respond to anyone who seeks Him (Acts 17:26, 27).

3. As sinners, the only thing we deserve is God's eternal wrath in hell. The Bible does not teach that God owes us anything or that we even deserve a chance to be saved. It teaches that we don't in any sense deserve to be saved. Salvation is by *grace*. This means that God does not owe anyone anything (Rom. 4:1–5). God does not have to save anyone at all. It is all of grace.

CONCLUSION

Throughout our study of immortality and eternal punishment, we have pointed out such texts as Matt. 12:31, 32; 25:46; 26:24; Mark 8:36–38; Heb. 9:27, which should rule out the Universalist's scheme. While the dream of the Universalist is a pleasant and comforting one, it is not scripturally correct. The gospel is both good news and bad news: Good news in that "whoever believes shall be saved" and bad news in that "whoever does not believe shall be condemned."

The Universalist actually cheapens and weakens the gospel by pulling out its fangs of a final, irreversible, eschatological judgment. It is only upon the black background of eternal punishment that the brilliant jewel of eternal salvation can be appreciated for all that it is. God's grace can be appreciated only to the extent that we understand the depths of God's wrath.

NOTES

1. McCLintock and Strong, Vol. X, p. 658.

2. P. Schaff, *History of the Christian Church,* Vol. 2, pp. 782f.

3. See: Clement, Fragments, No. 6, Melissa, A.N.F., Vol. 2, p. 580.

For Clements' Universalism, see *Anti-Nicean Fathers,* Vol. 3, Stromata, bk. 7, ch. 6.

4. McClintock and Strong, ibid.

5. See Pusey's discussion of the evidence in *What Is of Faith as to Everlasting Punishment?* pp. 136f.

6. McClintock and Strong, Vol. X, p. 659.

7. I.S.B.E., Vol. IV, p. 2503.

8. A. Dallimore, *George Whitefield* (London: Banner of Truth Trust, 1970).

9. H. Cheetman, *Unitarianism and Universalism* (Boston: Beacon Press, 1902), p. 82.

10. Ibid., p. 87.

11. E. Cassara, *Hosea Ballou* (Boston: Beacon Press, 1961).

12. Cheetman, ibid., p. 89.

13. J. Gerstner, *Jonathan Edwards on Heaven and Hell* (Grand Rapids: Baker Book House, 1980); *The Works of Jonathan Edwards* (London: Banner of Truth Trust, 1974), Vol. I, p. 668; Vol. II, pp. 7, 78, 80, 83, 122, 125, 190–200, 207–212, 515*, 878; T. Dwight, *Dwight's Theology* (New Haven: S. Converse, 1825), Vol. IV, pp. 456f.

14. Charles G. Finney, *Charles G. FInney: An Autobiography* (New York: Fleming H. Revell, 1876), pp. 48–51.

15. G. Machen, *Christianity and Liberalism* (Grand Rapids: Wm. B. Eerdmans Pub. Co., 1923), pp. 122–132.

16. See: R. Nash, *The New Evangelicalism* (Grand Rapids: Zondervan Pub. House, 1963), pp. 35, 46, 51.

17. See: H. Lindsell, *The Battle for the Bible* (Grand Rapids: Zondervan Pub. House, 1976).

18. C. Van Til, *Karl Barth and Evangelicalism* (Philadelphia: Pres. & Ref. Pub. Co., 1965), p. 32.

19. C. Van Til, *The New Modernism* (New Jersey: Pres. & Ref. Pub. Co., 1973), pp. 75, 103, 157, 346; C. Brown, *Karl Barth and the Christian Message* (Chicago: InterVarsity, 1967), pp. 130f.; H. Whitney, *The New "Myth"-ology* (New Jersey: Pres. & Ref. Pub. Co., 1969), pp. 75f., etc.

20. G. Berkouwer, *The Triumph of Grace in the Theology of Karl Barth* (Grand Rapids: Wm. B. Eerdmans Pub. Co., 1956), p. 116.

21. B.B. Warfield, *The Plan of Salvation* (Grand Rapids: Wm. B. Eerdmans Pub. Co., 1977), pp. 71, 72.

22. C. VanTil, *Karl Barth and Evangelicalism*, p. 38.

23. N. Punt, *Unconditional Good News* (Grand Rapids: Wm. B. Eerdmans Pub. Co., 1980), p. 135.

24. R. Morey, *Reincarnation and Christianity* (Minnesota: Bethany House Pub., 1980).

25. Machen, ibid., p. 12.

26. Warfield, ibid., p. 74.

27. A.W. Pink, *The Attributes of God* (Grand Rapids: Baker Book House), p. 90.

28. I.S.B.E., Vol. IV, p. 2502.

29. C. Henry, *Christian Personal Ethics* (Grand Rapids: Baker Book House, 1957), p. 556.

30. C. Henry, *Evangelicals in Crisis*, p. 27.

31. M. Luther, *The Bondage of the Wall* (New Jersey: Fleming H. Revell Co., 1957).

32. Warfield, ibid., p. 33.

33. McClintock and Strong, Vol. VIII, p. 790.

34. Punt, ibid., p. 1.

35. Warfield, ibid., p. 72.

36. Berkouwer, ibid., p. 362.

37. C. VanTil, *Christianity and Barthianism* (Philadelphia: Pres. & Ref. Pub. Co., 1965), p. 117.

38. C. Henry, *Christian Personal Ethics*, p. 555.

39. F. Bruce, *Answers to Questions*, p. 61.

40. L. Andrews, *The Two Opinions* (Macon, Ga. N.P., 1837).

41. R. Lenski, *The Interpretation of St. John's Gospel* (Minnesota: Augsburg Pub. House, 1969), p. 52.

42. J.A. Alexander, *Commentary on the Acts of the Apostles* (Grand Rapids: Zondervan Pub. House, 1956), p. 117.

43. G. Machen, *New Testament Greek for Beginners* (New York: The Macmillan Co., 1923), pp. 132, 197.

Chapter 10

OCCULTISM

In Chapter 6, we presented a brief historical overview of how certain rituals or practices such as séances, where mediums attempt to communicate with the spirits of the dead, were first viewed during the Middle Age as witchcraft and were punishable by death. Then as it became an organized religion in the early 19th century, witchcraft was renamed spiritualism, spiritism or theosophy. It had hundreds of thousands of followers. Later in that same century, spiritualism was renamed once again. This time it was called "psychic studies" by such groups as The Society of Psychical Research (SPR).

The SPR attempted to investigate all "psychic" experiences and either prove them fraudulent or valid according to scientific procedures.

In the 20th century during the 1950s, J. B. Rhine and others brought the aims and procedures of the SPR into the scientific community itself. Alson Smith correctly points out that

> Psychical research rode into the camp of Science on the coattails of psychology and when it got there it changed its name to "parapsychology."[1]

Parapsychology was, of course, hailed as a "new" science and, as Gary North rightly points out, none dared call it witchcraft.[2]

Although, as we have previously pointed out, there was nothing "new" about the practices which were being investigated, witchcraft or spiritualism had been secularized by simply dropping all the religious terminology and relabeling everything with secular terms.

Thus, the Christian is faced today with occultic writers outside of the church who state that parapsychology is neutral toward all religions, and Christianity is not really opposed to it at all.[3] Even within the church, there are clergymen involved in Spiritual Frontiers, which is a spiritualist organization operating within mainline Protestant denominations. There are even theologians who encourage Christians to get involved in psychic studies and develop their ESP potentials.[4]

Séances

One example of the influence of "witchcraft" or parapsychology within the Christian Church is Bishop Pike's attempt to communicate with the spirit of his dead son by attending séances held by Arthur Ford and other spiritistic mediums.[5] When a bishop in the Episcopal church goes to mediums for answers instead of going to the God of Scripture, we cannot but remember that King Saul attempted this in his own day. Also, we cannot but be amazed when we realize that the bishop and his mediums would have been put to death only a few centuries ago for their involvement in witchcraft.

That a cult leader like Moon would attend séances with Arthur Ford is not surprising considering the fact that he has always claimed to be a witch or shaman. But when a bishop in a Christian church attends séances and is not officially excommunicated, we are utterly astonished.

Of course, we are aware that some people like Bishop Pike claim that the Bible does not condemn such things as séances. Let us, therefore, examine the pertinent scriptures which speak to these issues and see for ourselves what the Bible has to say.

The Biblical Material

The pagan religions which surrounded Israel utilized mediums whose function was to contact the spirits of the departed in order to obtain answers to the questions which usually concerned the future.[6]

Just before Israel entered the promised land, God gave the following warning:

> "When you enter the land which the Lord your God gives you, you shall not learn to imitate the detestable things of those nations. There shall not be found among you anyone who makes his son or his daughter pass through the fire, one who uses divination, one who practices witchcraft, or one who interprets omens, or a sorcerer, or one who casts a spell, or a medium, or a spiritist, or one who calls up the dead. For whoever does these things is detestable to the Lord; and because of these detestable things the Lord your God will drive them out before you. For those nations, which you shall dispossess, listen to those who practice witchcraft and to diviners, but as for you, the Lord your God has not allowed you to do so." (Deut. 18:9–12, 14)

In the above passage, Moses used every contemporary word which had anything to do with the occult arts of the pagans who lived in the promised land. He could not have been clearer in his condemnation of such practices.

Among the practices which Moses condemned was mediumship. In the Hebrew text there are two words which encompassed all attempts to contact departed souls in the netherworld.

First, Moses condemned the attempt to contact *ohy*. This Hebrew word, which is incorrectly translated "medium" in the NASB, actually means "departed spirits or souls."[7] It is used 15 times in the Old Testament to refer to the spirits in the netherworld.[8]

Second, the word *yid-dgohnee* is always put after *ohy* where the attempt to contact the spirits is through a medium. Thus the word *yid-dgohnee* should have been translated "medium." It is referred to 11 times in the Old Testament.[9]

Given the universal condemnation of any and all attempts to contact the spirit world, the passages where these words are used can be legitimately applied to Ouija boards, pendulums, spells, signs, etc., as well as to séances. Any attempt to contact the dead is an abomination to God.

Let the reader pause to examine the following sample passage.

> "Do not turn to mediums or spiritists; do not seek them out to be defiled by them. I am the Lord your God." (Lev. 19:31)
> So Saul died for his trespass which he committed against the Lord, because of the word of the Lord which he did not keep; and also because he asked counsel of a medium, making inquiry of it. (1 Chron. 10:13)
> And when they say to you, "Consult the mediums and wizards who whisper and mutter," should not a people consult their God? Should they consult the dead on behalf of the living? (Isa. 8:19, 20)

The sin of consulting mediums or spirits was grave enough to warrant the death penalty (Lev. 20:27). It was connected with all the other black arts such as astrology and human sacrifice (2 Kings 21:5, 6). The practice of consulting mediums appeared when Israel fell into idolatry, and disappeared whenever the revival of true religion took place (2 Kings 23:24).

Mediumship was not only forbidden by divine law, but it was revealed to be futile because once the spirit of a person passed into the netherworld, that spirit could not return until the resurrection.

> "When a cloud vanishes, it is gone, so he who goes down to Sheol does not come up. He will not return again to his house, nor will his place know him any more." (Job 7:9, 10)
> "Before I go—and I shall not return—to the land of darkness and deep shadow." (Job 10:21)
> "But now he has died; why should I fast? Can I bring him back again? I shall go to him, but he will not return to me." (2 Sam. 12:23)

The Septuagint translates *ohy* and *yid-dgohnee* as *eggastrimuthos* which is the Greek word for "ventriloquist."

The Greek mediums were noted for strange or multiple voices coming out of their bodies at different places or from nearby objects such as jars or pots. These voices claimed to be the spirit or soul which the medium contacted to answer the question of the one who consulted the medium.

In the New Testament, the general word "sorcery" (Gal. 5:19–21; Rev. 21:8) embraced all of the occult arts. Mediumship was understood in terms of demon possession. Thus the customer was deceived by the demon in the medium into thinking that it was the departed spirit of the loved one. The Apostle Paul dealt with such a medium.

> And it happened that as we were going to the place of prayer, a certain slave-girl having a spirit of divination met us, who was bringing her masters much profit by fortunetelling. Following after Paul and us, she kept crying out, saying, "These men are bond-servants of the Most High God, who are proclaiming to you the way of salvation." And she continued doing this for many days. But Paul was greatly annoyed, and turned and said to the spirit, "I command you in the name of Jesus Christ to come out of her." And it came out at that very moment. (Acts 16:16–18)

From the above passage, it is clear that mediumship was a species of fortune-telling and a money-making racket then as well as now. The attempt of some to deny that the girl was demon possessed and to state that she was only a ventriloquist is impossible, because, as Meyer points out, Luke as well as Paul "regards this condition of hers as that of demonic."[10] In verse 18, Paul casts out the demon and the girl is freed from her bondage to it. Nevius, in *Demon Possession* (Kregel, 1968), gives multiple examples of modern parallels to Acts 16:16–18.

The New Testament authors assumed that once one passed into the netherworld, he remained there until the resurrection (1 Thess. 4:13–17). When the rich man in Hades asked that Lazarus be allowed to return to warn his brothers, this was denied (Luke 16:27–31). Although popular superstition believed in ghostly visits (Luke 24:37), there is no indication that this was a teaching of Scripture.

Let the reader here note what is stated in Luke 16:30, 31:

> "But he said, 'No, Father Abraham, but if someone goes to them from the dead, they will repent!' But he said to him, 'If they do not listen to Moses and the Prophets, neither will they be persuaded if someone rises from the dead.' "

True saving faith will never be produced by occultic events

such as ghostly apparitions. If someone will not believe in the gospel through the Scriptures, then all the occult evidences in the world will never produce true faith.

Everald Feilding (1867–1936) is an excellent example of this truth. Originally a professing Christian, his faith was badly shaken when his favorite sister died in 1895. He began to suffer from religious doubts and turned to the SPR for help. His biography points out:

> Assailed by religious doubts, he saw in psychical research a possible means by which mere faith in survival after death might be supported by scientifically collected evidence.[11]

Feilding spent the rest of his life attending séances in the hope of regaining his faith. Each time he thought he had at last found a true medium, he ultimately realized he had been deceived. He died having never come to a true knowledge of Jesus Christ or his salvation, which is by faith alone.

Additional Considerations

Even if one rejects the condemnation of Scripture, the claim of mediums that they can contact the spirit world is highly questionable on rational grounds.

First, we have only the medium's word, and there is no way to verify if the medium is telling the truth.

Second, fraud has been discovered in so many instances that the burden of proof rests on the medium to prove his case. Thus, we need not disprove spiritism because the burden of proof is on their shoulders and nothing yet has been submitted as proof that a competent magician cannot duplicate by trickery.

Third, mediums admit the existence of evil or bad spirits who will lie if given the chance.[12] If they exist, how can it be known if a lying spirit is pretending to be the spirit of a departed relative, or if the spirit of the loved one is speaking?

The above considerations alone render the practice of mediumship worthless so far as proving survival after death.

LIFE AFTER LIFE

When the work *Life After Life* appeared in 1975, both Moody and Kübler-Ross were propelled into the public spotlight. Here were two professionals in the medical field who risked the anger of the materialist establishment to put forth exciting "new" evidence which seemed to establish that man's conscious mind, or ego, survives the death of the body.

After the initial excitement died down, certain questions naturally arose. For example, is the "life after life" concept related to the "out-of-body experiences" (OBE) which those in the occult have claimed to have experienced through drugs, meditation, mediumship, or hypnosis? Are the leaders of the "life after life" teaching involved in spiritualism? In other words, are we simply being fed SPR material as some "new" discovery?

Both Moody and Kübler-Ross worked closely with Robert Monroe, who is the head of a cultic/occultic group called "M-5000." Monroe has been experimenting with "OBE" since the 1960s and is heavily involved in Eastern mysticism. Kübler-Ross is on the board of directors of M-5000, and she herself is so entrenched in the religion of spiritualism that she claims she has "spirit guides" who help her in her work.[13] Moody is involved with spirit beings as well.[14]

Have Moody and Kübler-Ross mislabeled the experiences which they relate in their books? They call these experiences "after death experiences" and speak of people as being "dead." But is this really accurate?

The people were not "dead" for hours or days but only officially "dead" for minutes. Death is abstractly defined for legal purposes, and no one has ever defined the exact moment and criteria of death. Is it not more reasonable to call these experiences "near death experiences"? After all, there is a great difference between being dead and being near death.

Even "near death experience" is not really accurate. People can go to Monroe's M-5000 and for a fee have an out-of-body experience, or astral projection, any time they want it. People who used many drugs such as LSD have frequently talked about their OBE's.[15] Eastern mystics have claimed that they were able to leave their bodies at will through meditation and yoga. Would it not be better just to call them "out-of-body experiences"? Not even Moody or Kübler-Ross deny that people can "feel" that they have left their bodies as a side effect of various drugs.[16] Even the lack of oxygen can cause hallucinations.

Is there not the possibility of demonic deception? In his first book, Moody clearly gave the impression that no one who had "died" saw a hell or heaven as the Bible describes.[17] Taking his book at face value, one was left with the impression that there is no reason for repentance in this life, for there is no judgment to avoid in the next life. All will be light and peace for all humanity.

In his second book, *Reflections on Life After Life*, Moody does meekly admit that some people saw a "hell" in some sense or the other. But this weak admittance does not do justice to the wealth of such material, some of which was collected in *Beyond Death's Door* by Dr. Maurice Rawlings.

While each case must be weighed on its own merits, we submit that the OBE's related by Moody can be fairly understood as either (1) drug experiences, (2) stress and pain responses, (3) hallucinations, (4) dreams, or (5) demonic deceptions. Given the fact that we only have what the patient "feels" happened, there is no scientific way to discern anything beyond the fact that some kind of psychological illusion took place.

Lastly, as Wilson and Weldon point out, "there is a clear parallel to occult phenomena in these experiences."[18] They document that there is nothing "new" in Moody's work. The terminology and interpretations are clearly occultic and stand under the condemnation of Scripture. We are once again confronted with occultic concepts under the guise of a 20th-century para-science.

REINCARNATION

One of the most aggressive forms of modern occultism is the theory of reincaration. This westernized concept states that each soul must go through a series of rebirths in order to be successively cleansed of moral evil. Once one's soul has paid off all its Karmic debt, it is reabsorbed into the infinite cosmic mind or energy and loses its self-consciousness and self-existence. Thus, there is no hell or heaven in the biblical sense, for one is merely recycled into another human body and lives once again on the earth.

Having elsewhere examined in detail the history, nature, arguments and defects of the theory of reincarnation,[19] we will merely summarize our conclusion at this point.

First, there are only four basic arguments which are put forward as proving reincarnation:

1. It solves the problem of evil.

2. People remember their past lives spontaneously and through hypnosis or psychic means.

3. The Jews and early Christians believed in it.

4. The Bible teaches it.

The first argument is self-refuting in that it either ends in a first life whose sufferings cannot be the punishment for past evils in a past life, or an infinite regression of lives that merely extends the problem of evil for all eternity.

The second argument does not hold up either. Intuitive recall or *deja vu* can be experienced with objects or buildings which were built in one's lifetime. Such feelings can hardly be interpreted as proving that the building existed in a prior life. Professional hypnotists are still divided over hypnotic recall. We have already seen how, in the case of Bridey Murphy, memories and dreams can be changed into recall experiences. Occultic recall can never be sure that it is not a demonic deception.

That some Hellenized Jews such as Philo may have adopted Greek ideas of reincarnation does not tell us anything about the beliefs of biblical Judaism. When the rabbinic writings are read, it becomes clear the Orthodox Jews believed that the wicked and righteous went to Sheol at death, awaiting the resurrection. The early Christians condemned reincarnation as a Gnostic heresy. Thus the third argument cannot stand historical scrutiny.

As to the fourth argument that the Bible teaches reincarnation, we have hopefully demonstrated otherwise throughout this volume. The attempt to use such passages as John 3:3, 5 is refuted merely by observing the context. At no point does the Old Testament or New Testament teach reincarnation.

We established in our study on Dan. 12:1–3, John 5:28, 29, etc., that the Scriptures teach resurrection, not reincarnation. The atonement of Christ undercuts the concept of paying off one's Karmic debt through one's own suffering in future lives by having Christ's substitutionary suffering on the cross absolve believing sinners from all moral guilt and evil (Heb. 10:1–4). Christ's suffering makes Karmic suffering unnecessary.

In short, the theory of reincarnation has no scientific or philosophical merit and is condemned by the clear teaching of Scripture that there is a hell to shun and a heaven to gain.

CONCLUSION

The Christian should not call upon the occult for proof that the soul survives the body, because the Scriptures alone are sufficient for all matters of faith, life and practice.

It is to be regretted that some Christians have not understood the true origin and nature of the occult. They have called upon it as a witness to immortality. They do not realize that the occult is always dramatically opposed to the only true immortality which has been brought to light through the gospel of Jesus Christ.

Occultic immortality and biblical immortality are two totally different things. Once this is recognized, then there will be no need for mediums, parapsychologists or reincarnationists.

NOTES

1. A. Smith, *Immortality, The Scientific Evidence* (New Jersey: Prentice-Hall, n.d.), p. 138.

2. G. North, *None Dare Call It Witchcraft* (New York: Arlington House, 1977).

3. R. Buckland, *Here Is the Occult* (New York: House of Collectibles, Inc., 1974), p. 15.

4. M. Kelsy, *The Christian and the Supernatural* (Minnesota: Augsburg Pub. House, 1976).

5. M. Unger, *The Haunting of Bishop Pike* (Illinois: Tyndale House Pub., 1968).

6. T. Davis, *Magic, Divination and Demonology Among the Hebrews and Their Neighbors* (New York: KTAV Pub. House, 1969).

7. R. Girdlestone, *Synonyms of the Old Testament*, pp. 298f.; I.S.B.E., Vol. II, p. 1094 and Vol. V, pp. 3097f.; *The Zondervan Bible Dictionary*, p. 275; Keil & Delitzsch, *Commentary on the Pentateuch*, Vol. II, p. 425.

8. See: Lev. 19:31; 20:6, 27; Deut. 18:11; 1 Sam. 28:3, 7–9; 2 Kings 21:6; 23:24; 1 Chron. 10:13; 2 Chron. 33:6; Isa. 8:19; 19:3; 29:4.

9. See: Lev. 19:31; 20:6, 27; Deut. 18:11; 1 Sam. 28:3, 9; 2 Kings 23:24; 2 Chron. 33:6; Isa. 8:19; 19:3.

10. J. Meyer, *Acts of the Apostles*, p. 313.

11. E. Feilding, *Settings with Eusopio Pelladino and Other Studies* (New York: University Books, 1963), p. VII.

12. H. Boswell, *Master Guide to Psychism* (New York: Parker Pub., 1969).

13. L. Kronisch, "Yoga Journal," Nov-Dec. 1976, p. 20.

14. *Thanatology: Death and Dying* (*Spiritual Counterfeits Journal*, April, 1977), p. 8.

15. R. Morey, *The Bible and Drug Abuse* (New Jersey: Pres. & Ref. Pub. Co., 1975).

16. *Life After Life*, pp. 156f.

17. Ibid., pp. 75f.

18. Wilson & Weldon, *Occult Shock and Psychic Forces* (California: Master Books, 1980), pp. 91–100.

19. R. Morey, *Reincarnation and Christianity* (Minnesota: Bethany House Pub., 1980).

APPENDIX I

On Eternal Punishment, According to the Rabbis and the New Testament

by Dr. Alfred Edersheim

The parables of the Ten Virgins and the Unfaithful Servant close with a discourse on "The Last Things," the final judgment and the fate of those at Christ's right hand and at His left (Matt. XXV. 31–46). This final judgment by our Lord forms a fundamental article in the Creed of the Church. It is the Christ who comes, accompanied by the angelic host, and sits down on the throne of His glory, when all nations are gathered before Him. Then the final separation is made, and joy or sorrow awarded in accordance with the past of each man's history. And that past, as in relationship to the Christ—whether it has been "with" Him or "not with" Him, which latter is now shown to be equivalent to an "against" Him. And while, in the deep sense of a love to Christ which is utterly self-forgetful in its service and utterly humble in its realization of Him to whom no real service can be done by man, to their blessed surprise, those on "the right" find work and acknowledgment where they had never thought of its possibility, every ministry of their life, however small, is now owned of Him as rendered to himself— partly, because the new direction, from which all such ministry sprang, was of "Christ in" them, and partly, because of the iden- tification of Christ with His people. On the other hand, as the lowest service of him who has the new inner direction is Christ- ward, so does ignorance, or else ignoration, of Christ ("When saw we Thee. . .") issue in neglect of service and labor of love, and neglect of service proceed from neglect and rejection of Christ. And so is life either "to" Christ or "not to" Christ, and necessarily ends in "the kingdom prepared from the foundation of the world" or in "the eternal fire which is prepared for the devil and his angels."

Thus far the meaning of the Lord's words could only be im- paired by any attempt at commentation. But they also raise questions of the deepest importance, in which not only the head, but perhaps much more the heart, is interested, as regards the precise meaning of the term "everlasting" and "eternal" in this and other connections, so far as those on the left hand of Christ are concerned. The subject has of late attracted renewed attention. The doctrine of the Eternity of Punishments, with the proper explanations and limitations given to it in the teaching of the Church, has been set forth by Dr. Pusey in his treatise: "What is of Faith as to Everlasting Punishment?" Before adverting, however briefly, to the New Testament teaching, it seems desirable with some fulness to set forth the Jewish views on this subject. For the views held at the time of Christ, whatever they were, must have been those which the hearers of Christ entertained; and whatever these views, Christ did not contradict or intend to correct them. And here we have happily sufficient materials for a history of Jewish opinions at different periods on the eternity of punishments; and it seems the more desirable carefully to set it forth, as statements both inaccurate and incomplete have been put forward on the subject.

Leaving aside the teaching of the Apocrypha and Pseudepigraphic Writings (to which Dr. Pusey has sufficiently referred), the first rabbinic utterances come to us from the time immediately before that of Christ, from the Schools of Shammai and Hillel (Rosh hash. 16b last four lines, and 17a). The former arranged all mankind into three classes: the perfectly righteous, who are immediately written and sealed to eternal life; the perfectly wicked, who are immediately written and sealed to Gehenna; and an intermediate class, who go down to Gehinnom, and moan, and come up again, according to Zech. 13:9, and which seemed also indicated in certain words in the Song of Hannah (1 Sam. 2:6). The careful reader will notice that this statement implies belief in eternal punishment on the part of the School of Shammai. For (1) the perfectly wicked are spoken of as written and sealed unto Gehenna; (2) the School of Shammai expressly quotes, in support of what it teaches about these wicked, Dan. 12:2, a passage which undoubtedly refers to the final judgment after the Resurrection; (3) the perfectly wicked, so punished, are expressly distinguished from the third, or intermediate class, who merely go down to Gehinnom, but are not written and sealed, and come up again.

Substantially the same, as regards eternity of punishment, is the view of the School of Hillel (u.s.17a). In regard to sinners of Israel and of the Gentiles it teaches, indeed, that they are tormented in Gehenna for twelve months, after which their bodies and souls are burnt up and scattered as dust under the feet of the righteous; but it significantly excerpts from this number certain classes of transgressors who go down to Gehinnom and are punished there to ages of ages. That the Nipal form of the verb used must mean punished and not judged, appears, not only from the context, but from the use of the same word and form in the same tractate (Rosh hash.12a, lines 7 &c. from top), when it is said of the generation of the Flood that they were punished—surely not judged—by hot water. However, therefore, the School of Hillel might accentuate the mercy of God, or limit the number of those who would suffer eternal punishment, it did teach eternal punishment in the case of some. And this is the point in question.

But, since the Schools of Shammai and Hillel represented the theological teaching in the time of Christ and His Apostles, it follows that the doctrine of eternal punishment was that held in the days of our Lord, however it may afterward have been modified. Here, so far as this book is concerned, we might rest the case. But for completeness sake it will be better to follow the historical development of Jewish theological teaching, at least a certain distance.

The doctrine of the eternity of punishment seems to have been held by the Synagogue throughout the whole first century of our era. This will appear from the sayings of the Teachers who flourished during its course. The Jewish parable of the fate of those who had not kept their festive garments in readiness or appeared in such as were not clean (Shabb.152b, 153a) has been already quoted in our exposition of the parables of the Man Without the Wedding Garment and of the Ten Virgins. But we have more than this. We are told (Ber. 28b) that when that great rabbinic authority of the first century, Rabbi Jochanan ben Zakkai—"the light of Israel, the right hand pillar, the mighty hammer"—lay dying and wept, he accounted for his tears by fear as to his fate in judgment, illustrating the danger by the contrast of punishment by an earthly king "whose bonds are not eternal bonds nor his death eternal death," while as regarded God and His judgment: "If He is angry with me, His wrath is an eternal wrath; if He binds me in fetters, His fetters are eternal fetters; and if He kills me, His death is an eternal death." In the same direction is this saying of another great rabbi of the first century, Elieser (Shabb, 152b, about the middle), to the effect that "the souls of the righteous are hidden under the throne of glory," while those of the wicked were to be bound and in unrest, one angel hurling them to another from one end of the world to the other—of which latter strange idea he saw confirmation in 1 Sam. 25:29. To the fate of the righteous he applied, among other beautiful passages, Isa. 57:2, to that of the wicked Isa. 57:21. Evidently, the views of the rabbis of the first century were in strict accordance with those of Shammai and Hillel.

In the second century of our era, we mark a decided difference in rabbinic opinion. Although it was said that after the death of

Rabbi Meir, the ascent of smoke from the grace of his apostate teacher had indicated that the rabbi's prayers for the deliverance of his master from Gehenna had been answered (Chag.15b), most of the eminent teachers of that period propounded the idea, that in the last day the sheath would be removed which now covered the sun, when its fiery heat would burn up the wicked (Ber.R.6). Nay, one rabbi maintained that there was no hell at all, but that that day would consume the wicked; and yet another, that even this was not so, but that the wicked would be consumed by a sort of internal conflagration.

In the third century of our era, we have once more a reaction, and a return to the former views. Thus (Kethub.104a, about the middle) Rabbi Eleaser speaks of the three bands of angels, which successively go forth to meet the righteous, each with a welcome of their own; and of the three bands of angels of sorrow, which similarly receive the wicked in their death—and this, in terms which leave no doubt as to the expected fate of the wicked. And here Rabbi Jose informs us (Tos. Ber. vi. 15) that "the fire of Gehenna which was created on the second day is not extinguished for ever." With this view accord the seven designations which, according to Rabbi Joshua ben Levi, attach to Gehenna (Erub. 19 a, line 11, &c, from bottom—but the whole page bears on the subject). This doctrine was only modified when Ben Lakish maintained that the fire of Gehenna did not hurt sinners from among the Jews (Kethub. u.s.). Nor does even this other saying of his (Nedar. 8b, last four lines) necessarily imply that he denied the eternity of punishment: "There is no Gehinnom in the world to come"—since it is qualified by the expectation that the wicked would be punished, not annihilated, by the heat of the sun, which would be felt as healing by the righteous. Lastly, if not universal beatification, yet a kind of universal moral restoration seems implied in the teaching of Rabbi Jehudah to the effect that in the *saeculum futurum*, God would destroy the Yetser haRa.

Tempting as the subject is, we must here break off this historical review for want of space, not of material. Dr. Pusey has shown that the Targumim also teach the doctrine of eternal punishment—though their date is a matter of discussion—and to the passages quoted by him in evidence others might be added. And if on the other side the saying of Rabbi Akiba should be quoted (Eduy. ii. 10) to the effect that the judgment of the wicked in Gehenna was one of the five things that lasted for twelve months, it must be remembered that, even if this be taken seriously (for it is really only a *jeu d'esprit*), it does not necessarily imply more than the teaching of Hillel concerning that intermediate class of sinners who were in Gehenna for a year—while there was another class the duration of whose punishment would be for ages of ages. Even more palpably inept is the quotation from Bab Mez. 58 b (lines 5, &c., from the bottom). For, if that passage declares that all are destined to come up again from Gehenna, it expressly excepts from this these three classes of persons: adulterers, those who put their fellowmen publicly to shame, and those who apply an evil name to their neighbors.

But there can at least be no question that the passage which has been quoted at the outset of these remarks (Rosh haSh. 16 b, 17 a) proves beyond the possibility of gainsaying that both the Great Schools, into which rabbinic teaching at the time of Christ was divided, held the doctrine of eternal punishments. This, of course, entirely apart from the question who—how many, or rather, how few—were to suffer this terrible fate. And here the cautions and limitations, with which Dr. Pusey has shown that the Church has surrounded her teaching, cannot be too often or earnestly repeated. It does, indeed, seem painfully strange that, if the meaning of it be at all realized, some should seem so anxious to contend for the extension to so many of a misery from which our thoughts shrink in awe. Yet of this we are well assured, that the Judge of all the earth will judge, not only righteously, but mercifully. He alone knows all the secrets of heart and life, and He alone can apportion to each the due need. And in this assured conviction may the mind trustfully rest as regards those who have been dear to us.

But if on such grounds we shrink from narrow and harsh dogmatism, there are certain questions which we cannot quite evade, even although we may answer them generally rather than specifically. We put aside, as an unhealthy and threatening sign of certain religious movements, the theory, lately broached, of a so-called "Conditional Immortality." So far as the reading of the present writer extends, it is based on bad philosophy and even worse exegesis. But the question itself, to which this "rough-and-ready" kind of answer has been attempted, is one of the most serious. In our view, an impartial study of the words of the Lord, recorded in the Gospels—as repeatedly indicated in the text of these volumes— leads to the impression that His teaching in regard to reward and punishment should be taken in the ordinary and obvious sense, and not in that suggested by some. And this is confirmed by what is now quite clear to us, that the Jews, to whom He spoke, believed in eternal punishment, however few they might consign to it.

APPENDIX II

Additional Readings from Early Church Fathers

1. *The soul continues to exist consciously after death and is separate from the body.*

The Second Apology of Justin Martyr

Since Christians believe they ascend to God at death, pagans are pictured by Justin as saying, "Go then all you and kill yourself and pass even now to God, and do not trouble us" (Chap. IV).

Justin's Dialogue with Trypho

"But I do not say, indeed, that all souls die; for that were truly a piece of good fortune to the evil. What then? The souls of the pious [after death] remain in a better place, while those of the unjust and wicked are in a worse [place], waiting for the time of judgment. Thus some which have appeared worthy of God never die; but others are punished so long as God wills them to exist and to be punished" (Chap. V).

Justin's Hortatory Address to the Greeks

The Christian teachers "with one mouth and one tongue, they have in succession, and in harmony with one another, taught us both concerning God, and the creation of the world, and the formation of man, and concerning the immortality of the human soul, and the judgment which is to be after this life, and concerning all things which it is needed for us to know. . ." (Chap. VIII).

Justin on the Resurrection

"The resurrection is a resurrection of the flesh which died. For the spirit dies not; the soul is in the body, and without a soul it cannot live. The body, when the soul forsakes it, is not. For the body is the house of the soul; and the soul the house of the Spirit" (Chap. 10).

Irenaeus' *Against Heresies*

"Men . . . consist of a body and a soul" (Bk.11, chap. XIII, 3).

"The Lord has taught with very great fulness, that souls not only continue to exist [after death], not by passing from body to body, but that they preserve the same form [in their disembodied state] as the body had to which they were adopted, and that they remember the deeds which they did in this state of existence, and from which they have now ceased, [as] in that narrative which is recorded respecting the rich man and Lazarus who found repose in the bosom of Abraham. . . . Dives knew Lazarus after death . . . each continued in his own proper position . . . Dives also, and who enjoined those who did not wish to come into that place of torment to believe Moses and the prophets. . . . It is plainly declared that souls continue to exist [after death], and that they do not pass from body to body, that they possess the form of a man, so that they may be recognized, and retain the memory of things in this world . . . that each class [of souls] receives a habitation such as it has deserved, even before the judgment" (Bk. II, chap. XXXIV, 1).

"If any persons at this point maintain that those souls, which only began a little while ago to exist, cannot endure for any length of time [after death] . . . that they should die with the body itself— let them learn that [souls] extend their existence into long series, of ages in accordance with the will of God their Creator; so that he grants them that they should be thus formed at the beginning, and that they should so exist afterwards [after death]" (Bk. II, chap. XXXIV, 2).

"The soul, and the [physical] life which it possesses, must be understood as being separate existences. When God therefore bestows life and perpetual duration, it comes to pass that souls . . . henceforth endure [forever], since God has both willed that they should exist, and should continue in existence [after death]" (Bk. II, chap. XXXIV, 4).

Using Matt. 22:29f., "He is not the God of the dead, but of the living," Irenaeus demonstrates the doctrine of the resurrection and also that "the fathers . . . do indubitably live to God, and have not passed out of existence, since they are children of the resurrection" (Bk. IV, chap. V, 2).

That Irenaeus believed that souls went to Hades after death and were conscious there is clear from the fact that he believed "the Lord descended into the regions beneath the earth, preaching his advent there also, and [declaring] the remission of sins received by those who believe in him" (Bk. IV, chap. XXVII, 2).

"Now the soul and the spirit are certainly a part of the man, but certainly not the man" (Bk. V, chap. VI, 1).

"Souls are incorporeal. . . . Therefore David says, My soul also shall live to Him, just as if its substance were immortal. Neither, on the other hand, can they say that the spirit is the mortal body . . . it is [the flesh] which does and is decomposed, but not the soul or the spirit. For to die is to lose vital power, and to become henceforth breathless, inanimate, and devoid of motion, and to melt away into those [component parts] from which also it derived the commencement of [its] substance. But this event happens neither to the soul, for it is the breath of life; nor to the spirit, for the spirit is simple and not composite, so that it cannot be decomposed, and is itself the life of those who receive it. We must therefore conclude that it is in reference to the flesh that death is mentioned; which after the soul's departure, becomes inanimate, and is decomposed gradually into the earth from which it was taken. This [flesh], then, is what is mortal" (Bk. V, chap. VII, 1).

"He uses these words [mortal, corruptible] most manifestly in reference to the flesh; for the soul is not mortal, neither the spirit" (Bk. V, chap. XIII, 3).

"For three days He dwelt in the place where the dead are. . . . For as the Lord went away in the midst of the shadow of death, where the souls of the dead were, yet afterwards arose in the body, and after the resurrection was taken up [into heaven], it is manifest that the souls of His disciples also, upon whose account the Lord underwent these things, shall go away into the invisible place allotted to them by God, and there remain until the resurrection" (Bk. V, chap. XXXI, 2).

Note: To Irenaeus, God alone had absolute immortality, for He alone was without beginning or end. When the Gnostics claimed that the souls partook of God's absolute immortality and thus had no beginning, Irenaeus emphasized the soul was not immortal in the sense of no beginning. God created the soul at conception. On the other hand, when the Stoics and other materialists insisted the soul was only the physical life of the body and that it died when the body died, Irenaeus emphasized the soul was immortal as a gift of God and thus did not cease to exist after the death of the body. It continued on consciously in bliss or torment. The annihilationists quote Irenaeus when he is speaking against the Gnostics and misapply his statements to attack the orthodox position.

2. *The wicked will suffer conscious eternal torment after the resurrection and judgment.*

The Second Apology of Justin Martyr

"The unjust and intemperate shall be punished in eternal fire" (Chap. I).

"There shall be punishment in eternal fire inflicted upon those who do not live temperately" (Chap. II).

"The wicked angels and demons and men shall cease to exist [on earth]. . . . They will justly suffer in eternal fire the punishment of whatever sins they have committed" (Chap. VII).

"They, having been shut up in eternal fire, shall suffer their just punishment and penalty. For if they are even now overthrown by men through the name of Jesus Christ, this is an intimation of the punishment in eternal fire which is to be inflicted on themselves and those who follow them" (Chap. VIII).

"Our assertions that the wicked are punished in eternal fire" (Chap. IX).

Justin's Hortatory Address to the Greeks

When Plato described the future, eternal, conscious punishment of the wicked, "he plainly and manifestly wrote what he had learned from the [Old Testament] prophets about the judgment" (Chap. XXVII).

In Chap. XXV, Justin refers to conscious torment in Hades after death for the soul and after the resurrection and judgment, eternal, conscious torment for the body as well as the soul.

Justin on the Resurrection

"For what is man but the reasonable animal composed of body and soul? Is the body by itself man? No, but the soul of man. Would the body be called man? No, but it is called the body of man" (Chap. VIII).

"The resurrection is a resurrection of the flesh which died. For the spirit dies not; the soul is in the body, and without a soul it cannot live. The body, when the soul forsakes it, is not. For the body is the house of the soul; and the soul the house of the spirit" (Chap. X).

Fragments from the Last Writings of Justin

"Learning plainly from the discourses of Christ and his apostles that eternal fire was prepared for him who voluntarily departed from God" (Irenaeus, *Against Heresies*, Chap V, 26).

"When the Lord appeared, and the devil clearly understood

that eternal fire was laid up and prepared for him and his angels" (John of Antioch).

Irenaeus' *Against Heresies*

When Christ returns he will "raise up anew all flesh of the whole human race . . . that he should execute just judgment towards all," that he may send "spiritual wickedness; and the angels who transgressed and became apostates, together with the ungodly, and unrighteous, and wicked, and profane among men, into everlasting fire" (Bk. I, chap. X).

"He shall send the unrighteous, and those who do not the works of righteousness, into everlasting fire where their worm shall not die, and the fire shall not be quenched" (Bk. I, chap. XXXII).

"Those, on the other hand, who are worthy of punishment, shall go away into it, they too having their own souls, and their own bodies, in which they stood apart from the grace of God" (Bk. II, chap. XXXIV).

"He himself . . . shall come in glory, the Savior of those who are saved, and the Judge of those who are judged, and sending into eternal fire those who transform the truth" (Bk. III, chap. IV).

"The heretics . . . [shall] remain among those in hell (*epud inFeros*)" (Bk. IV, chap. XXVI).

"Inasmuch, then, as in both Testaments there is the same righteousness of God [displayed] when God takes vengeance, in the one case [Old Testament] indeed typically, temporarily, and more moderately; but in the other [New Testament], really, enduringly, and more rigid; for the fire is eternal" (Bk. IV, chap. XXVIII).

"The punishment of those who do not believe the Word of God . . . is increased; being not merely temporal but rendered also eternal. For to whomsoever the Lord shall cry, 'Depart from me, ye cursed, into everlasting fire,' there shall ye be damned forever" (Bk. IV, chap. XXVIII).

"The Lord, who judges for eternity those whom he doth judge, and lets go for eternity those whom he does let go" (Bk. IV, chap. XXVIII).

"Those who fly from eternal rest, have a habitation in accordance with their fleeing . . . for those persons who shun rest shall justly incur punishment, and those who avoid the light shall justly dwell in darkness . . . themselves the curse to themselves of their inhabiting eternal darkness, destitute of all good things, having become to themselves the cause of [their consignment to] an abode of that nature" (Bk. IV, chap. XXXIV).

"The same God . . . prepared the eternal fire for the ringleader of the apostasy, the devil, and those who revolted with him, into which [fire] the Lord has declared those men shall be sent who have been set apart by themselves on his left hand . . . preparing . . . eternal fire and outer darkness, which are evils indeed to those persons who fall into them. . . . [He] shall send them into a furnace of fire; there shall be weeping and gnashing of teeth" (Bk. IV, chap. XL).

"Inasmuch, then, as in this world some . . . shun the light, and separate themselves from God, the Word of God comes preparing a fit habitation for both . . . in darkness, that they may partake of its calamities. . . . He will send into eternal fire" (Bk. V, chap. XXVII).

3. *The theory of reincarnation or transmigration entails the belief that the soul is immortal in the sense of having no beginning. Reincarnationists believe the soul pre-existed its conception in the womb and was previously in other animal or human bodies. The Christian position has always opposed such views because souls come into existence at conception and thus do not pre-exist the body. Neither do souls migrate from body to body but after death are in either bliss or torment awaiting the resurrection.*

Justin Martyr's Dialogue with Trypho

Reincarnationists "neither dreading punishment nor hoping for any benefit from God . . . affirm that the same things shall always happen . . . believe that though they have committed evil they will not suffer punishment . . . and that the soul, in consequence of its immortality, needs nothing from God." They believe that the soul is immortal in the sense of having no beginning and it is part of God and is incapable of feeling pain (Chap. I).

They believe that all souls are part of God whether they be animal or human souls (Chap. IV).

The folly of reincarnation is demonstrated in that one cannot remember what he is being punished or rewarded for in his present life (Chap. IV).

"Therefore souls neither see God nor transmigrate into other bodies" (Chap. IV). They believe that souls are "both unbegotten and immortal" (Chap. V). But Christians believe that "if the world is begotten, souls are necessarily begotten" (Chap. V).

After the death of the body, "the souls of the pious remain in a better place, while those of the unjust and wicked are in a worse, waiting for the time of judgment" (Chap. V).

Irenaeus' *Against Heresies*

In Bk. II, Chap. XXXIII, Irenaeus refutes the theory of reincarnation on the grounds that since no one remembers their past lives, no benefit can be derived. Also, they disparage the body which is God's creation. He then uses the doctrine of the resurrection as the final answer. He also points out that, "Souls not only continue to exist [after death], not by passing from body to body, but that they preserve the same form" (Bk. II, chap. XXXIV).

Irenaeus then interprets the parable of the rich man in Hades as teaching conscious torment or bliss after death (Bk. II, chap. XXXIV).

SELECTED BIBLIOGRAPHY

While our research involved over one thousand works, we have reduced the bibliography to those works which directly deal with the issues of death, immortality and eternal punishment.

Alford, H. *The State of the Blessed Dead.* New York: Randolph & Co.

Alger, W. *A Critical History of the Doctrine of a Future Life.* New York: W.J. Widdleton, Pub., 1866.

Allis, O.T. *The Five Books of Moses.* Philadelphia: Pres. & Ref. Pub. Co., 1964.

The Apocryphal New Testament, ed. James. Oxford: Clareden Press, 1924.

The Apocrypha and Pseudepegrapha of the Old Testament, ed. Charles. Oxford: Clarendon Press, 1913.

Arndt and Gingrich. *Greek-English Lexicon of the New Testament and Other Early Christian Literature.* Chicago: The University of Chicago Press, 1963.

Arndt, W. *Bible Difficulties.* St. Louis, Mo.: Concordia Publishing House, 1962.

Atkinson, B. *Life and Immortality: An Examination of the Nature and Meaning of Life and Death as They Are Revealed in the Scriptures.* England: Phoenix Press, n.d.

The Babylonian Talmud. London: The Soncino Press, 1952.

Badham, P. *Christian Beliefs About Life After Death.* New York: Barnes & Noble, 1976.

Baker's Dictionary of Theology. Grand Rapids: Baker Book House, 1960.

Bailey, L. *Biblical Perspectives on Death.* Philadelphia: Fortress Press, 1979.

Baille, J. *And the Life Everlasting.* New York: Charles Scribner's Sons, 1933.

Bartlett, S. *Life and Death Eternal: A Refutation of the Theory of Annihilation.* Boston: American Tract Society, 1866.

Bechersteth, E. *Hades and Heaven.* New York: Carter & Bros., 1869.

Beecher, E. *History of Opinions on the Scriptural Doctrine of Retribution.* New York: D. Appleton and Co., 1878.

Berkhof, L. *Principles of Biblical Interpretation.* Grand Rapids: Baker Book House, 1950.

Berkhof, L. *Systematic Theology.* London: The Banner of Truth Trust, 1966.

Berkhof, L. *The History of Christian Doctrines.* London: The Banner of Truth Trust, 1969.

Berkouwer, G. *Man: The Image of God.* Grand Rapids: Wm. B. Eerdmans Pub. Co., 1962.

Berkouwer, G. *The Return of Christ.* Grand Rapids: Wm. B. Eerdmans Pub. Co., 1972.

Boettner, L. *Immortality.* Philadelphia: Presbyterian and Ref. Pub. Co., 1967.

Boyce, J. *Abstract of Systematic Theology.* Christian Gospel Foundation; reprint of 1887 Edition.

Brandon, S. *The Judgment of the Dead.* New York: Charles Scribner's Sons, 1967.

Braun, J. *Whatever Happened to Hell?* New York: Thomas Nelson Pub., 1979.

Brown, C. *Karl Barth and the Christian Message.* Illinois: InterVarsity Press, 1967.

Brown, Driver, and Briggs. *A Hebrew and English Lexicon of the Old Testament.* London: Oxford Univ. Press., 1966.

Bruce, F. *Answers to Questions.* Grand Rapids: Zondervan Pub. House, 1972.

Bruce, F.F. *New Testament History.* New York: Anchor Books, 1972.

Budge, W. *Egyptian Ideas of the Future Life.* New York: Bell Pub. Co., 1959.

Buis, H. *The Doctrine of Eternal Punishment.* Philadelphia: Pres. & Ref. Pub. Co., n.d.

Calloway, G. *The Idea of Immortality.* Edinburgh: T. & T. Clark, 1919.

Calvin, J. *Institutes of the Christian Religion.* Philadelphia: The Westminster Press, 1967.

Calvin, J. *Tracts and Treatises.* Grand Rapids: Eerdmans Pub. Co., 1958.

Cavendish, R. *The Black Arts.* New York: Capricorn Books, 1968.

Chambers, A. *Our Life After Death.* Philadelphia: George Jacobs & Co., 1897.

Charles, R. *A Critical History of the Doctrine of a Future Life.* London: Adam and Charles Block, 1913.

Clark, D. *Man All Immortal.* Cincinnati: Poe & Hitchcock, 1864.

Clarke, I. *True Tales of the Occult.* New York: A.S. Barnes & Co., 1973.

Coombs. *Life After Death.* Illinois: InterVarsity Press, 1978.

Coon, P. *The Doctrine of Future and Endless Punishment Proved.* Cincinnati: J.A. & V.P. James, 1850.

Constable, Henry. *Duration and Nature of Future Punishment*. London: Hobbs, 1886.

Cosgrove, M. *The Essence of Human Nature*. Grand Rapids: Zondervan/Probe, 1977.

Cremer, H. *Beyond the Grave*. New York: Harpers & Brothers, 1886.

Cullmann, O. *Immortality of the Soul or Resurrection of the Dead?* London: The Epworth Press, 1958.

Custance, A. *The Mysterious Matter of Mind*. Grand Rapids: Zondervan/Probe, 1980.

Dabney, R. *Lectures in Systematic Theology*. Grand Rapids: Zondervan Pub. House, 1972.

David, T. *Magic, Divination and Demonology Among the Hebrews and Their Neighbors*. New York: KTAV Pub. House, 1969.

Delitzsh, F. *Babel and Bible*. New York: Williams and Norgate, 1903.

Dwights Theology, Vol. 4. New Haven: S. Converse, 1825.

Edersheim, A. *The Life and Times of Jesus the Messiah*. Grand Rapids: Eerdmans Pub. Co., 1962.

Edwards and Pap, ed. *A Modern Introduction to Philosophy*. New York: The Free Press, 1965.

Edwards, J. *The Works of Jonathan Edwards*, Vol. I & II. London: The Banner of Truth Trust, 1974.

Elg, S. *Beyond Belief*. New York: Tower Pub., 1967.

The Encyclopedia of Philosophy, ed. Paul Edwards. New York: Macmillan Pub. Co., 1967.

Essays on Greco-Roman and Related Talmudic Literature. New York: KTAV Pub. House, 1977.

Feilding, E. *Settings with Eusopia Palladina and Others*. New York: University Books, 1963.

Flavel, J. *The Works of John Flavel*, Vol. I. London: The Banner of Truth Trust, 1968.

Flew, A. *Body, Mind and Death*. New York: Macmillan, 1964.

Flew & MacIntyre, ed. *New Essays on Philosophical Theology*. London: SCM Press, 1966.

Froom, L. *The Conditionalist Faith of Our Fathers*. Washington, D.C.: Review and Harald Pub., 1966.

Fudge, E. *The Fire That Consumes*, Verdict Pub., 1982.

Fyfe, J. *The Hereafter*. Edinburgh: T. & T. Clark, 1890.

Gerstner, J. *Jonathan Edwards and Heaven and Hell*. Grand Rapids: Baker Book House, 1980.

Gilbert, L. *Side-Lights on Immortality*. New York: Fleming H. Revell Co., 1903.

Gill, J. *Body of Divinity*. Atlanta, Ga: Turner Lassetter, 1965.

Gilson, E., ed. *Recent Philosophy*. New York: Random House, 1966.

Gordon, G. *The Witness to Immortality*. New York: Houghton, Mifflin & Co., 1893.

Grant, F. *Can We Still Believe in Immortality?* Louisville: Cloister Press, 1944.

Grant, F. *Facts and Theories as to a Future State.* New York: Loizeaux Bros., 1889.

Guillebaud, H. *The Righteous Judge.* England: Phoenix Press, n.d.

Hanhart, A. *The Intermediate State in the New Testament.* T. Wever, Franeker, 1966.

Hanson, A. *The Wrath of the Lamb.* London: S.P.C.K., 1957.

Harbaugh, H. *Heaven.* Philadelphia: Lindsay & Blakeston, 1856.

Hart, W. *Eternal Purpose.* Philadelphia: J.B. Lippencott & Co., 1882.

Hellwig, M. *What Are They Saying About Death and Christian Hope?* New York: Paulist Press, 1978.

Hendriksen, W. *The Bible on the Life Hereafter.* Grand Rapids: Baker Book House, 1977.

Hennecke, E. *New Testament Apocrypha.* Philadelphia: The Westminster Press, 1969.

Henry, C.F. *Christian Personal Ethics.* Grand Rapids: Baker Book House, 1957.

Hick, J. *Life and Death Eternal.* New York: Harper & Row, 1976.

Hick, J. *Philosophy of Religion.* New Jersey: Prentice-Hall, 1963.

Hodge, A. *Evangelical Theology.* London: The Banner of Truth Trust, 1976.

Hodge, A. *Immortality Not Conditional.* Philadelphia: Pres. Board of Pub., 1882.

Hodge, A. *Outlines of Theology.* Grand Rapids: Zondervan Pub. House, 1972.

Hodge, C. *Systematic Theology,* Vol. III. London: James Clarke & Co. Ltd., 1960.

Hodge, J.A. *Recognition After Death.* New York: American Tract Society, 1889.

Hough, R. *The Christian After Death.* Chicago: Moody Press, 1947.

Hovey, A. *The State of the Impenitent Dead.* Boston: Gould & Lincoln, 1859.

Hudson, C. *Debt and Grace, as Related to the Doctrine of a Future Life.* New York: Rudd & Carleton, 1861.

The International Standard Bible Encyclopedia, ed. J. Orr. Grand Rapids: Wm. B. Eerdmans Pub. Co., 1939.

Into the Unknown. New York: *Reader's Digest,* 1981.

Is This Life All There Is? New York: Watchtower Bible and Tract Society, Inc., 1974.

Jackson, W. London: *The Doctrine of Retribution,* Hodden & Stoughton, 1875.

James, M. *The Apocryphal New Testament.* Oxford, 1924.

Jungel, E. *Death: The Riddle and the Mystery.* Philadelphia: Westminster Press, 1974.

Juris, P. *The Other Side of Purgatory*. Hopkins, Mn.: pub. by author, 1981.

Keil and Delitzsch. *Biblical Commentary on the Old Testament*. Grand Rapids: Eerdmans Pub. Co., n.d.

Kellog, S. *From Death to Resurrection*. New York: Anson D.F. Randolph & Co., 1885.

Kelsey, M. *The Christian and the Supernatural*. Minnesota: Augsburg Pub. House, 1976.

Kester, J. *The Life Beyond Death*. Nashville: Southern Baptist Convention, 1930.

King's College Lectures on Immortality. University of London Press, 1920.

Kline, M. *Images of the Spirit*. Grand Rapids: Baker Book House, 1980.

Koch, K. *Christian Counseling and Occultism*. Grand Rapids: Kregel Pub., 1965.

Koch, K. *Occult ABC*. Germany: Literature Mission, 1978.

Koestler, A. *The Ghost in the Machine*. New York: Macmillan, 1968.

Kübler-Ross, E. *Questions and Answers on Death and Dying*. New York: Macmillan, 1974.

Landis, R. *The Immortality of the Soul and the Final Condition of the Wicked*. New York: Carlton & Porter, 1859.

Let God Be True. New York: Watchtower Bible and Tract Society, 1946.

Leuba, J. *The Belief in God and Immortality*. Chicago: The Open Court Pub. Co., 1921.

Lewis, C.S. *Miracles*. New York: Macmillan Co., 1966.

Lewis, C.S. *The Abolition of Man*. New York: Macmillan Co., 1947.

Lewis, E. *Life and Immortality*. London: Ellest Stock, 1924.

Lockyer, H. *Last Words of Saints and Sinners*. Grand Rapids: Kregel Pub., 1975.

Lord, F. *Conquest of Death*. New York: Abingdon & Cokesburg Press, 1942.

Luther, M. *The Bondage of the Will*. New Jersey: Fleming H. Revell Co., 1957.

Macartney, C. *Putting on Immortality*. New York: Fleming H. Revell Co., 1926.

Make Sure All Things. New York: Watchtower Bible and Tract Society, 1965.

Marchant, J., ed. *Immortality*. New York: G.P. Putman's Sons, 1924.

Martin and Klann. *Jehovah of the Watchtower*. Minnesota: Bethany House Pub., 1981.

Martin, W. *The Truth About Seventh Day Adventism*. Grand Rapids: Zondervan Pub. House, 1960.

McDowell, J. *More Evidence That Demands a Verdict*. Campus Crusade for Christ International, 1975.

Merrill, S. *The New Testament Idea of Hell*. New York: Hitchcock and Walden, 1978.

Mickelson, B. *Interpreting the Bible*. Grand Rapids: Wm. B. Eerdmans Pub. Co., 1979.

The Midrash. London: Soncino Press, 1939.

Mills, D. *Overcoming Religion*. New Jersey: Citadel Press, 1981.

Mills, L., ed. *Perspectives on Death*. New York: Abingdon Press, 1969.

Moody. *Life After Life*. New York: Bantam Books, 1977.

Moody, R. *Reflections on Life After Life*. New York: Bantam Books, 1978.

Morey, R. *A Christian's Handbook for Defending the Faith*. Pres. & Ref. Pub. Co., 1979.

Morey, R. *Horoscopes and the Christian*. Minnesota: Bethany House Pub., 1981.

Morey, R. *Reincarnation and Christianity*. Minnesota: Bethany House Pub., 1980.

Morey, R. *The Bible and Drug Abuse*. New Jersey: Pres. & Ref. Pub. Co., 1973.

Morey, R. *The Saving Work of Christ*. Sterling, Va.: Grace Abounding Ministry, Box 25, 1980.

Morris, E. *Is There Salvation After Death?* New York: Armstrong & Son, 1887.

Morris, L. *The Biblical Doctrine of Judgment*. Grand Rapids: Wm. B. Eerdmans Pub. Co., 1960.

Motzer, J. *After Death*. Philadelphia: The Westminster Press, 1965.

Myers, F. *Human Personality and Its Survival of Bodily Death*. London, 1903.

Nash, R. *The New Evangelicalism*. Grand Rapids: Zondervan Pub. House, 1963.

Neusner, J. *Understanding Rabbinic Judaism*. New York: KTAV Pub. House, Inc., 1974.

Newall, V. *The Encyclopedia of Witchcraft and Magic*. New York: A. & W. Visual Library, 1974.

Nickelsbury. *Jewish Literature Between the Bible and the Mishnah*. Philadelphia: Fortress Press, 1981.

North, G. *None Dare Call It Witchcraft*. New York: Arlington House Pub., 1977.

Oehler, G. *Theology of the Old Testament*. New York: Funk and Wagnalls, 1883.

Oses & Haraldson. *At the Hour of Death*. New York: Avon, 1977.

Ostwald, W. *Individuality and Immortality*. Cambridge: Houghton Mifflin & Co., 1906.

Parrinder, G. *The Bhagavad Gita*. London: Sheldon Press, 1974.

Parrinder, G. *Witchcraft: European and African*. London: Faber and Faber, 1963.

Patterson, R. *Paradise*. Philadelphia: Pres. Board of Pub., 1879.

Pelikan, J. *The Shape of Death*. New York: Abingdon Press, 1961.

Penfield, W. *The Mystery of the Mind*. New Jersey: Princeton Univ. Press., 1975.

Perowne, S. *Immortality*. London: Deighton, Bell, and Co., 1869.

Petry, R. *Christian Eschatology and Social Thought*. New York: Abingdon Press, 1956.

Pink, A.W. *Eternal Punishment*. Pennsylvania: Reiner Pub., Swengel, n.d.

Pink, A.W. *The Attributes of God*. Grand Rapids: Baker Book House, n.d.

Plumtre, E. *The Spirits in Prison*. New York: Thomas Whittaker, 1885.

Popper, K., & Eccles., J. *The Self and Its Brain*. Springer Verlay International, 1977.

Price, H. *Fifty Years of Psychical Research*. New York: Longman, Green & Co.

Primitive Conceptions of Death and the Netherworld in the Old Testament. Rome: Biblica Et Orientalia–N.21, 1969.

Psychic Discoveries Behind the Iron Curtain. New York: Prentice-Hall, 1970.

Punt, N. *Unconditional Good News*. Grand Rapids: Wm. B. Eerdmans Pub. Co., 1980.

Pusey, E. *What Is of Faith as to Everlasting Punishment?* London: James Parker & Co., 1880.

Rahner, K. *On the Theology of Death*. Herder and Header, 1962.

Ramm, B. *Hermeneutics*. Grand Rapids: Baker Book House, 1980.

Ramm, B. *Protestant Biblical Interpretation*. Boston: W.A. Wilde Co., 1956.

Ramm, B. *Protestant Christian Evidences*. Chicago: Moody Press, 1966.

Ramm, B. *The Christian View of Science and Scripture*. London: The Patermaster Press, 1964.

Rawlings, M. *Beyond Death's Door*. Nashville: Thomas Nelson Pub., 1978.

Recent Philosophy, ed. Gilson, Langan & Maurer. New York: Random House, 1966.

Reichenbach, B. *Is Man the Phoenix?* Grand Rapids: Wm. B. Eerdmans Pub. Co., 1978.

Rimner, H. *The Evidences for Immortality*. Grand Rapids: Wm. B. Eerdmans Pub. Co., 1935.

Rowell, G. *Hell and the Victorians: A Study of the Nineteenth Century Theological Controversies Concerning Eternal Punishment and the*

Future Life. Oxford: Clarendon Press, 1974.

Ryle, J. *Shall We Know One Another in Heaven?* Wilmington, Del.: Great Christian Books, Inc., 1977.

Ryle. G. *The Concept of the Mind.* London: Hutchinson's University, 1949.

Runes, D. *Dictionary of Psychology.* New Jersey: Littlefields, Adams & Co., 1967.

Salmond, S. *The Christian Doctrines of Immortality.* Edinburg: T. & T. Clark, 1895.

Schaeffer, F. *Back to Freedom and Dignity.* Illinois: InterVarsity Press, 1973.

Schaff, P. *History of the Christian Church.* Grand Rapids: Wm. B. Eerdmans Pub. Co., 1971.

Schener, S. *The History of the Jewish People in the Age of Jesus Christ.* London: T. & T. Clark, 1979.

Schwarz, H. *Beyond the Gates of Death.* Minnesota: Augsburg Pub. House, 1981.

Shedd, W. *The Doctrine of Endless Punishment.* New York: Charles Scribner's Sons, 1880.

A Modern Introduction to Philosophy, eds. Edwards & Arthur Pep. New York: The Free Press, 1965.

Smith, A. *Immortality, The Scientific Evidence.* New Jersey: Prentice-Hall, Inc., n.d.

Spirit Mediumship and Society in Africa. London: Routledge & Kegan Pub., 1969.

Sproul, R. *If There Is a God, Why Are There Atheists?* Minnesota: Bethany House Pub., 1978.

Stoner, R. *What Do We Know About Life After Death?* Grand Rapids: Zondervan Pub. Co., 1941.

Strange Stories, Amazing Facts. New York: *Reader's Digest,* 1976.

Streeter, B. *Immortality.* London: Macmillan & Co., 1930.

Striker, W. *What Happens After Death?* New York: American Tract Society, 1935.

Strong, A. *Systematic Theology.* Valley Forge, Pa.: Judson Press, 1976.

Sutcliffe, E. *The Old Testament and the Future Life.* London: Burns, Oates & Washtourne, 1947.

Sturat, M. *Future Punishment.* Philadelphia: Pres. Pub. Committee, 1867.

Swehart, P. *The Edge of Night.* Illinois: InterVarsity Press, 1978.

Taylor, A. *The Christian Hope of Immortality.* New York: Macmillan Co., 1947.

Taylor, R. *Metaphysics.* New Jersey: Prentice-Hall, 1963.

Terry, M. *Biblical Hermeneutics.* Grand Rapids: Zondervan Pub. House, n.d.

That Unknown Country. Massachusetts: CA Nichols Co., 1888.

Thayer, J. *Greek-English Lexicon of the New Testament.* Grand Rapids: Zondervan Pub. House, 1965.

The Septuagint Version of the Old Testament and Apocrypha. London: Samuel Bagster and Sons Ltd., n.d.

Theological Dictionary of the New Testament, ed. Kittel. Grand Rapids: Wm. B. Eerdmans Pub. Co., 1969.

Thiessen, H. *Lectures in Systematic Theology.* Grand Rapids: Wm. B. Eerdmans Pub. Co., 1963.

Tromp, N. *Primitive Conceptions of Death and the Netherworld in the Old Testament.* Rome: Pontifical Biblical Institute, 1969.

Unger, M. *The Haunting of Bishop Pike.* Illinois: Tyndale House, 1968.

Walker, D. *The Decline of Hell.* Chicago: University of Chicago Press, 1969.

Van Til, C. *Christianity and Barthianism.* Pres. & Ref. Pub. Co., 1965.

Van Til., C. *Karl Barth and Evangelicalism.* Pres. & Ref. Pub. Co., 1964.

Van Til, C. *The New Modernism.* Pres. & Ref. Pub. Co., 1973.

Vos, G. *Biblical Theology.* Grand Rapids: Wm. B. Eerdmans Pub. Co., 1966.

Warfield, B. B. *Selected Shorter Writings of Benjamin B. Warfield.* Nutley, N.J.: Pres. & Ref. Pub. Co., 1970.

Warfield, B.B. *The Plan of Salvation.* Grand Rapids: Wm. B. Eerdmans Pub. Co., 1977.

Wenham, J. *The Goodness of God.* Illinois: InterVarsity Press, 1974.

White, Edward. *Life In Christ.* London: Elliot Stock, 1878.

White, E.G. *The Great Controversy Between Christ and Satan.* Washington, D.C.: Review and Herald Pub. Assoc., 1911.

Wilson, C. *The Occult.* New York: Random House, 1971.

Wilson, R. *A Scientific Investigation of the Old Testament.* Chicago: Moody Press, 1959.

Wilson and Weldon. *Occult Shock and Psychic Forces.* California: Master Books, 1980.

Windelband, W. *A History of Philosophy.* New York: Harper & Row Pub., 1958.

Woodson, L. *What the Bible Says About Hell.* Grand Rapids: Baker Book House, 1976.

Young, E. *The Study of Old Testament Theology.* London: James Clarke and Co., Ltd., 1958.

Zeller, E. *Outlines of the History of Greek Philosophy.* New York: Meridian Books, 1967.

SCRIPTURE INDEX
OLD TESTAMENT

Exodus

Leviticus

Numbers

Deuteronomy

Proverbs

SCRIPTURE INDEX
NEW TESTAMENT

302

1 Corinthians

306

SUBJECT INDEX

I.   General Topics
II.   Names
III.   Apocryphal Writings
IV.   Patristic References

I. General Topics

---

*Asterisked numbers in this index means full treatment of the subject is given on these pages.

II. Names

III. Apocryphal Writings

IV. Patristic References